Preface to
the Second Edition

I was in London on 7 July 2005. I live and work near Tavistock
Square, where the bus was blown up, and Russell Square, the
scene of what was probably the worst of the underground
bombs. The streets were bizarrely quiet; there was no traffic
except for the emergency services. Telephones were not working
and I could not reach my family and friends. But even before
I had discovered what had happened, e-mail messages of
concern were pouring in from India, the United States, even
Baghdad and Jerusalem.

In a way, this was typical of our current security dilemmas.
Time and space are distorted in 'new wars'. We are more aware
than ever before of violence taking place in different parts of
the world and often we know more about what is happening
far away than is taking place in our immediate vicinity. These
perceptions of violence shaped by television and the Internet
affect our responses as much as the everyday experience of the
situation on the ground.

Since I wrote the first edition of this book, there has actually
been a decline in the number of wars in the world and a decline
in the number of people killed in wars.[1] In Africa, some of the
most terrible wars have ended, at least for the moment – in the
Democratic Republic of the Congo, where some 4 million
people died, in Southern Sudan, where the war lasted over
twenty years causing untold devastation and human tragedy, or
in Angola, Sierra Leone and Liberia – even though many wars

are continuing, such as in Darfur. Wars in other places, such as the Balkans, Sri Lanka or Aceh, have also been halted. We are very conscious of the continuing wars in Iraq, Palestine and Afghanistan, but so far the death toll has not reached the heights of the wars in the early 1990s in Bosnia or Rwanda. Indeed, the first five years of the twenty-first century are probably one of the most peaceful half decades in history.

Yet, paradoxically, the atmosphere of fear and our sense of insecurity has greatly increased since 11 September 2001. How do we explain this paradox? First of all, terrorist incidents have greatly increased, as has the number of people killed in terrorist incidents.[2] Although far fewer people die in terrorist attacks than in wars, and although most terrorist incidents take place in the Middle East or Asia, the attacks in New York, Madrid or London draw attention to the pervasiveness and apparent arbitrariness of contemporary violence. Those of us living in the wealthy parts of the world are painfully learning that violence can no longer be contained by national borders. Moreover, the idea of a 'War on Terror', and especially the invasion of Iraq, implicates us once again in a narrative of global conflict.

Secondly, the changes in patterns of violence described in this book have been accentuated by terrorism and by contemporary conflicts. Civilians continue to be the main victims, because violence is deliberately inflicted on civilians, because civilians do not have the same protection as military forces, and because it is difficult to distinguish between combatants and non-combatants. Casualties in war and terrorist incidents (both deaths and wounded) are mainly civilian. Uprooting of people (refugees and displaced persons) remains a continuing feature of contemporary conflicts as a result either of deliberate ethnic cleansing or of material and physical insecurity. Detention, torture and rape, both as a weapon of war and as a side-effect of war, as well as the destruction of historic buildings and symbols are widespread in contemporary conflicts. Contemporary conflicts are also characterized by a rise in crime, so that often it is difficult to distinguish between criminal and political violence. Hostage-taking, kidnapping, smuggling, loot and pillage are all ways in which political violence is financed, and, at the same time, political causes provide a cover for purely criminal acts.

New & Old Wars

Second Edition

New & Old Wars

Second Edition

MARY KALDOR

Stanford University Press
Stanford, California

© Polity Press
© 1998, 2006 Mary Kaldor
Originating publisher: Polity Press, Cambridge.

First published in the USA by Stanford University Press, 1998
Printed in Great Britain

ISBN-13: 978-0-8047-5645-7 (cloth)
ISBN-13: 978-0-8047-5646-4 (pbk)

Printed on acid-free paper

Contents

Thirdly, identity politics seems even more prevalent than it was in the mid-1990s. The growth of exclusive and/or fundamentalist religious and nationalist movements has not abated.[3] The main outcome of the 'new wars' is political mobilization around exclusivist causes; what often starts as top-down instrumentalist nationalism or religious fundamentalism is transformed into passionate grass-roots sentiments as a result of the experience of war and complicity in war crimes. Moreover, the rise of the Christian right in the United States or anti-immigrationism in Western Europe has apparently been fuelled by the insecurity associated with 9/11, the Madrid and London bombings, or race riots in Britain and France. As I show in the new chapter of this book, what began in Iraq as resistance to Western occupation has been transformed into sectarian conflict between Sunnis on the one side, and Shi'ites and Kurds on the other.

In other words, political violence at the beginning of the twenty-first century is more omnipresent, more directed at civilians, involves a blurring of the distinctions between war and crime, and is based on and serves to foment divisive identity politics – these are the characteristics of 'new wars'. Terrorism has to be understood as one variant of 'new wars' – the logical outcome of the tactics developed in contemporary conflicts. Moreover insecurity is not just the result of political violence. Natural disasters and disease kill many more people than do war and terrorism and compound a global risk environment in which war, poverty, or climate change are all intertwined.

Looking back at the period when I first wrote this book, it was a time of optimism. It was after the end of the Cold War, the last of the great 'old wars' of the twentieth century. The 1990s witnessed the emergence of global governance – stronger and more active international institutions, more multilateralist behaviour by states, a new discourse of human rights and humanitarianism, and the rise of a global civil society pressing for treaties on land mines, climate change or the International Criminal Court. I do believe that this explains the decline in the number of wars. This has been achieved through various forms of political and economic pressure on the warring parties, through the readiness to deploy troops and humanitarian agencies and to use them in new ways, or through various mechanisms for controlling the finance of wars, the Kimberly process for the certification of diamonds, for example, or restrictions on diaspora funding in places such as Sri Lanka.

What the international community has succeeded in doing is freezing conflicts, in stabilizing the level of war-related violence. However, in most conflict-affected regions, there are still high levels of human rights violations and crime; a variety of armed actors remain at large; there is high unemployment and a large informal or illegal economy; and very little has been done to confront identity politics. Big weaknesses in all international interventions are the provision of public security (policing and the rule of law) and reconstruction (infrastructure, public works, public services), even though there are ongoing efforts to redress these weaknesses. But, in my view, the biggest weakness has been the failure to promote a cosmopolitan politics. In this book I argue that the key to resolving new wars is the construction of legitimate political authority. Much of the literature, nowadays, emphasizes the need for state-building.[4] I prefer the term 'legitimate political authority', not only because this covers local and international institutions as well as states but mainly because the focus on legitimacy encompasses politics and civil society as well as institutions. International agencies tend to act in top-down ways. They talk mainly to the elites who are often the warring parties; they pay lip-service to concepts such as participation and partnerships; they are reluctant to seek local advice or to rely on local capacities. When I first wrote the chapter on Bosnia–Herzegovina, I was still hopeful that the international community could ally with local democrats and reduce the power of the nationalists. Today, as I explain in the revised chapter, the choice is between a benign imperialism, which has tried to put in place the appropriate institutions of governance and act on behalf of all ethnic groups, and local nationalists, who are as powerful as ever. The losers have been the local cosmopolitan groups and parties who were formerly a significant element in the region.

Can the efforts of the international community to stabilize 'new wars' be sustained? In the present climate of fear and division, I am doubtful. The wars in Afghanistan and Iraq may have discredited the very notion of humanitarian intervention and peacekeeping. The space for political and legal approaches to 'new wars' and terrorism has been narrowed. On the other hand, the early years of the twenty-first century have also been a moment of renewed political mobilization – the growth of social movements concerned about war, democracy, poverty or climate change. Is it possible to build on these public sentiments and regain some of the confidence of the 1990s? It is only if we are able to reverse the current atmosphere and reinstate a mood of hope and reason that we can assist those people, mainly in conflict zones, who currently lead intolerable lives.

Since I wrote this book, I have moved from the University of Sussex to the London School of Economics. I want to thank my colleagues at the Centre for the Study of Global Governance, who have contributed to this edition of the book. These include my co-Director, David Held, who proposed both the original book and the second edition, and has been unfailingly supportive; Yahia Said, who has helped me both with the big ideas and with his encyclopaedic knowledge of Iraq; Vesna Bojičić and Denisa Kostovicova, who keep me up to date on Bosnia and Kosovo, and who have both provided great insights into the changes in the region and beyond; Jen Otoadese, who has helped me to put together the various chapters and provided administrative support which has given me time to finish this project; and Sabine Selchow, who has found references and sources of information and who has offered important critical conceptual comments. I would also like to thank Julian Robinson and Josh Kaldor-Robinson for reading some or all of the book and for discussing the world.

Parts of chapter 3 were incorporated into a chapter written by me and Vesna Bojičić, 'The political economy of war in Bosnia–Herzegovina', in Mary Kaldor and Basker Vashee (eds), *Restructuring the Global Military Sector: New Wars* (London: Cassell/Pinter, 1997). An earlier version of chapter 4 was published as 'Cosmopolitanism versus nationalism: the new divide?', in Richard Caplan and John Feffer (eds), *Europe's New Nationalisms* (Cambridge: Cambridge University Press, 1996).

Mary Kaldor
April 2006

Abbreviations

ABiH	Army of Bosnia–Herzegovina
ANC	African National Congress
AU	African Union
BRA	Bourgainville Revolutionary Army
BSA	Bosnian Serb Army
CIS	Commonwealth of Independent States
ECHO	European Community Humanitarian Office
ECOMOG	Economic Community of West African States Ceasefire Monitoring Group
ECOWAS	Economic Community of West African States
EU	European Union
GDP	Gross Domestic Product
HCA	Helsinki Citizens' Assembly
HDZ	Croatian Democratic Party
HOS	Paramilitary wing of HSP
HSP	Croatian Party of Rights
HV	Croatian Army
HVO	Croatian Defence Council
ICC	International Criminal Court
ICFY	International Conference on Former Yugoslavia
ICRC	International Committee of the Red Cross
IDP	Internally displaced person
IFOR	Implementation Force
IFP	Inkatha Freedom Party

IISS	International Institute for Strategic Studies
IMF	International Monetary Fund
IRA	Irish Republican Army
JNA	Yugoslav National Army
MOS	Muslim Armed Forces
MPRI	Military Professional Resources Incorporated
NACC	NATO Coordination Council
NATO	North Atlantic Treaty Organization
NGO	Non-governmental organization
OAU	Organization of African Unity
OSCE	Organization for Security and Cooperation in Europe
PASOK	Panhellenic Socialist Movement (Greece)
RENAMO	Resistência Nacional Moçambiçana
SCR	Security Council Resolution
SDA	(Muslim) Party of Democratic Action
SDS	Serbian Democratic Party
SFOR	Stabilization Force
SPLA	Sudan People's Liberation Army
TO	Territorial Defence Units
UN	United Nations
UNHCR	United Nations High Commissioner for Refugees
UNICEF	United Nations Children's Fund
UNPROFOR	United Nations Protection Force
UNU	United Nations University
WEU	Western European Union
WIDER	World Institute for Development Economics Research

1

Introduction

In the summer of 1992, I visited Nagorno-Karabakh in the Transcaucasian region in the midst of a war involving Azerbaijan and Armenia. It was then that I realized that what I had previously observed in the former Yugoslavia was not unique; it was not a throwback to the Balkan past but rather a contemporary predicament especially, or so I thought, to be found in the post-communist part of the world. The wild west atmosphere of Knin (then the capital of the self-proclaimed Serbian republic in Croatia) and Nagorno-Karabakh, peopled by young men in home-made uniforms, desperate refugees and thuggish, neophyte politicians, was quite distinctive. Later, I embarked on a research project on the character of the new type of wars and I discovered from my colleagues who had first-hand experience of Africa that what I had noted in Eastern Europe shared many common features with the wars taking place in Africa and perhaps also other places, for example South Asia. Indeed, the experience of wars in other places shed new light on my understanding of what was happening in the Balkans and the former Soviet Union.[1]

My central argument is that, during the the last decades of the twentieth century, a new type of organized violence developed, especially in Africa and Eastern Europe, which is one aspect of the current globalized era. I describe this type of violence as 'new war'. I use the term 'new' to distinguish such wars from prevailing perceptions of war drawn from an earlier

era, which I outline in chapter 2. I use the term 'war' to emphasize the political nature of this new type of violence, even
though, as will become clear in the following pages, the new
wars involve a blurring of the distinctions between war (usually
defined as violence between states or organized political groups
for political motives), organized crime (violence undertaken by
privately organized groups for private purposes, usually financial gain) and large-scale violations of human rights (violence
undertaken by states or politically organized groups against
individuals).

In most of the literature, the new wars are described as
internal or civil wars or else as 'low-intensity conflicts'. Yet
although most of these wars are localized, they involve a myriad
of transnational connections so that the distinction between
internal and external, between aggression (attacks from abroad)
and repression (attacks from inside the country), or even
between local and global, are difficult to sustain. The term
'low-intensity conflict' was coined during the Cold War period
by the US military to describe guerrilla warfare or terrorism.
Although it is possible to trace the evolution of the new wars
from the so-called low-intensity conflicts of the Cold War
period, they have distinctive characteristics which are masked
by what is in effect a catch-all term. Some authors describe
the new wars as privatized or informal wars;[2] yet, while the
privatization of violence is an important element of these wars,
in practice, the distinction between what is private and what
is public, state and non-state, informal and formal, what is done
for economic and what for political motives, cannot easily be
applied. A more appropriate term is perhaps 'post-modern',
which is used by several authors.[3] Like 'new wars', it offers a
way of distinguishing these wars from the wars which could
be said to be characteristic of classical modernity. However,
the term is also used to refer to virtual wars and wars in
cyberspace;[4] moreover, the new wars involve elements of pre-
modernity and modernity as well. Finally, Martin Shaw uses
the term 'degenerate warfare'. For him there is a continuity
with the total wars of the twentieth century and their genocidal aspects; the term draws attention to the decay of the
national frameworks, especially military forces.

Critics of the 'new war' argument have suggested that many
features of the new wars can be found in earlier wars and that

the dominance of the Cold War overshadowed the significance of 'small wars' or 'low intensity' conflicts.[5] There is some truth in this proposition. The main point of the distinction between new and old wars was to change the prevailing perceptions of war, especially among policy-makers. In particular, I wanted to emphasize the growing illegitimacy of these wars and the need for a cosmopolitan political response – one that put individual rights and the rule of law as the centrepiece of any international intervention (political, military, civil or economic). Nevertheless, I do think that the 'new war' argument does reflect a new reality – a reality that was emerging before the end of the Cold War. Globalization is a convenient catch-all to describe the various changes that characterize the contemporary period and have influenced the character of war.[6]

Among American strategic writers, there is a discussion about what is known as the Revolution in Military Affairs, or Defence Transformation.[7] The argument is that the advent of information technology is as significant as was the advent of the tank and the aeroplane, or even as significant as the shift from horsepower to mechanical power, with profound implications for the future of warfare. In particular, it is argued that these changes have made modern war much more precise and discriminate. However, the Revolution in Military Affairs is conceived by these writers within the inherited institutional structures of war and the military. They envisage wars on a traditional model in which the new techniques develop in a more or less linear extension from the past. Moreover, they are designed to sustain the imagined character of war which was typical of the Cold War era and utilized in such a way as to minimize own casualties. The preferred technique is spectacular aerial bombing or rapid and dramatic ground manoeuvres which reproduces the appearance of classical war for public consumption but which is rather clumsy as an instrument for influencing the reality on the ground. Hence Baudrillard's famous remark that the Gulf War did not take place.[8] These complex sophisticated techniques were used in the Gulf War of 1991, in the last phases of the war in Bosnia–Herzegovina, in Kosovo, in Afghanistan and, most recently, in Iraq. In most of these cases, they did achieve limited clearly defined goals, but they failed to control the situation on the ground and they caused many civilian casualties.

I share the view that there has been a revolution in military affairs, but it is a revolution in the social relations of warfare, not in technology, even though the changes in social relations are influenced by and make use of new technology. Beneath the spectacular displays are real wars, which, even in the case of the 1991 Iraq war in which hundreds and thousands of Kurds and Shi'ites died, are better explained in terms of my conception of new wars. In this second edition, I have added a new chapter on the ongoing war in Iraq to show the clash between what I call technology-updated 'old war' and the 'new war' that is taking place.

The new wars have to be understood in the context of the process known as globalization. By globalization, I mean the intensification of global interconnectedness – political, economic, military and cultural – and the changing character of political authority. Even though I accept the argument that globalization has its roots in modernity or even earlier, I consider that the globalization of the 1980s and 1990s was a qualitatively new phenomenon which can, at least in part, be explained as a consequence of the revolution in information technologies and dramatic improvements in communication and data-processing. This process of intensifying interconnectedness is a contradictory process involving both integration and fragmentation, homogenization and diversification, globalization and localization. It is often argued that the new wars are a consequence of the end of the Cold War; they reflect a power vacuum which is typical of transition periods in world affairs. It is undoubtedly true that the consequences of the end of the Cold War – the availability of surplus arms, the discrediting of socialist ideologies, the disintegration of totalitarian empires, the withdrawal of superpower support to client regimes – contributed in important ways to the new wars. But equally, the end of the Cold War could be viewed as the way in which the Eastern bloc succumbed to the inevitable encroachment of globalization – the crumbling of the last bastions of territorial autarchy, the moment when Eastern Europe was 'opened up' to the rest of the world.

The impact of globalization is visible in many of the new wars. The global presence in these wars can include international reporters, mercenary troops and military advisers, and diaspora volunteers as well as a veritable 'army' of international agencies ranging from non-governmental organizations (NGOs) such as Oxfam, Save the Children, Médecins Sans Frontières, Human Rights Watch and the International Red Cross to international institutions such as the United Nations High Commissioner for Refugees (UNHCR), the European Union (EU), the United Nations Children's Fund (UNICEF), the Organization for Security and Cooperation in Europe (OSCE), the African Union (AU) and the United Nations (UN) itself, including peacekeeping troops. Indeed, the wars epitomize a new kind of global/local divide between those members of a global class who can speak English, have access to faxes, the Internet and satellite television, who use dollars or euros or credit cards, and who can travel freely, and those who are excluded from global processes, who live off what they can sell or barter or what they receive in humanitarian aid, whose movement is restricted by roadblocks, visas and the cost of travel, and who are prey to sieges, forced famines, landmines, etc.

In the literature on globalization, a central concern has to do with the implications of global interconnectedness for the future of territorially based sovereignty – that is to say, for the future of the modern state.[9] The new wars arise in the context of the erosion of the autonomy of the state and in some extreme cases the disintegration of the state. In particular, they occur in the context of the erosion of the monopoly of legitimate organized violence. This monopoly is eroded from above and from below. It has been eroded from above by the transnationalization of military forces which began during the two world wars and was institutionalized by the bloc system during the Cold War and by innumerable transnational connections between armed forces that developed in the post-war period.[10] The capacity of states to use force unilaterally against other states has been greatly weakened. This is partly for practical reasons – the growing destructiveness of military technology and the increasing interconnectedness of states, especially in the military field. It is difficult to imagine nowadays a state or group of states risking a large-scale war which could be even more destructive than what was experienced during the two world wars. Moreover, military alliances, international arms production and trade, various forms of military cooperation and exchanges, arms control agreements, etc., have created a form of global military integration. The weakening of states' capacity to use unilateral force is also due to the evolution of international norms. The principle that unilateral aggression is illegitimate was first codified in the Kellogg–Briand pact of 1928, and reinforced after World War II in the UN Charter and through the reasoning used in the war crimes trials in Nuremberg and Tokyo.

At the same time, the monopoly of organized violence is eroded from below by privatization. Indeed, it could be argued that the new wars are part of a process which is more or less a reversal of the processes through which modern states evolved. As I argue in chapter 2, the rise of the modern state was intimately connected to war. In order to fight wars, rulers needed to increase taxation and borrowing, to eliminate 'wastage' as a result of crime, corruption and inefficiency, to regularize armed forces and police and to eliminate private armies, and to mobilize popular support in order to raise money and men. As war became the exclusive province of the state, so the growing destructiveness of war against other states was paralleled by a process of growing security at home; hence the way in which the term 'civil' came to mean internal. The new wars occur in situations in which state revenues decline because of the decline of the economy as well as the spread of criminality, corruption and inefficiency, violence is increasingly privatized both as a result of growing organized crime and the emergence of paramilitary groups, and political legitimacy is disappearing. Thus the distinctions are breaking down between external barbarity and domestic civility, between the combatant as the legitimate bearer of arms and the non-combatant, or between the soldier or policeman and the criminal. The barbarity of war between states may have become a thing of the past. In its place is a new type of organized violence that is more pervasive, but also perhaps less extreme.

In chapter 3, I use the example of the war in Bosnia–Herzegovina to illustrate the main features of the new wars, mainly because it is the war with which I am most familiar. The war in Bosnia–Herzegovina shares many of the characteristics of wars in other places. But in one sense it is exceptional; it became the focus of global and European attention during the 1990s. More resources – governmental and non-governmental – have been concentrated there than in any other new war up until the current war in Iraq. On the one hand, this means that, as a case study, it has atypical features. On the other hand, it also means that it has become the paradigm case from which different lessons are drawn, the example which is used to argue out different general positions, and, at the same time, a laboratory in which experiments in the different ways of managing the new wars have taken place.

The new wars can be contrasted with earlier wars in terms of their goals, the methods of warfare and how they are financed. The goals of the new wars are about identity politics in contrast to the geo-political or ideological goals of earlier wars. In chapter 4, I argue that, in the context of globalization, ideological and/or territorial cleavages of an earlier era have increasingly been supplanted by an emerging political cleavage between what I call cosmopolitanism, based on inclusive, universalist, multicultural values, and the politics of particularist identities.[11] This cleavage can be explained in terms of the growing divide between those who are part of global processes and those who are excluded, but it should not be equated with this division. Among the global class are members of transnational networks based on exclusivist identity, while at the local level there are many courageous individuals who refuse the politics of particularism.

By identity politics, I mean the claim to power on the basis of a particular identity – be it national, clan, religious or linguistic. In one sense, all wars involve a clash of identities – British against French, communists against democrats. But my point is that these earlier identities were linked either to a notion of state interest or to some forward-looking project – ideas about how society should be organized. Nineteenth-century European nationalisms or post-colonial nationalisms, for example, presented themselves as emancipatory nation-building projects. The new identity politics is about the claim to power on the basis of labels – in so far as there are ideas about political or social change, they tend to relate to an idealized nostalgic representation of the past. It is often claimed that the new wave of identity politics is merely a throwback to the past, a resurgence of ancient hatreds kept under control by colonialism and/or the Cold War. While it is true that the narratives of identity politics depend on memory and tradition, it is also the case that these are 'reinvented' in the context of the

failure or the corrosion of other sources of political legitimacy
– the discrediting of socialism or the nation-building rhetoric
of the first generation of post-colonial leaders. These backward-
looking political projects arise in the vacuum created by the
absence of forward-looking projects. Unlike the politics of ideas
which are open to all and therefore tend to be integrative, this
type of identity politics is inherently exclusive and therefore
tends towards fragmentation.

There are two aspects of the new wave of identity politics
which specifically relate to the process of globalization. First,
the new wave of identity politics is both local and global,
national as well as transnational. In many cases, there are
significant diaspora communities whose influence is greatly
enhanced by the ease of travel and improved communication.
Alienated diaspora groups in advanced industrial or oil-rich
countries provide ideas, funds and techniques, thereby imposing their own frustrations and fantasies on what is often a very
different situation. Second, this politics makes use of the
new technology. The speed of political mobilization is greatly
increased by the use of the electronic media. The effect of
television, radio or videos on what is often a non-reading public
cannot be overestimated. The protagonists of the new politics
often display the symbols of a global mass culture – Mercedes
cars, Rolex watches, Ray-Ban sunglasses – combined with the
labels that signify their own brand of particularistic cultural
identity.

The second characteristic of the new wars is the changed
mode of warfare[12] – the means through which the new wars
are fought. The strategies of the new warfare draw on the
experience of both guerrilla warfare and counter-insurgency,
yet they are quite distinctive. In conventional or regular war,
the goal is the capture of territory by military means; battles
are the decisive encounters of the war. Guerrilla warfare developed as a way of getting round the massive concentrations of
military force which are characteristic of conventional war. In
guerrilla warfare, territory is captured through political control
of the population rather than through military advance, and
battles are avoided as far as possible. The new warfare also
tends to avoid battle and to control territory through political
control of the population, but whereas guerrilla warfare, at
least in theory as articulated by Mao Tse-tung or Che Guevara,

aimed to capture 'hearts and minds', the new warfare borrows from counter-insurgency techniques of destabilization aimed at sowing 'fear and hatred'. The aim is to control the population by getting rid of everyone of a different identity (and indeed of a different opinion) and by instilling terror. Hence the strategic goal of these wars is to mobilize extremist politics based on fear and hatred. This often involves population expulsion through various means such as mass killing and forcible resettlement, as well as a range of political, psychological and economic techniques of intimidation. This is why, in all these wars, there has been a dramatic increase in the number of refugees and displaced persons, and why most violence is directed against civilians. At the turn of the twentieth century, the ratio of military to civilian casualties in wars was 8:1. Today, this has been almost exactly reversed; in the wars of the 1990s, the ratio of military to civilian casualties is approximately 1:8. Behaviour that was proscribed according to the classical rules of warfare and codified in the laws of war in the late nineteenth century and early twentieth century, such as atrocities against non-combatants, sieges, destruction of historic monuments, etc., constitutes an essential component of the strategies of the new mode of warfare. The terrorism experienced in places such as New York, Madrid or London, as well as in Israel or Iraq, can be understood as a variant of new strategy – the use of spectacular, often gruesome, violence to create fear and conflict.

In contrast to the vertically organized hierarchical units that were typical of 'old wars', among the units that fight these wars are a disparate range of different types of groups, such as paramilitary units, local warlords, criminal gangs, police forces, mercenary groups and also regular armies, including breakaway units from regular armies. In organizational terms, they are highly decentralized and they operate through a mixture of confrontation and cooperation even when on opposing sides. They make use of advanced technology even if it is not what we tend to call 'high technology' (stealth bombers or cruise missiles, for example). In the last fifty years, there have been significant advances in lighter weapons – undetectable landmines, for example, or small arms which are light, accurate and easy to use so that they can even be operated by children. Modern communications – cellular phones or computer links

– are also used in order to coordinate, mediate and negotiate among the disparate fighting units.

The third way in which the new wars can be contrasted with earlier wars is what I call the new 'globalized' war economy, which is elaborated in chapter 5 along with the mode of warfare. The new globalized war economy is almost exactly the opposite of the war economies of the two world wars. The latter were centralized, totalizing and autarchic. The new war economies are decentralized. Participation in the war is low and unemployment is extremely high. Moreover, these economies are heavily dependent on external resources. In these wars, domestic production declines dramatically because of global competition, physical destruction or interruptions to normal trade, as does tax revenue. In these circumstances, the fighting units finance themselves through plunder, hostage-taking and the black market or through external assistance. The latter can take the following forms: remittances from the diaspora, 'taxation' of humanitarian assistance, support from neighbouring governments, or illegal trade in arms, drugs or valuable commodities such as oil or diamonds or human trafficking. All of these sources can only be sustained through continued violence so that a war logic is built into the functioning of the economy. This retrograde set of social relationships, which is entrenched by war, has a tendency to spread across borders through refugees or organized crime or ethnic minorities. It is possible to identify clusters of war economies or near war economies in places such as the Balkans, the Caucasus, Central Asia, the Horn of Africa, Central Africa or West Africa.

Because the various warring parties share the aim of sowing 'fear and hatred', they operate in a way that is mutually reinforcing, helping each other to create a climate of insecurity and suspicion – indeed, it is possible to find examples in both Eastern Europe and Africa of mutual cooperation for both military and economic purposes.[13] Often, among the first civilians to be targeted are those who espouse a different politics, those who try to maintain inclusive social relations and some sense of public morality. Thus though the new wars appear to be between different linguistic, religious or tribal groups, they can also be presented as wars in which those who represent particularistic identity politics cooperate in suppressing the values of civility and multiculturalism. In other words, they can be understood as wars between exclusivism and cosmopolitanism.

This analysis of new wars has implications for the management of conflicts, which I explore in chapter 6. There is no possible long-term solution within the framework of identity politics. And because these are conflicts with extensive social and economic ramifications, top-down approaches are likely to fail. In the early 1990s there was great optimism about the prospects for humanitarian intervention to protect civilians. However, the practice of humanitarian intervention has, I would argue, been shackled by a kind of myopia about the character of the new warfare. On the one hand, the persistence of inherited mandates, the tendency to interpret these wars in traditional terms, has been the main reason why humanitarian intervention has often failed to prevent the wars and may actually have helped to sustain them in various ways – for example, through the provision of humanitarian aid, which is an important source of income for the warring parties, or through the legitimation of war criminals by inviting them to the negotiating table, or through the effort to find political compromises based on exclusivist assumptions. On the other hand, humanitarian intervention has been used to legitimize updated 'old wars' such as in Kosovo or Iraq.

The key to any long-term solution is the restoration of legitimacy, the reconstitution of the control of organized violence by public authorities, whether local, national or global. This is both a political process – the rebuilding of trust in and support for public authorities – and a legal process – the re-establishment of a rule of law within which public authorities operate. This cannot be done on the basis of particularistic politics. An alternative forward-looking cosmopolitan political project which would cross the global/local divide and reconstruct legitimacy around an inclusive, democratic set of values has to be counterposed against the politics of exclusivism. In all the new wars there are local people and places who struggle against the politics of exclusivism – the Hutus and Tutsis who called themselves Hutsis and tried to defend their localities against genocide, the non-nationalists in the cities of Bosnia–Herzegovina, particularly Sarajevo and Tuzla, who kept alive civic multicultural values, the elders in Northwest Somaliland who negotiated peace. What is needed is an alliance between local defenders of civility and transnational institutions which would guide a strategy aimed at controlling violence. Such a strategy would include political, military and economic components. It would operate within a framework of international law, based on that body of international law that comprises both the 'laws of war' and human rights law, which could perhaps be termed cosmopolitan law. In this context, peacekeeping could be reconceptualized as cosmopolitan lawenforcement. Since the new wars are, in a sense, a mixture of war, crime and human rights violations, so the agents of cosmopolitan law-enforcement have to be a mixture of soldiers and police. I also argue that a new strategy of reconstruction, which includes the reconstruction of social, civic and institutional relationships, should supplant the current dominant approaches of structural adjustment or humanitarianism.

The war in Iraq is a good illustration of the way in which misperceptions about the character of war exacerbate 'new wars'. The Bush administration believed that they could defeat Saddam Hussein rapidly, using new technology to substitute for manpower, and install a new regime, along the lines of the occupation of post-war Germany and Japan. They found themselves caught up in an ever worsening new war spiral, involving both state and non-state actors, identity politics, a criminalized war economy and growing numbers of civilian casualties. This is the subject of chapter 7, which has been written especially for this edition.

In the final chapter of the book, I discuss the implications of the argument for global order. Although the new wars are concentrated in Africa, Eastern Europe and Asia, they are a global phenomenon not just because of the presence of global networks, or because they are reported globally. The characteristics of the new wars I have described are to be found in North America and Western Europe as well. The right-wing militia groups in the United States are not so very different from the paramilitary groups in Eastern Europe or Africa. Indeed, in the United States it is reported that private security officers outnumber police officers by two to one. Nor is the salience of identity politics and the growing disillusionment with formal politics just a Southern and Eastern phenomenon. The violence in the inner cities of Western Europe and North

America can, in some senses, be described as new wars. The suicide bombers responsible for the attacks of 7 July on London were, after all, home-grown. It is sometimes said that the advanced industrial world is integrating and the poorer parts of the world are fragmenting. I would argue that all parts of the world are characterized by a combination of integration and fragmentation even though the tendencies to integration are greater in the North and the tendencies to fragmentation may be greater in the South and East.

Since 9/11 it has become clear that it is no longer possible to insulate some parts of the world from others. Neither the idea that we can re-create some kind of bipolar or multipolar world order on the basis of identity – Christianity versus Islam, for example – nor the idea that the 'anarchy' in places such as Africa and Eastern Europe can be contained is feasible if my analysis of the changing character of organized violence has some basis in reality. This is why the cosmopolitan project has to be a global project even if it is, as it must be, local or regional in application.

The book is based, first and foremost, on direct experience of the new wars, especially in the Balkans and the Transcaucasian region. As one of the chairs of the Helsinki Citizens' Assembly (HCA), I travelled extensively in these areas and learned much of what I know from the critical intellectuals and activists involved in local branches of the HCA. In particular, in Bosnia–Herzegovina, the HCA was given the status of an implementing agency of the UNHCR, which enabled me to move around the country during the war in support of local activists. I was also lucky enough to have access to the various institutions responsible for carrying out the policies of the international community; as chair of the HCA, it was one of my tasks, along with others, to present the ideas and proposals of local branches to governments and international institutions such as the EU, NATO, the OSCE and the UN. More recently, I have been involved in a project aimed at supporting civil society in Iraq. As an academic, I was able to supplement and put into context this knowledge through reading, through exchanges with colleagues working in related fields and through research projects undertaken for the United Nations University (UNU) and the European Commission.[14] In particular, I was greatly helped by the newsletters, news digests, pleas for help and monitoring reports that now can be received daily on the Internet.

The aim of this book is not simply to inform, although I have tried to provide information and to back my assertions with examples. The aim is to offer a different perspective, the perspective derived from the experiences of critically minded individuals on the ground, tempered by my own experience in various international fora. It is a contribution to the reconceptualization of patterns of violence and war that has to be undertaken if the tragedies that are encroaching in many parts of the world are to be halted. I am not an optimist, yet my practical suggestions may seem utopian. I offer them in hope, not in confidence, as the only alternative to a grim future.

2

Old Wars

As Clausewitz was fond of pointing out, war is a social activity.[1] It involves the mobilization and organization of individual men, almost never women, for the purpose of inflicting physical violence; it entails the regulation of certain types of social relationships and has its own particular logic. Clausewitz, who was arguably the greatest exponent of modern war, insisted that war could not be reduced either to art or to science. Sometimes he likened war to business competition, and he often used economic analogies to illustrate his points.

Every society has its own characteristic form of war. What we tend to perceive as war, what policy-makers and military leaders define as war, is, in fact, a specific phenomenon which took shape in Europe somewhere between the fifteenth and eighteenth centuries, although it has passed through several different phases since then. It was a phenomenon that was intimately bound up with the evolution of the modern state. It went through several phases, as I have tried to show in table 2.1, from the relatively limited wars of the seventeenth and eighteenth centuries associated with the growing power of the absolutist state, to the more revolutionary wars of the nineteenth century such as the Napoleonic Wars or the American Civil War, both of which were linked to the establishment of nation-states, to the total wars of the early twentieth century, and the imagined Cold War of the late twentieth century, which were wars of alliances and, later, blocs. Each of these

Table 2.1 *The evolution of old wars*

	17th and 18th centuries	19th century	Early 20th century	Late 20th century
Type of polity	absolutist state	nation-state	coalitions of states; multinational states; empires	blocs
Goals of war	reasons of state; dynastic conflict; consolidation of borders	national conflict	national and ideological conflict	ideological conflict
Type of army	mercenary/ professional	professional/ conscription	mass armies	scientific-military elite/professional armies
Military technique	use of firearms, defensive manoeuvres, seiges	railways and telegraph, rapid mobilization	massive firepower; tanks and aircraft	nuclear weapons
War economy	regularization of taxation and borrowing	expansion of administration and bureaucracy	mobilization economy	military-industrial complex

phases was characterized by a different mode of warfare, involving different types of military forces, different strategies and techniques, different relations and means of warfare. But, despite these differences, war was recognizably the same phenomenon: a construction of the centralized, 'rationalized', hierarchically ordered, territorialized modern state. As the centralized, territorialized modern state gives way to new types of polity emerging out of new global processes, so war, as we presently conceive it, is becoming an anachronism.

This chapter aims to provide a stylized description of old wars. Actual warfare never exactly fitted the stylized description. This type of war was predominantly European. There were always rebellions, colonial wars or guerrilla wars, both in Europe and elsewhere, which were sometimes given the description of 'irregular warfare' or else not called wars at all. Instead, they were called uprisings, insurgencies or, more recently, low-intensity conflicts. Nevertheless, it is the stylized notion of war that still profoundly affects our thinking about war and dominates, even today, the way policy-makers conceive of security.

War and the Emergence of the Modern State

Clausewitz defined war as 'an act of violence intended to compel our opponent to fulfill our will'.[2] This definition implied that 'we' and 'our opponent' were states, and the 'will' of one state could be clearly defined. Hence war, in the Clausewitzean definition, is war between states for a definable political end, i.e. state interest.

The notion of war as state activity was firmly established only towards the end of the eighteenth century. The only precedent for this type of war was ancient Rome, although even in this case it was one-sided; the state, i.e. Rome, fought against barbarians who had no notion of the separation of state and society. Van Creveld argues that war between the Greek city-states did not count as state warfare since there was no clear distinction between the state and the citizens. Wars were fought by citizen militias, and contemporary accounts of warfare tended to refer to war between 'the Athenians' and 'the Spartans' rather than to war between 'Athens' and 'Sparta'.[3]

Between the fall of the Roman Empire and the late Middle Ages, war was fought by a variety of actors – the Church, feudal barons, barbarian tribes, city-states – each with its own characteristic military formations. Hence, the barbarian mode of fighting was generally based on warrior cults, the individual warrior being the key military unit. Feudal barons depended on knights, with their codes of honour and chivalry, supported by serfs. The city-states of Northern Italy typically depended on citizen militias, much like the earlier Greek city-states.

In the early stages of European state formation, monarchs raised armies to fight wars from coalitions of feudal barons rather as the UN Secretary-General, today, has to mobilize voluntary contributions from individual states in order to raise a peacekeeping force. Gradually, they were able to consolidate territorial borders and to centralize power by using their growing economic assets, derived from customs duties, various forms of taxation and borrowing from the emergent bourgeoisie, to raise mercenary armies which gave them a certain degree of independence from the barons. However, mercenary armies turned out to be unreliable; their loyalty could not be counted on. Moreover, they were disbanded after wars or for the winter. The cost of disbandment and of re-enlistment was often prohibitive and, in the closed seasons, the mercenaries could always find other less savoury ways of making a living. Thus, mercenary armies came to be replaced by standing armies which enabled monarchs to create specialized, professional military forces. The introduction of drill and exercise, pioneered by Gustav Adolphus of Sweden and Prince William of Orange, kept the army occupied in periods when there was no open warfare. According to Keegan, the establishment of permanent infantry troops, the creation of *compagnies d'ordonnance* or regiments, became the 'device for securing the control of armed force by the state'. They were kept in garrison towns which became 'schools of the nation'.[4] Uniforms were introduced to distinguish soldiers from civilians. As Michael Roberts puts it, 'the soldier became the King's man for he wore the King's coat'[5] – literally, as it turned out, because kings increasingly tended to wear military uniforms to exhibit their roles as military commanders.

The new type of military organization was to become typical of the emerging administrative arrangements that were associated with modernity. The soldier was the agent of what Max Weber called rational-legal authority:

> The modern military officer is a type of appointed official who is clearly marked out by certain class distinctions . . . In this respect, such officers differ radically from elected military leaders; from charismatic condottieri; from the type of officers who recruit and lead mercenary armies as a capitalistic enterprise; and finally from the incumbents of commissions which have been purchased. There may be gradual transitions between these types. The patrimonial 'retainer' who is separated from the means of carrying out his function and the proprietor of a mercenary army for capitalistic purposes, have along with the private capitalistic entrepreneur, become pioneers of the modern type of bureaucracy.[6]

The establishment of standing armies under the control of the state was an integral part of the monopolization of legitimate violence which was intrinsic to the modern state. State interest became the legitimate justification for war, supplanting concepts of justice, *jus ad bellum*, drawn from theology. The Clausewitzean insistence that war is a rational instrument for the pursuit of state interest – 'the continuation of politics by other means' – constituted a secularization of legitimacy that paralleled developments in other spheres of activity. Once state interest had become the dominant legitimation of war, then claims of just cause by non-state actors could no longer be pursued through violent means.

In the same vein, there developed rules about what constituted legitimate warfare which were later codified in the laws of war. All types of warfare are characterized by rules; the very fact that warfare is a socially sanctioned activity, that it has to be organized and justified, requires rules. There is a thin dividing line between socially acceptable killing and what is ostracized by society. But that dividing line is defined differently in different periods. In the Middle Ages, the rules of warfare, *jus in bello*, were derived from papal authority. Under the modern state, a new set of secular rules had to be evolved. According to van Creveld:

> To distinguish war from mere crime, it was defined as something waged by sovereign states and by them alone. Soldiers

were defined as personnel licensed to engage in armed violence on behalf of the state . . . To obtain and maintain their license, soldiers had to be carefully registered, marked and controlled to the exclusion of privateering. They were supposed to fight only when in uniform, carrying their arms 'openly' and obeying a commander who could be held responsible for their actions. They were not supposed to resort to 'dastardly' methods such as violating truces, taking up arms again after they had been taken prisoner, and the like. The civilian population was supposed to be left alone, 'military necessity' permitting.[7]

In order to finance standing armies, administration, taxation and borrowing had to be regularized. Throughout the eighteenth century, military spending accounted for around three-quarters of state budgets in most European states. Administrative reform had to be undertaken to improve tax-raising capacities; corruption had to be limited, if not eliminated, to prevent 'leakage'.[8] War offices and secretaries of war had to be established to organize and improve the efficiency of expenditure. To extend borrowing, it was necessary to regularize the banking system and the creation of money, to separate the king's finance from the finance of the state and, ultimately, to establish central banks.[9]

Likewise, other means had to be found to establish law and order and justice within the territory of the state both to provide a secure basis for taxation and borrowing and for legitimacy. A kind of implicit contract was established whereby kings offered protection in exchange for funds. The elimination and/or outlawing of brigands, privateers and highwaymen eliminated private forms of 'protection', thus swelling the king's revenue-raising capacity, and created a basis for legitimate economic activity. Hence, parallel to the redefinition of war as war between states, as an external activity, was the process Anthony Giddens calls internal pacification, which included the introduction of monetary relations – e.g. wages and rent – in place of more direct coercion, the phasing out of violent forms of punishment such as flogging and hanging, and the establishment of civilian agencies for tax collection and domestic law-enforcement. Particularly important was the emerging distinction between the military and the civilian police responsible for domestic law and order.[10]

The process of monopolization of violence was by no means smooth and uninterrupted, nor did it take place at the same time or in the same way in different European states. The Prussian state, created after the Treaty of Westphalia out of the various pieces of territory held by the House of Hohenzollern, is often considered a model. This state, which was an entirely artificial creation, was able in the eighteenth century to match the military strength of France with only one-fifth of the population, owing to the vigorous combination of military reform and rational administration introduced by Frederick William, the Great Elector, and his successors. In contrast, French kings faced continual rebellions by the nobility and had enormous difficulty in regularizing administration and tax collection. Skocpol argues that a central consideration in explaining the French Revolution was the inability of the *ancien régime* to develop the administrative and financial capacity necessary to realize its military ambitions.[11]

Nor was the process as rational or as functional as this stylized description suggests. Michael Roberts insisted that it was military logic that led to the formation of standing armies. But it is difficult to distinguish the exigencies of war from the demands of domestic consolidation. Cardinal Richelieu favoured the establishment of a standing army because he saw it as a way to bring the nobles under control. Rousseau consistently argued that war was directed as much against subjects as against other states:

> Again, anyone can understand that war and conquest without and the encroachments of despotism within give each other mutual support; that money and men are habitually taken at pleasure from a people of slaves to bring others beneath the same yoke; and that conversely war furnishes a pretext for exactions of money and another, no less plausible, for keeping large armies constantly on foot, to hold people at awe. In a word, anyone can see that aggressive princes wage war at least as much on their subjects as on their enemies, and that the conquering nation is left no better off than the conquered.[12]

While rational state interest was claimed to be the goal of war, more emotive causes have always been required to instil loyalty and to persuade men to risk their lives. It was, after all, religious fervour that inspired Cromwell's New Model Army, which was the earliest example of a modern professional force. Prussian success is often attributed to the force of Lutheranism.

By the end of the eighteenth century, it was possible to define the specific socially organized activity which we perceive as war. It could be situated in the context of a whole series of new distinctions which were characteristic of the evolving state. These included:

- the distinction between public and private, between the sphere of state activity and non-state activity;
- the distinction between internal and external, between what took place within the clearly defined territory of the state and what took place outside;
- the distinction between the economic and the political which was associated with the rise of capitalism, the separation of private economic activity from public state activities, and the removal of physical coercion from economic activities;
- the distinction between the civil and the military, between domestic non-violent legal intercourse and external violent struggle, between civil society and barbarism;
- the distinction between the legitimate bearer of arms and the non-combatant or the criminal.

Above all, there emerged the distinction between war and peace itself. In place of more or less continuous violent activity, war became a discrete event, an aberration in what appeared to be a progressive evolution towards a civil society, not in today's sense of active citizenry and organized NGOs, but in the sense of day-to-day security, domestic peace, respect for law and justice. It became possible to conceive of 'perpetual peace'. Even though many of the great liberal thinkers understood the connection between state consolidation and war, they also anticipated that increasing interchange between states and growing accountability of states towards an informed public could usher in a more integrated Europe and a more peaceful world, an extension of civil society beyond national borders. It was Kant, after all, who pointed out in 1795 that the global community had shrunk to the point where a 'right violated anywhere could be felt everywhere'.[13]

Clausewitz and the Wars of the Nineteenth Century

Clausewitz began to write *On War* in 1816, one year after the ending of the Napoleonic Wars. He had participated in the wars on the losing side and had been taken prisoner, and the book is profoundly influenced by his experience. The Napoleonic Wars constituted the first people's war. Napoleon introduced conscription, the *levée en masse*, in 1793, and in 1794 he had 1,169,000 men under arms – the largest military force ever before created in Europe.

The central thesis of *On War*, particularly the first chapter, which was the only chapter Clausewitz considered to be completed, is that war tends towards extremes. War is composed of three levels – the level of the state or the political leaders, the level of the army or the generals, and the level of the people. Roughly speaking, these three levels operate through reason, through chance and strategy, and through emotion. From this trinitarian depiction of war, Clausewitz derived his concept of absolute war. Absolute war is best interpreted as a Hegelian abstract or ideal concept; it is the inner tendency of war that can be derived from the logic of the three different levels. It has its own existence, which is in tension with empirical realities.

The logic was expressed in terms of three 'reciprocal actions'. At a political level, the state always meets resistance in achieving its objectives and therefore has to press harder. At a military level, the aim has to be disarmament of the opponent in order to achieve the political objective, otherwise there is always a danger of counter-attack. And, finally, the strength of will depends on popular feelings and sentiments; war unleashes passion and hostility that may be uncontrollable. For Clausewitz, war was a rational activity even though emotions and sentiments were mobilized in its service. In this sense, it is also a modern activity based on secular considerations and not confined by prohibitions derived from pre-rational conceptions of the world.

Real war differs from abstract war for two main reasons – political and military. First, the political objective may be limited and/or popular backing may be insufficient:

> The more violent the excitement which precedes a War, by so much nearer will the War approach to its abstract form, so

much the more will it be directed to the destruction of the enemy, so much the nearer will the military and political ends coincide; so much the more purely military and less political the War appears to be, but the weaker the motives and the tensions, so much the less will be the natural direction of the military element – that is force – be coincident with the direction which the political element indicates; so much the more must, therefore, the War become diverted from its natural direction.[14]

Second, war is always characterized by what Clausewitz calls 'friction' – problems of logistics, poor information, uncertain weather, indiscipline, difficult terrain, inadequate organization and so on – all of which slow down war and make it different in reality from paper plans. War, says Clausewitz, is a 'resistant medium' in which uncertainty, inflexibility and unforeseen circumstance all play their part. Real war is the outcome of the tension between political and practical constraints and the inner tendency for absolute war.

As forces increased in scale, it became more and more difficult for organization and command to be carried out by a single person. Hence there was a growing need for a strategic theory which could provide the basis for a shared discourse about war through which war could be organized. As Simkin puts it, there was a need for a 'jargon' which could guide common military doctrines and what later became known as standard operating procedures.[15]

Clausewitz provided the basic building blocks of a body of strategic thinking that was developed during the nineteenth and twentieth centuries. The two main theories of warfare – attrition theory and manoeuvre theory – were initially developed in *On War* along with his discussion of offence and defence and of concentration and dispersion. Attrition theory means that victory is achieved by wearing down the enemy, by imposing on the enemy a higher casualty rate or 'attrition rate'; it is usually associated with defensive strategies and with high concentrations of force. Manoeuvre theory depends on surprise and pre-emption. In this case, mobility and dispersion are important to create uncertainty and to achieve speed. As Clausewitz pointed out, these two theories are necessarily complementary. It is very difficult to achieve a decisive victory through attrition. Yet, at the same time, a strategy based on manoeuvre ultimately needs a superiority of force to be successful.

The most salient conclusion of *On War* is the importance of overwhelming force and a readiness to use force. This apparently simple point was not obvious in the early nineteenth-century context in which Clausewitz was writing. In the eighteenth century wars were fought, by and large, prudently, in order to conserve professional forces. There was a tendency to avoid battle; defensive sieges were preferred to offensive assaults; campaigns were halted for the winter and strategic retreats were frequent. For Clausewitz, battle was the 'single activity of war'; it was the decisive moment, which he compared to cash payment in the marketplace. The mobilization of force and the application of force were the most important factors in determining the outcome of war:

> As the use of physical power to the utmost extent by no means excludes the cooperation of the intelligence, it follows that he who uses force unsparingly, without reference to the bloodshed involved, must obtain a superiority if his adversary uses less vigour in its application. The former then dictates the law to the latter and both proceed to extremities to which the only limitations are those imposed by the amount of counteracting force on each side.[16]

The Napoleonic model in which all citizens were mobilized was not to be repeated until World War I. However, several developments during the nineteenth century brought the Clausewitzean version of modern war closer to reality. One was the dramatic advance in industrial technology which began to be applied to the military field. Particularly important was the development of the railway and the telegraph, which enabled much greater and faster mobilization of armies; these techniques were used to great effect in the Franco-Prussian War, which ended with the unification of Germany in 1871. The mass production of guns, particularly small arms, was pioneered in the United States so that the American Civil War is often described as the first industrialized war. The development of military technology was one reason for the extension of state activity into the industrial sphere. The late nineteenth-century naval arms race marked the emergence of what was later to be described as the military-industrial complex in both Germany and Britain.

A second development was the growing importance of alliances. If overwhelming force was what mattered in war, then force could be augmented through alliances. By the end of the nineteenth century, alliances began to solidify – an important reason why the major powers were all drawn into World War I.

A third important development was the codification of the laws of war which began in the mid-nineteenth century with the Declaration of Paris (1856), which regulated maritime commerce in wartime. In the American Civil War, a prominent German jurist was employed to draw up the so-called Lieber Code, which laid down the rules and basic principles for war on land and treated the rebels as an international opponent. The Geneva Convention of 1864 (inspired by Henri Dunant, who founded the International Red Cross), the St Petersburg Declaration of 1868, the Hague Conferences of 1899 and 1907, and the London Conference of 1908 all contributed to a growing body of international law concerning the conduct of war – the treatment of prisoners, the sick and wounded, and non-combatants, as well as the concept of 'military necessity' and the definition of weapons and tactics that do not conform to this concept. While these rules were not always followed, they contributed importantly to a delineation of what constitutes legitimate warfare and the boundaries within which unsparing force could be applied. In a sense, they were an attempt to preserve the notion of war as a rational instrument of state policy in a context where the logic of war and the extremist tendencies of war, combined with growing techno-logical capacities, were leading to ever-increasing levels of destructiveness.[17]

To sum up, modern war, as it developed in the nineteenth century, involved war between states with an ever-increasing emphasis on scale and mobility, and an increasing need for 'rational' organization and 'scientific' doctrine to manage these large conglomerations of force.

The Total Wars of the Twentieth Century

In Clausewitz's work, there was always a tension between his insistence on reason and his emphasis on will and emotion. Men of genius and military heroes are central characters in *On War*; sentiments such as patriotism, honour and bravery are part of the fabric of the book. Equally significant, however, are his conclusions about the instrumental nature of war, the importance of scale and the need for an analytical conceptualization of war. Indeed, the tension between reason and emotion, art and science, attrition and manoeuvre, defence and offence, instrumentalism and extremism constitute the key components of Clausewitzean thought. This tension can be said to have reached breaking-point in the twentieth century.

First of all, the wars of the first half of the twentieth century were total wars involving a vast mobilization of national energies both to fight and to support the fighting through the production of arms and necessities. Clausewitz could not possibly have envisaged the awesome combination of mass production, mass politics and mass communications when harnessed to mass destruction. Nevertheless, war in the twentieth century came as close as can be conceived to Clausewitz's notion of absolute war, culminating in the discovery of nuclear weapons which, in theory, could wreak total destruction without 'friction'. But at the same time, some of the characteristics of the new wars were foreshadowed in the total wars of the twentieth century. In a total war, the public sphere tries to incorporate the whole of society, thus eliminating the distinction between public and private. The distinction between the military and the civil, between combatants and non-combatants, correspondingly starts to break down. In World War I, economic targets were considered legitimate military targets. In World War II, the term 'genocide' entered into legal parlance as a result of the extermination of the Jews.[18] On the Allied side, the indiscriminate bombing of civilians, creating a scale of devastation of genocidal proportions (even if it did not match the scale of extermination carried out by the Nazis), was justified on the grounds of breaking enemy morale – as 'military necessity', to use the language of the laws of war.

Second, as war involved more and more people, the justification of war in terms of state interest became increasingly hollow, if it ever had any convincing validity. War, as van Creveld points out, is a proof that men are not selfish. No individualistic utilitarian calculation can justify risking death. The main reason why mercenary armies were so unsatisfactory is that economic incentive is, of its nature, inadequate as a motivation for warfare. The same is true of 'state interest' – a concept that derives from the same school of positivistic thinking that gave rise to modern economics. Men go to war for a variety of individual reasons – adventure, honour, fear, comradeship, protection of 'home and hearth' – but socially organized legitimate violence needs a common goal in which the individual soldier can believe and which he shares with others. If soldiers are to be treated as heroes and not as criminals, then heroic justification is needed to mobilize their energies, to persuade them to kill and risk being killed.

In World War I, patriotism seemed sufficiently powerful to demand sacrifice, and millions of young men volunteered to fight in the name of King and Country. The terrible experience of that war led to disillusion and despair and an attraction to more powerful abstract causes – what Gellner calls secular religions.[19] For the Allied nations, World War II was literally a war against evil; whole societies were mobilized, knowing what war entailed in a way that their predecessors in World War I did not: the fight against Nazism and the protection of their own ways of life. They fought in the name of democracy and/or socialism against fascism. In the Cold War, the same ideologies were called upon to justify the ever-continuing arms race. To justify the threat of mass destruction, the Cold War was presented as a struggle of good against evil along the lines of the wartime experience. That this justification was either unconvincing or insufficient is probably the main explanation for the failure of post-war military interventions, particularly the American intervention in Vietnam and the Soviet intervention in Afghanistan. The obstacles to successful counter-insurgency have been extensively analysed, but the central point is that soldiers did not feel like heroes. These were faraway countries where the rights and wrongs of the situation were not self-evident. Those who participated in the wars felt, at best, like pawns in a game of high politics they could not comprehend and, at worst, like murderers. In the United States – although not in Russia, which was to repeat the same mistake in

Chechnya – where political leaders are highly conscious of public opinion, this experience led to a deep reluctance to risk American casualties. The consequence has been the development of strategies, based largely on air power in which force can be applied without risking loss of life on the American side, which Edward Luttwak calls 'Post-Heroic Warfare'.[20] In Iraq, the emphasis on force protection has greatly hampered the ability to stabilize the situation, even though it has not prevented casualties.

Gabriel Kolko, in his monumental work on twentieth-century warfare,[21] argues that wars are always started by a 'handful of men' who suffer from 'socially sanctioned blindness'. Political leaders operate within an elite consensus that excludes dissenters, and consequently this allows for the transmission of false information and misleading illusions about what a war involves. His argument offers strong support for the thesis that democracies are less likely to be involved in wars. Undoubtedly, more accountable leaders would be less likely to embark on impossible adventures. In the case of World War I, however, the blindness of political leaders seems to have been shared by ordinary men and women. In the case of World War II, at least in Britain, public opinion was probably more belligerent than the appeasing political leaders. But embarking on wars is only the beginning; what matters in sustaining war is the extent to which the goal of war is recognized by those who participate in the war as legitimate. War is a paradoxical activity. On the one hand, it is an act of extreme coercion, involving socially organized order, discipline, hierarchy and obedience. On the other hand, it requires loyalty, devotion and belief from each individual. What has become clear in the post-war period is that, at least in Western countries, there are few causes that constitute a legitimate goal for war for which people are prepared to die.

In fact, the idea that war is illegitimate already began to gain acceptance after the trauma of World War I. The Kellogg–Briand Pact of 1928 renounced war as an 'instrument of policy' except in self-defence. This prohibition was reinforced by the Nuremberg and Tokyo trials, in which German and Japanese leaders were prosecuted for 'planning aggressive war', and codified in the UN Charter. Nowadays, it does seem to have become widely accepted that the use of force is only justifiable either in self-defence or if it is sanctioned by the international community – in particular, the UN Security Council. Even the US administration, under George W. Bush, felt the need to justify the war in Iraq in terms of a new doctrine of 'pre-emptive self-defence' and to have at least the appearance of a 'coalition of the willing'.

Third, the techniques of modern war have developed to a point of sharply diminishing utility. The great battleships of the late nineteenth century turned out to be more or less irrelevant in World War I. What mattered was mass-produced firepower. World War I was a defensive war of attrition in which rows of young men, directed by generals schooled in nineteenth-century strategic thought to use force unsparingly, were mowed down by machine guns. Towards the end of the war, the introduction of tanks and aircraft enabled an offensive breakthrough which made possible the type of manoeuvre warfare which was to characterize World War II. In the post-war period, the increase in the lethality and accuracy of all munitions, due at least in part to the revolution in electronics, has greatly increased the vulnerability of all weapons systems. The weapons platforms of World War II have become extraordinarily complex and expensive, thus diminishing their utility because of cost and logistical requirements, combined with ever-diminishing improvements in performance.[22] The problems of mobilization and inflexibility, and the risks of attrition, have been magnified in the post-war period, making it almost prohibitive to mount a major operation except against a clearly inferior enemy, as in the Falklands/Malvinas War of 1982 or the Gulf operation of 1991.

The logical endpoint of the technological trajectory of modern war is, of course, weapons of mass destruction, particularly nuclear weapons. A nuclear war would be one in which force is applied in the extreme in a matter of minutes. But what rational purpose could ever justify their use? In the post-war period, many strategic thinkers have grappled with this problem. Do not nuclear weapons nullify the premise of modern warfare – state interest?[23]

Finally, in the post-war period, alliances have been rigidified so that the distinction between what is internal and what is external is also eroded. Already in World War II, it became apparent that individual nation-states could not fight wars unilaterally. This lesson was applied in the construction of the post-war alliances – NATO and the Warsaw Pact. Integrated command systems established a military division of labour in which only the superpowers had the independent capacity to wage full-scale wars. Essentially, European countries, in the post-war period, abandoned one of the essential attributes of sovereignty – the monopoly of legitimate organized violence – and, at least in Western Europe, what was effectively a trans-national civil society was extended to a group of nations. There is a widespread discussion about the social-science finding that democracies do not go to war with each other.[24] One explanation for this finding, which interestingly is rarely discussed in the literature, is the integration of military forces on a transnational basis which provides a practical constraint against war. Claus Offe makes a similar point about the 1989 revolutions in Eastern Europe; the reason they were so peaceful, he argues, was because of the integration of military forces in the Warsaw Pact, and this also explains the Romanian exception.[25]

Outside the European alliances, a network of military connections was established through looser alliances, the arms trade, the provision of military support and training, creating a set of patron–client relationships which also inhibited the capacity to wage war unilaterally. Since 1945, there have been very few inter-state wars, and these (India and Pakistan, Greece and Turkey, Israel and the Arab states) were generally restrained by superpower intervention. The exception, which proves the rule, was the Iran–Iraq War. This war lasted for eight years and could be waged unilaterally because of the availability of oil revenues. Both sides learned the disutility of modern conventional warfare. To quote van Creveld again:

A million or so casualties later, the belligerents found them-selves back at their starting points. The Iranians were taught that, in the face of massive firepower assisted by gas, their fanatic young troops would not be able to achieve a break-through except on the road to heaven. The Iraqis learnt that conventional superiority alone was incapable of inflicting a meaningful defeat on a large country with almost three times their own population.[26]

The erosion of the distinctions between public and private, military and civil, internal and external, also calls into question the distinction between war and peace itself. World War II was a total war, representing a fusion between war, state and society – a fusion which continued to characterize totalitarian societies. The Cold War sustained a kind of permanent war psychosis based on the theory of deterrence which is best encapsulated in the slogan 'War is Peace' in Orwell's *Nineteen Eighty-Four*. The Cold War kept alive the idea of war while avoiding its reality. The maintenance of large standing armies integrated in military alliances, the continued technological arms race, and the levels of military spending hitherto never experienced in peacetime were supposed to have guaranteed peace because no war of the stylized type described in this chapter broke out on European soil. At the same time, many wars took place all over the world, including Europe, in which more people died than in World War II. But because these wars did not fit our conception of war, they were discounted.

The irregular, informal wars of the second half of the twentieth century, starting with the wartime resistance movements and the guerrilla warfare of Mao Tse-tung and his successors, represent the harbingers of the new forms of warfare. The actors, techniques and counter-techniques which emerged out of the cracks of modern warfare were to provide the basis for new ways of socially organizing violence. During the Cold War, their character was obscured by the dominance of the East–West conflict; they were conceived as a peripheral part of the central conflict. Even before the end of the Cold War, when the threat of another 'modern war' really began to recede, we began to become aware of what Luttwak calls the new bellicosity.

3

Bosnia–Herzegovina: A Case Study of a New War

The war in Bosnia–Herzegovina lasted from 6 April 1992 until 12 October 1995, when a ceasefire agreement, brokered by the US Assistant Secretary of State Richard Holbrooke, came into effect. Some 260,000 people died and around two-thirds of the population were displaced from their homes. Violations of human rights took place on a massive scale, including forced detention, torture, rape and castration. Many historic monuments of incalculable value were destroyed.

The war in Bosnia–Herzegovina became the archetypal example, the paradigm of the new type of warfare in the 1990s. There are many other wars in the world, as Boutros Boutros-Ghali insensitively pointed out to Sarajevans when he visited the city on 31 December 1992. If human tragedies can be measured in numbers, it can even be asserted, as Boutros-Ghali did, that more terrible things have happened in other places.[1] But the war in Bosnia–Herzegovina impinged on global consciousness more than any other war in the last decade of the twentieth century.

The war mobilized a huge international effort, including high-level political talks involving all the major governments and the humanitarian efforts of international institutions and NGOs, as well as far-ranging media attention. Individual careers were made or broken, world status in the post-Cold War era was, at least partially, determined – the dismal inadequacy of the EU foreign policy-making capacity, the floundering of the UN, the US comeback, the redefinition of Russia's role, even the origin of the widespread belief that Muslims are the world's victims. Both the initial large-scale deployment of troops from NATO and Partnership for Peace countries and the subsequent EU military mission have had far-reaching implications for the role of NATO and for the institutional framework of European security as well as for the way in which we conceive of peacekeeping.

For these reasons, the war in Bosnia–Herzegovina could be considered one of those defining events in which entrenched political assumptions, strategic thinking and international arrangements are both challenged and reconstructed. While the 1991 Gulf War was significant as the first post-Cold War international crisis, the Bosnian crisis lasted longer and was more representative of wars of the 1990s. When the war began, the central actors in the so-called international community had not had time to adjust their inherited mindsets either about the character of war or about their perception of Yugoslavia. The international reaction was at best confused and sometimes stupid, at worst culpable for what happened. But during the war some attitudes changed, especially among those operating on the ground. A few far-sighted individuals, both from Bosnia itself and from within international institutions, were, in perhaps marginal ways, able to influence and encourage new ways of thinking. In particular, the experience of the war in Bosnia–Herzegovina helps to explain some of the profound differences between the United States and Europe on security issues.

This chapter traces the deficiencies of inherited ways of perceiving the war and sets out the need for a new type of analysis in relation to political and military assumptions about why and how wars are fought in the new century and the implications for international involvement.

Why the War was Fought – Political Goals

Bosnia–Herzegovina was the most ethnically mixed republic of former Yugoslavia; according to the 1991 census, the population consisted of Muslims (43.7 per cent), Serbs (31.4 per cent) and Croats (17.3 per cent), with the balance being made up of

Yugoslavs, Jews, Roma and people who described themselves in a variety of other ways, such as 'giraffes' or 'lampshades'. In fact, around a quarter of the population were intermarried and, in urban areas, a secular pluralistic culture flourished. The main difference between the ethnic groups was religion – the Serbs were Orthodox and the Croats were Catholic. In the first democratic elections of November 1990, parties which claimed to represent the different ethnic groups received over 70 per cent of the votes and controlled the National Assembly. These parties were the SDA (the Party of Democratic Action), which was the Muslim nationalist party, the SDS (the Serbian Democratic Party) and the HDZ (the Croatian Democratic Party). Although they promised during the election campaign that their aim was for the three communities to live peacefully together, these three groups became the parties to the conflict.

The political goal of the Bosnian Serbs and the Bosnian Croats, backed by Serbia and Croatia, respectively, was 'ethnic cleansing'. This phenomenon has been defined by the UN Commission of Experts as 'rendering an area ethnically homogeneous by using force or intimidation to remove from a given area persons from another ethnic or religious group.'[2] They wanted to establish ethnically homogeneous territories which would eventually become part of Serbia and Croatia, and to divide the ethnically mixed Bosnia–Herzegovina into a Serbian and a Croat part. To justify these goals, they used the language of self-determination which was drawn from the earlier communist rhetoric about wars of national liberation in the third world. The goal of the Bosnian government, which was controlled by the Bosnian Muslims, was the territorial integrity of Bosnia–Herzegovina, since Muslims were a majority in Bosnia–Herzegovina and had most to lose from partition; from time to time, the Bosnian government was prepared to consider a rump Muslim state or ethnic cantonization.

Ethnic cleansing was a characteristic of East European nationalism in the twentieth century. The term was first used to describe the expulsion of Greeks and Armenians from Turkey in the early 1920s. Ethnic cleansing takes a variety of forms, ranging from economic and legal discrimination to appalling forms of violence. The milder form was practised by Croatia after the elections of 1990 when Serbs began to lose their jobs and when Serb policemen in Serb majority areas were replaced. The form of violent ethnic cleansing that was to be typical of the war in Bosnia–Herzegovina was initiated by the Serbs in Croatia together with the JNA (the Yugoslav National Army) and sundry paramilitary groups, systematized by the Bosnian Serbs and their allies in Bosnia–Herzegovina, and copied by the Croats both in Bosnia–Herzegovina and in Croatia.

How is this form of virulent ethnic nationalism to be explained? The dominant perception of the war is expressed in the terms 'Balkanization' or 'tribalism'. The Balkans, it is argued, situated at the confluence of civilizations and caught historically between the shifting borders of the Ottoman and Austro-Hungarian empires, has always been characterized by ethnic divisions and rivalries, by ancient hatreds that persist just beneath the surface. These divisions were temporarily suppressed during the communist period, only to burst forth again in the first democratic elections. 'A Letter from 1920', a short story written by Ivo Andrić between the two world wars, is widely quoted as evidence for this view. In the story, a young man decides to leave Bosnia for ever, because it is 'a country of fear and hate'.[3]

This perception of the war, evident, for example, in David Owen's book, pervaded European policy-making circles and the high-level negotiations.[4] It was deliberately fostered by some of the parties to the conflict themselves. Thus Karadžić, the Bosnian Serb leader, said that Serbs, Croats and Muslims were like 'cats and dogs', while Tudjman, the Croatian president, repeatedly emphasized that Serbs and Croats could not live together because Croats were Europeans while Serbs were Easterners, like Turks or Albanians.[5] (Interestingly enough, he seems, at least from time to time, to think it is possible to live with Muslims since, in his view, they are really Croats, and Croatia and Bosnia–Herzegovina were traditionally united. On the other hand, the Serbs consider Muslims to be like Turks, in other words, like themselves, according to Croat conceptions!)

It is a view which corresponds to the primordial view of nationalism, that nationalism is inherent and deeply rooted in human societies deriving from organically developed 'ethnies'.[6] What it does not explain is why there are long periods of coexistence of different communities or nationalities, or why waves of nationalism take place at particular times. It does not explain the undoubted existence of alternative conceptions of Bosnian and indeed Yugoslav society as a rich unified culture, as opposed to multiculturalism, which includes the various religious communities and languages and also important elements of secularity.[7] Undoubtedly, Bosnia–Herzegovina has a grim history, especially during the twentieth century, but so do other parts of Europe. The view that aggressive nationalism is somehow peculiar to the Balkans allows us to assume that the rest of Europe is immune to the Bosnian phenomenon. The former Yugoslavia, despite the fact that it was earlier considered to be the most liberal of the communist regimes and first on the list of potential new members of the EU, has become a black spot in the middle of Europe surrounded by other supposedly more 'civilized' societies – Greece to the south, Bulgaria and Romania to the east, Austria, Hungary and Italy to the north and west. But what if the current wave of nationalism has contemporary causes? Does not the primordial view amount to a kind of myopia, an excuse for inaction, or worse?

There is an alternative view which holds that nationalism has been reconstructed for political purposes. This view corresponds more closely to the 'instrumentalist' conception of nationalism, according to which nationalist movements reinvent particular versions of history and memory to construct new cultural forms that can be used for political mobilization.[8] What happened in Yugoslavia was the disintegration of the state both at a federal level and, in the case of Croatia and Bosnia–Herzegovina, at a republican level. If we define the state in the Weberian sense as the organization which 'successfully upholds the monopoly of legitimate organized violence', then it is possible to trace, first, the collapse of legitimacy and, second, the collapse of the monopoly of organized violence. The emergence of virulent nationalism, which did indeed construct itself on the basis of certain traditional social divisions and prejudices – divisions which by no means encompassed the whole of contemporary Yugoslav society – has to be understood in terms of the struggle, on the part of increasingly desperate (and corrupt) elites, to control the remnants of the state. Moreover, in a post-totalitarian society, control is much more extensive than in more open societies, extending to all major social institutions – enterprises, schools, universities, hospitals, media and so forth.

To understand why the state ruptured along national lines can best be explained in terms of the recent history of Yugoslavia rather than by delving into the pre-communist past. The Titoist regime was a totalitarian regime in the sense of centralized control over all aspects of social life. It was more liberal than other regimes in Eastern Europe and allowed a certain degree of economic pluralism: from the 1960s Yugoslav citizens were allowed to travel and hold foreign currency accounts; artistic and intellectual freedom was much greater than in other communist countries. The political identity of the Yugoslav regime was derived, in part, from the struggle of the partisans during World War II; in part, from its capacity to provide reasonable living standards for the population; and, in part, from its special inter-national position as a bridge between East and West, with its own indigenous brand of socialism, and its role as leader of the non-aligned movement. As the memory of World War II faded and as the economic and social gains of the post-war period began to disappear, it was inevitable that its legitimacy would be called into question. The fall of the Berlin Wall, the democracy move-ments in the rest of Eastern Europe, and the end of the East–West division added a final blow to former Yugoslav identity.

Although the Yugoslav partisans had fought on the slogan 'Brotherhood and Unity' and the aim was to develop a new socialist Yugoslav man or woman, as in the Soviet Union, the regime had built into its functioning a complicated system of checks and balances to ensure that no ethnic group became dominant; in effect, it institutionalized ethnic difference. In order to counterbalance the numerical dominance of Serbs, six republics were established, each (with the exception of Bosnia–Herzegovina) with a dominant nationality – Serbia, Montene-gro, Croatia, Bosnia–Herzegovina, Slovenia and Macedonia. In addition, there were two autonomous provinces inside Serbia – Kosovo (where there was an Albanian majority) and Vojvo-dina (with a mixed population of Serbs, Croats and Hungari-ans). Despite this, polls consistently showed, up until the 1980s, growing support for Yugoslavism. This system was aug-mented by the 1974 constitution which devolved power to republics and autonomous provinces and established a mecha-nism for elite rotation based on ethnic arithmetic. Although the League of Communists retained its monopoly position, after 1974 the party itself increasingly divided along national lines. In a situation in which other political challenges were disallowed, a nationalist political discourse became the only form of legitimate debate. In effect, there were ten communist parties – one for each republic and autonomous province, one for the federation and one for the JNA. As Ivan Vejvoda points out, the 1974 constitution empowered collective actors, notably *nomenklatura* at the republican and provincial levels, while further disenfranchising individual citizens. It was decentralization of totalitarianism.[9] In this context, national communitarian identities were the obvious candidates to fill the vacuum created by the loss of Yugoslavism.

Yugoslavia experienced the strains of economic transition some ten years earlier than other East European countries.[10] During the 1950s and 1960s, the country experienced fast economic growth based on a model of rapid defence-oriented heavy industrialization that was typical of centrally planned economies. In the Yugoslav case, this was somewhat modified by the self-management model and the fact that agriculture, for the most part, remained in private hands. During this period, Yugoslavia received substantial amounts of foreign assistance because it was seen as a buffer against a possible Soviet attack on Southeast Europe. In the 1970s, Western aid began to decline and was replaced by commercial loans, which were relatively easy to acquire following the oil crisis. As in the case of other centrally planned economies, Yugoslavia had great difficulty restructuring its economy; this was compounded by the slowdown in growth in Western countries, which inhibited the growth of exports and reduced the earnings from remittances from Yugoslavs working abroad, and by the growing autonomy of the republics and self-governing provinces who felt no responsibility for the balance of payments and competed with each other to create money.

By 1979, the debt had reached crisis proportions – some $US 20 billion. An International Monetary Fund (IMF) Recovery Plan was agreed in 1982 which included both liberalization and austerity. The main effect of this plan was to intensify the competition for resources at the level of the republics and to contribute to the growing criminalization of the economy. The federation was unable to control the creation of money, and by

December 1989 the monthly inflation rate had reached 2500 per cent. Unemployment averaged 14 per cent throughout the decade; particularly hard hit were urban middle classes, largely dependent on state salaries and pensions, and rurally based industrial workers, who were forced to survive on what they could produce from their small agricultural plots. A series of corruption scandals in the late 1980s, especially in Bosnia–Herzegovina, revealed the growing links between the degenerate ruling elite and a new class of mafia types. Typical in this respect was the Agromerc scandal which revealed the nefarious activities of Fikret Abdić, longtime party boss in Bihać, who was later to become a key figure in the war. Nationalist arguments were a way of coping with economic discontent, appealing to the victims of economic insecurity and concealing the growing *nomenklatura*–mafia alliance.

By the end of the 1980s the unravelling of Yugoslav statehood had gathered pace. The last federal prime minister, Antje Marković, tried to reimpose control at a federal level with a programme of 'shock therapy' introduced in January 1990. Despite the success of the programme in reducing inflation, it caused immense resentment at the level of republics because it effectively removed their 'license to print money'.[11] By November 1990, Yugoslavia as a single economic space was challenged by various unilateral economic actions – above all, massive Serbian borrowing to pay for the imposition of Serbian rule in Kosovo, known as the 'Great Bank Robbery', but also the Slovene refusal to contribute to the Fund for Underdeveloped Regions and the unilateral Croatian abolition of excise tax on cars, effectively bribing voters with the promise of cheaper foreign cars.

Yugoslavia as a single communicative space also unravelled. By the 1970s, each republic and province controlled its own television and radio. There was occasional rotation of news programmes on the first channel and news from other republics and autonomous provinces could be seen (by rotation) on the second channel. This broke down in the late 1980s.[12] Despite the last-ditch attempt by Marković to establish an all-Yugoslav television, *Yutel*, the media were effectively nationalized, providing a powerful basis for nationalist propaganda.

By 1990 federal legitimacy had been challenged, at the level both of legislatures and of the judiciary. The first democratic elections were held in the republics and not at a federal level. When the federal constitutional court challenged decisions taken by the newly elected republican parliaments, such as the Slovene decision not to contribute to the Fund for Underdeveloped Regions or the Slovene and Croatian declarations of sovereignty, these legal opinions were ignored. A similar disregard for constitutional decisions taken at a republican level was shown by those Serbs in Croatia who wanted to declare a 'Serbian Autonomous Region'.

Finally, the last vestige of Yugoslav statehood was removed in 1991, when the monopoly of organized violence broke down. The JNA had been the bastion of Yugoslavism.[13] Already by the 1970s Territorial Defence Units (TOs) were established in the republics as a result of a new 'Generalized Popular Defence System' introduced after the Soviet invasion of Czechoslovakia in 1968. By 1991 the JNA was increasingly being used as a tool of Slobodan Milošević, the President of Serbia, while the Slovenes and Croats were secretly organizing and arming their own independent forces based on the TOs and the police through the growing black market for surplus arms then emerging in Eastern Europe. At the same time, the Serbs were creating their own paramilitary groups. In particular, they initiated their plan 'RAM' (Frame), secretly to arm and organize the Serbs in Croatia and Bosnia–Herzegovina. The JNA utterly failed in its efforts to disarm the paramilitaries (the Croats and Slovenes claimed that their forces were not paramilitary groups but legal defence forces) and ended up siding with the Serb paramilitary groups in Croatia and Bosnia.[14]

The emergence of a new form of nationalism paralleled the disintegration of Yugoslavia. It was new in the sense that it was associated with the disintegration of the state, in contrast to earlier 'modern' nationalisms which aimed at state-building, and that, unlike earlier nationalisms, it lacked a modernizing ideology. It was also new in terms of the techniques of mobilization and the forms of organization. It was Milošević who was the first to make extensive use of the electronic media to propagate the nationalist message. His 'anti-bureaucratic revolution', which aimed to remove the Titoist system of checks and balances perceived as discriminating against Serbs, provided the basis for a populist political appeal over the heads of the existing communist hierarchy. Through mass rallies, he legitimized his hold on power. The victim mentality often characteristic of majorities who feel themselves minorities was nurtured with an electronic diet of tales of 'genocide' in Kosovo, first by the Turks in 1389 and more recently by the Albanians, and of holocaust in Croatia and Bosnia–Herzegovina, with clips of World War II interspersed with current developments. In effect, the Serbian public experienced a virtual war long before the real war was to take place – a virtual war that made it difficult to distinguish truth from fiction so that war became a continuum in which the 1389 battle of Kosovo, World War II and the war in Bosnia were all part of the same phenomenon. David Rieff describes how Bosnian Serb soldiers, after a day of shooting from the hills around Sarajevo, would ring their Muslim friends in the town. This extraordinarily contradictory behaviour made perfect sense to the soldiers because of the psychological dissonance produced by this virtual reality. They were not shooting at their private friends, but at Turks. 'Before the summer ends', one soldier told Rieff, 'we will have driven the Turkish army out of the city, just as they drove us from the field of Kosovo in 1389. That was the beginning of Turkish domination of our lands. This will be the end of it, after all these cruel centuries . . . We Serbs are saving Europe even if Europe does not appreciate our efforts.'[15]

If Milošević perfected the media technique, it was Tudjman who developed the horizontal transnational form of organization. Unlike Milošević, he came from a dissident background, having spent time in prison in the early 1970s for his nationalist views, although formerly he had been a JNA general. His party – the HDZ – had little time to prepare for the first democratic elections, and did not control the media. Tudjman, however, had been mobilizing support among the Croatian diaspora in North America. He claimed that the HDZ had branches in thirty-five North American cities, each with fifty to several hundred members and some with up to two thousand members. The diaspora was always regarded with great suspicion by the communist authorities; émigrés were largely considered to be former *Ustashe* (the wartime Croatian fascists). Tudjman said later that the most crucial political decision he had ever made was to invite the émigrés back for the HDZ Congress in February 1990.[16] This transnational form of organization was a highly significant source of funds and election techniques and, subsequently, arms and mercenaries. It induced another form of virtual reality arising from the time–space distantiation of diaspora party members, who were, in effect, imposing on a contemporary situation an image of Croatia which dated from when they had left.

The process of disintegration and the rise of a new form of virulent nationalism was encapsulated in Bosnia–Herzegovina, which had always been a mixed society. The differentiation of communities along religious lines (Orthodox, Catholic, Muslim and Jewish) had been institutionalized during the latter part of Ottoman rule through the millet system and, in various forms, this 'institutionalized communitarianism', as Xavier Bougarel calls it,[17] was sustained throughout Austro-Hungarian rule (1878–1914) and during the first and second Yugoslavias. Nevertheless, in the post-war period there were many mixed marriages and, particularly in cities, the communitarian logic was supplanted by a modern secular culture. Yugoslavism was particularly strong in Bosnia–Herzegovina. It was in this republic that *Yutel* was most popular and that Marković was to choose to launch his reform party.

Bougarel distinguishes 'institutionalized communitarianism' from political and territorial nationalism. The former depends on a balance between communities which is known as *komsiluk* (good neighbourliness) and which is threatened by political or military mobilization, as happened during the two world wars. The re-emergence of political nationalism in the late 1980s occurred, as was the case earlier, for instrumental reasons. It was a response, according to Bougarel, to discontent arising from uneven development and to the growing divide between the economic and scientific elite and backward rural regions. This divide was especially acute in Bosnia–Herzegovina and was exacerbated during the 1980s. It was also a response to the loss of legitimacy of the ruling party.

Six months before the 1990 elections, a poll conducted in Bosnia–Herzegovina showed that 74 per cent of the population favoured the banning of nationalist parties. Yet, when the election did take place, 70 per cent of the voters supported these parties. This discrepancy can be explained in terms of Bougarel's argument. Most people feared the threat to *komsiluk* represented by the nationalist parties. But once political mobilization took place, they found it necessary to rally to their community. Even so, other factors also need to be taken into account. On the one hand, the League of Communists in Bosnia–Herzegovina was traditionally considered hard line and slow to adapt to the wave of democracy that was affecting the rest of Eastern Europe – the nationalist parties represented the most obvious alternative to the communists. Moreover, it was discredited by a series of corruption scandals in the late 1980s. On the other hand, the speed of nationalist mobilization is explained partly by the role of Croatia and Serbia. The HDZ, the Croat nationalist party, was actually a branch of Tudjman's party, and the SDS, the Serb nationalist party, was a branch of the Serbian nationalist party that was established in the Krajina, the Serb-dominated part of Croatia. In addition, *Matica Hrvatska*, the Croatian cultural centre in Zagreb, and the Serbian Academy of Sciences, responsible for the notorious 1986 memorandum which first set out a Serb nationalist pro-gramme, both played an active role in mobilizing nationalist sentiment, together with the religious institutions.

The elections were won by the nationalist parties and they formed an uneasy coalition – not surprisingly, given the con-flicting nature of their political goals. In particular, the SDS members of the Assembly were repeatedly outvoted by the SDA and the HDZ. The non-nationalist civic parties won 28 per cent of the vote; they were supported largely by urban intellectuals and industrial workers. The war was precipitated by the decision of the international community to recognize Slovenia and Croatia and any other former Yugoslav republic provided it held a referendum and recognized minority rights (something that was ignored in the Croatian and Bosnian cases). The SDA and HDZ favoured independence; the Serbs did not.

Bougarel concludes that the contradictory portrayals of Bosnia–Herzegovina as a land of tolerance and coexistence and as a country of fear and hate are, in fact, both true. Fear and hate are not endemic but, in certain periods, are mobilized for political purposes. The very scale of the violence can be inter-preted not as a consequence of 'fear and hate', but rather as a reflection of the difficulty of reconstructing 'fear and hate'. As Živanović, an independent-minded liberal who remained in Serb-controlled areas throughout the war, put it: 'The war had to be so bloody because the ties between us were so strong.'[18]

This mobilization of 'fear and hate' takes specific forms in specific periods and has to be explained in terms of specific causes. In other words, the new nationalism is a contemporary phenomenon arising from recent history and shaped by the current context.

It is sometimes argued that Muslim nationalism is a different phenomenon from Serb and Croatian nationalism. Those who oppose the dominant perception of the war as a civil war often argue that this was a war of Serbian and, to a lesser extent, Croatian aggression. It is certainly true that Bosnian Serb nationalists, aided and abetted by the Serbian and Yugoslav governments, were the aggressors in this war, and it was they who initiated and applied most systematically and extensively the policy of ethnic cleansing. Likewise, Croat nationalists, backed by the Croatian government, followed their example, albeit on a lesser scale. It is also the case that the SDA, the Muslim nationalist party, was always in favour of a unified multicultural Bosnia–Herzegovina. However, multicultural-ism, for the Muslim nationalists, meant political organization along communitarian lines – hence, Izetbegović's attempts to organize 'acceptable' ethnic groupings such as the Serb Civic Council or the Croat Peasants' Party. Moreover, the SDA did display some of the inclinations of other nationalist parties – such as the tendency to impose rigid political control over all institutions, or the use of the media to generate a virtual war against other communities: the SDA magazine, *Dragon of Bosnia*, was especially shrill in its calls for nationalist violence.[19] The UN Commission of Experts says that Bosnian forces did not engage in ethnic cleansing, although they committed war crimes. However, Croatians were certainly expelled or chose to leave from parts of Central Bosnia captured by Bosnian forces during the Muslim–Croat conflict, and this was also true of Serbs in areas captured during the last days of the war. In other words, this was a war of Serbian and Croatian aggression, but it was a new nationalist war as well.

That fear and hate were not endemic to Bosnian society became apparent in the outburst of civic activism during the run-up to the war.[20] A mass peace movement developed with strong support from the Bosnian media, trade unions, intel-lectuals, students and women's groups. Tens of thousands of people formed a human chain across every single bridge in

Mostar in July 1991. A *Yutel*-organized rally in Sarajevo in August 1991 was attended by 100,000 people. In September, 400 European peace activists, travelling as the Helsinki Citizens Assembly Peace Caravan, joined thousands of Bosnians in a human chain which linked the mosque, the Orthodox church, the Catholic church and the synagogue in Sarajevo. Similar demonstrations were organized in Tuzla and in Banja Luka and other towns and villages.

The highpoint and the end of the movement came in March and April 1992. On 5 March, peace activists succeeded in pulling down barricades erected by Muslim and Serb nationalist groups after a Serb bridegroom had been shot at his wedding. On 5 April, 50,000 to 100,000 demonstrators marched through Sarajevo to the parliament building to demand the resignation of the government and to ask for an international protectorate. Thousands more came in busloads from Tuzla, Zenica and Kakanj but could not enter the city because of Serb and Muslim barricades. The war began when Serb snipers fired on the demonstrators from the Holiday Inn – the first person to die was a twenty-one-year-old medical student from Dubrovnik.[21] The following day, Bosnia–Herzegovina was recognized by European states and the Serbs left the Bosnian Assembly. The state was recognized at the very moment of its disintegration.

According to Bougarel, the Bosnian war was a civil war in the sense that it was a war *against* the civilian population and *against* civil society.[22] And Tadeusz Mazowiecki, the Special Rapporteur for the UN Commission on Human Rights, reports the belief of some observers that 'the attacking forces are determined to "kill" the city [Sarajevo] and the tradition of tolerance and ethnic harmony that it represents'.[23] Or to put it another way, the war could be viewed as a war of exclusivist nationalists against a secular multicultural pluralistic society.

How the War was Fought – Military and Economic Means

Yugoslavia was probably the most militarized country in Europe outside the Soviet Union. Until 1986, military spending amounted to 4 per cent of GNP – more than any other non-Soviet European country except Greece.[24] The JNA itself consisted of some 70,000 regular officers and staff, plus around 150,000 conscripts. In addition, each republic and autonomous province was responsible for organizing and equipping the TOs, largely reserve forces, which were reportedly 1 million strong.

The JNA remained a Yugoslav entity up to 1991. The army controlled a network of interconnected bases, weapons stores and enterprises, which, in contrast to the rest of the economy, were organized on a Yugoslav-wide basis. Even though the partisan strategy which informed JNA organization was based on decentralized local combat formations, control remained centralized at a Yugoslav level. Among JNA officers, 70 per cent of whom were Serbian or Montenegrin, Yugoslavism continued to grow at a time when it was declining in other spheres of social life. The JNA accounted for the bulk of the federal budget and, by 1991, it seemed as though the JNA and the League of Communists were virtually all that was left of the Yugoslav idea – hence, Yugoslavism came to be associated with totalitarianism and militarism.

From 1986 to 1991 military spending fell dramatically, from $US 2491 million in constant 1988 prices to $US 1376 million,[25] thus contributing to a growing sense of victimization and paranoia about internal and external enemies within the JNA. (The arrest of young Slovenian journalists who had criticized arms exports to the third world in 1988, and the subsequent notorious trial, was an expression of this paranoia.) The story of the wars in Slovenia, Croatia and, above all, Bosnia–Herzegovina is also the story of the break-up of the Yugoslav military-industrial complex. The JNA and the TOs disintegrated into a combination of regular and irregular forces augmented by criminals, volunteers and foreign mercenaries competing for control over the former Yugoslavia's military assets.

At the outset of the war in Bosnia–Herzegovina, there was a bewildering array of military and paramilitary forces. In theory, there were three parties to the conflict – the Serbs, Croats and Bosnians. In practice, different forces cooperated with each other in differing combinations throughout the war. Thus, in the early stages of the war, the Croats and Bosnians cooperated against the Serbs. Then, after the publication of the Vance–Owen Plan in 1993, which was based on ethnic cantonization, the Croats and Muslims started fighting each other, since the Croats wanted to establish control of 'their' cantons. Then came the Washington Agreement between the Muslims and Croats, imposed by the Americans, and, in the final stages of the war, the Muslims and Croats cooperated again, at least officially. During the course of the war, the forces of each party to the conflict were increasingly centralized and regularized. By the end of the war, the main regular forces were the Bosnian Serb Army (BSA), the Croatian Defence Council (HVO) and the Army of Bosnia–Herzegovina (ABiH).

After the ten-day war in Slovenia in June 1991, the JNA withdrew to Croatia (leaving their weapons behind). By mid-July 1991, the JNA had moved an estimated 70,000 troops into Croatia. Together with some 12,000 irregular Serb forces, both local volunteers and (often criminal) groups imported from Serbia proper, they experimented with the strategies that were to be used in Bosnia–Herzegovina. After the ceasefire in Croatia the JNA withdrew to Bosnia–Herzegovina, taking with them their equipment. In May 1992, the JNA formally withdrew from Bosnia–Herzegovina. In practice, only some 14,000 troops withdrew to Serbia and Montenegro; approximately 80,000 troops transferred to the Bosnian Serb Army.

The HVO was formed out of the militia attached to the HDZ. It operated together with the Croatian army (HV), which was formed on the basis of Croatian territorial defence forces and built up during the course of the war with training assistance from a private company formed by American retired generals called Military Professional Resources Incorporated (MPRI).[26]

There was no Bosnian army when the war broke out. Essentially, the defence of Bosnian territory was locally organized. Sarajevo was defended by a motley crew of patriotic leagues and other paramilitary groups, largely organized by the Sarajevo underground. Tuzla was defended by the local police force augmented by a locally organized patriotic league. Although Izetbegović announced the formation of a regular army in May 1992, it was not until Silajdžić became prime minister in the autumn of 1993 that the various gangster groups were control-led and the army command was centralized. Even at that time, the UN Commission of Experts estimated that, of 70,000 troops, only 44,000 were armed.[27]

The BSA was much better equipped than the other regular forces, as can be seen from table 3.1. In particular, it had a considerable advantage in heavy weapons – tanks, artillery, rocket launchers and mortars. It inherited the JNA's equipment and, more importantly, it controlled most of the JNA's weapons stores; these had been situated in the hills of Bosnia–Herzegovina, because this was envisaged to be the heartland of any guerrilla-based defence of Yugoslavia, and had been well stocked in anticipation of a long war. The ABiH, which was the least well equipped and suffered, in particular, from a dearth of heavy weapons, was dependent on Croatian supply routes to acquire arms.[28] The HVO received equipment from Croatia. In addition to equipment taken from weapons stocks in Croatia, various black-market sources were used to acquire mainly surplus ex-Warsaw Pact equipment. (Interestingly, there was some evidence that ex-JNA enterprises in Croatia, Slovenia and Serbia continued to cooperate to produce spare parts and equipment.)[29]

It is possible to identify, in addition to the regular forces, three main types of irregular force: paramilitary organizations, generally under the control of an individual; foreign mercenary groups; and local police augmented by armed civilians. The UN Commission of Experts identified eighty-three paramilitary groups on the territory of former Yugoslavia – some fifty-six were Serbian, thirteen were Croatian and fourteen were Bosnian. The estimated size of these forces was 20,000 to 40,000, 12,000 to 20,000 and 4000 to 6000 respectively. The vast majority of these acted locally, but certain groups operated

Table 3.1 *Regular forces in Bosnia–Herzegovina 1995*

	Armed forces	Main battle tanks	Artillery	Multiple rocket launchers	Mortars
ABiH	92,000	31	100	2	200
HVO	50,000	100	200	30	300
BSA	75,000	370	700	70	900

Source: *Military Balance 1995–6*, International Institute for Strategic Studies, London, 1996.

much more widely in conjunction with regular forces and gained considerable notoriety.

On the Serb side, the two most well-known groups were Arkan's 'Tigers' and Šešelj's Chetniks or 'White Eagles'. Arkan, whose real name was Željko Ražnjatović, was a big figure in the Belgrade underworld. He owned a string of ice-cream parlours, allegedly a cover for his smuggling activities, which expanded considerably during the war. Before the war, he had apparently been recruited by a special unit in the Yugoslav government in order to assassinate émigrés. He also owned the fan club of the Belgrade Red Star football team and his Tigers were recruited from the club. The Tigers initially operated in Croatia; in Bosnia–Herzegovina they were reported as operating in twenty-eight counties. According to reports collected by the UN Commission: 'Their hair was cut short and they wore black woollen caps, black gloves cut off mid-finger, and black badges on the upper arm. According to other reports, they wore multicoloured uniforms, red arrows, knit caps, a badge showing the Serbian flag on the right arm, and an emblem showing a tiger and the words "Arkanove delije" on the shoulder.'[30] The Tigers were well armed, including tanks and mortars. Šešelj had been a dissident. He had taught at the University of Sarajevo and, reportedly, spent a year at the University of Michigan.[31] He was imprisoned in the early 1980s for his anti-communist writings. After he was released, he moved to Belgrade, where he joined the Serbian nationalists. His party, the Serbian National Renewal Party, gained seats in the 1990 elections and was particularly successful in the federal elections of May 1992, when he won 33 out of 138 seats. Like the Tigers, the Chetniks were initially active in Croatia. In Bosnia–Herzegovina, they were reported to operate in thirty-four counties. The Šešeljovci were 'bearded men'. They wore Serbian military berets with a Serbian military flag on the front, or black fur hats with a Serbian cockade. They were reportedly always drunk and they recruited additional 'weekend fighters'.

Both Arkan and Šešelj seem to have operated together with the JNA. According to the UN Commission: 'In many of these counties, Šešelj and Arkan exercised control over other forces operating in the area. These forces consisted of local paramilitary groups, and sometimes the JNA. In some counties, Šešelj's and Arkan's forces operated under the command of the JNA.'[32]

Šešelj always insisted that his forces were armed and equipped by Milošević.

The most well-known Croatian paramilitary group was HOS, a wing of the Croatian Party of Rights (HSP). Its members wore black uniforms and the Croatian chequered shield like the wartime *Ustashe*. Up to 1993, when their leader Dobroslav Paraga was arrested for trying to overthrow the Croatian government, HOS operated in conjunction with the HVO. Another Croatian paramilitary group was the 'Wolves' led by Jusuf Prazina, known as Juka. He was an underworld figure from Sarajevo before the war broke out and had been in prison five times. The Wolves wore 'crew-cuts, black jump-suits, sun glasses and sometimes masks'.[33] They operated together with the ABiH until August 1992 and then worked with the HVO.

The two notorious gangsters, Ćaco and Celo, operated in Sarajevo up until the autumn of 1993. Ćaco had been a club musician called Musan Topalović, and Celo was a criminal who had just come out of prison after serving eight years for rape. Most paramilitary groups on the Bosnian side were referred to as Green Berets or Muslim Armed Forces (MOS) and reportedly operated under the command of the ABiH.

The names of other paramilitary groups include Black Swans, Yellow Ants (which referred to their looting abilities), Mečet's Babies, Mosque Pigeons, Knights, Serbian Falcons, and so on. Among mercenaries, the most well known were the *Mujahidiin*, mostly veterans from the Afghan wars. They were supposed to have been expelled under the Dayton Agreement. They reportedly operated in Zenica, Travnik, Novi Travnik, Mostar and Konjic. According to Croat intelligence, they were organized by a man named Abdulah, who owned the 'Palma' video shop in Travnik. The UN Commission suggests that the *Mujahidiin* acted more or less independently of the ABiH. Other mercenaries included the Garibaldi Unit (Italians fighting alongside the Croats) and Russians fighting on the Serbian side, as well as mercenaries from Denmark, Finland, Sweden, Britain and the United States. British soldiers made redundant in the post-Cold War cuts took up positions training both Bosnian and Croatian forces.

Local militia were organized by municipalities, as in Tuzla, or by big enterprises, as in Velika Klusa, in Fikret Abdić's

Agromerc, or in Zenica, where the former communists still controlled the steelworks.

During the war, the formal economy collapsed. This was the result of a combination of factors: physical destruction, impossibility of acquiring inputs, and loss of markets. Industrial production was estimated at 10 per cent of its pre-war level and unemployment was between 60 and 90 per cent. The currency collapsed; exchange was based on a combination of barter and Deutschmarks. For the most part, people faced a painful choice: they could live insufficiently off humanitarian aid; they could volunteer for the army or become a criminal or both; or they could try to leave. Many people left, especially the young and educated, so that the population decline was even more dramatic than the figures on ethnic cleansing suggest.

The various military forces were totally dependent on outside sources of assistance. These included direct support from outside governments, 'taxation' of humanitarian assistance, and remittances from individuals. The regular forces were largely funded and equipped by sponsor governments. The BSA was funded by the Serbian government up to the embargo, imposed by Milošević in August 1994. The HVO was funded by Croatia, and the ABiH received support from Islamic states and, covertly, from the USA. The paramilitaries were funded from loot and extortion of expelled people, as well as confiscation of equipment, etc., from conquered territories, 'taxation' of humanitarian aid, which they collected at many checkpoints, and the black market. The local militia were funded by municipalities who received the 'taxes' from humanitarian assistance collected on their territory and also continued to tax citizens, including those who were abroad, and enterprises on their territory. All three types of force cooperated with each other both militarily and economically.

The strategy adopted by this combination of regular and irregular forces – a strategy practised most consistently and systematically by the Bosnian Serbs as well as by the Bosnian Croats – was territorial gain through political control rather than military offence. Violence was used to control populations rather than to capture territory. The difficulty of acquiring territory through military offence was made plain quite early on in the war in Croatia. The JNA experienced the classic problems of offence which have become typical of modern war, as was illustrated by the Iran–Iraq War. The two-month siege of Vukovar, a town in East Slovonia, Croatia, from September to October 1991, showed how massive superiority in both firepower and manpower was insufficient to capture a relatively small town. When Vukovar eventually fell, on 20 November 1991, it had been reduced to rubble. The attempt to take Dubrovnik, which, according to the memoirs of the then minister of defence, General Kadijević, was part of a plan to occupy Split and the Dalmatian Coast, failed.[34] A characteristic feature of the war in Bosnia was the siege of the main Bosnian cities. Although they could not be captured, they could be shelled continuously and cut off from supplies.

Except in the early stage of the war in Bosnia–Herzegovina, when the Bosnian Serbs faced very little opposition, and in the last stages of the war, when they had become very weak, little territory changed hands. Essentially, the war was directed not against opposing sides, but against civilian populations. This explains why there was no continuous front. Instead, different areas were controlled by different parties, and forces were interspersed in what the UN Commission describes as a 'chequered' military map, with confrontation lines in and around cities encircling the areas of control. Indeed, in late 1993, before the Washington Agreement between Muslims and Croats, territory under Bosnian control basically consisted of a few enclaves surrounded by hostile forces, what some described as a 'leopard skin' territory. With the exception of Banja Luka, which was under Serb control, and Mostar, which was divided between Croats and Muslims, most towns remained under Bosnian control while the countryside was divided between Serbs and Croats.

Apart from a few strategic points, e.g. the Brcko corridor, which connected Serb territories and which potentially provided a communication route from Northern Bosnia to Zagreb, there was relatively little fighting between the opposing sides. There were, indeed, various examples of cooperation, mostly in the black market, but also differing short-term and local military cooperation between different parties. On one occasion, UNPROFOR (the United Nations Protection Force) intercepted a telephone conversation between the local Muslim commander in Mostar and the local Serb commander discussing the price in German marks to be paid if the Serbs would shell the Croats. The nadir was reached when the Serbs took Mount Igman, overlooking Sarajevo, in July 1993; the paramilitary groups at that time defending Mount Igman were ready to 'sell' their positions in order to control the black-market routes. Most of the violence was directed against civilians – the shelling of cities and towns combined with sniper fire and various forms of atrocity within the towns and villages – and became, in effect, what was known as ethnic cleansing.

The Bosnian Serbs wanted to create an autonomous Bosnian Serb territory. But since there were almost no areas except Banja Luka where Serbs were numerically dominant and, perhaps more importantly, where extremist Serbs were numerically dominant, this had to be brought about through ethnic cleansing. The areas seem to have been chosen for strategic reasons, to link the Serb-held territories in Krajina with Serbia and to control JNA bases and weapons stores. The tactic of establishing 'Serb autonomous areas' seems to have followed a consistent pattern first worked out in the war in Croatia. Descriptions of the process can be found in numerous reports of journalists, UN agencies and independent NGOs such as Helsinki Watch.

The typical pattern applied to rural areas – villages and small towns. First, the regular forces would shell the area and issue frightening propaganda so as to instil a mood of panic. Reports of terror in neighbouring villages would add to the panic. Then the paramilitary forces would close in and terrorize the non-Serb residents with random killing, rape and looting. Control over local administration would then be established. In the more extreme cases, non-Serb men were separated from the women and killed or taken to detention centres. Women were robbed and/or raped and allowed to go or taken to special rape detention centres. Houses and cultural buildings such as mosques were looted, burned or blown up. The paramilitary groups also seem to have had lists of prominent people – community leaders, intellectuals, SDA members, wealthy people – who were separated from the rest and executed. 'It was the conscious elimination of an articulate opposition and of political moderation. It was also the destruction of a community from the top down.'[35] The television journalist Michael Nicholson refers to this process as 'elitocide' and the mayor of Tuzla talked about 'intellectual cleansing'.

The existence of detention centres became known in August 1992. The UN Commission of Experts identified some 715, of which 237 were operated by Bosnian Serbs, 89 by the ABiH and government and 77 by Bosnian Croats. According to the Commission, they were the scene of 'the worst inhumane acts', including mass executions, torture, rape and other forms of sexual assault. (Although grave breaches of the Geneva Conventions were reported in the Bosnian camps, the allegations were fewer and less systematic than in the Serbian and Croatian camps.) A specific aspect of the process of ethnic cleansing has been widespread rape. Although mass rape has taken place in other wars, its systematic character, in detention centres and in particular places and at particular times, suggests that it may have been part of a deliberate strategy.[36]

In urban areas, in particular Banja Luka, ethnic cleansing was a slower, more legalistic process. The lives of non-Serbs were made untenable. For example, they were removed from their jobs, with no access to medical care; communication was cut off; they were not allowed to meet in groups of more than four. In many towns, variously described Bureaux for Population Exchange were established through which non-Serbs or non-Croats could surrender their property and pay large sums to be allowed to leave.[37]

Similar techniques were adopted in Croat-controlled areas. In Bosnian-controlled areas the evidence does not suggest deliberate ethnic cleansing, although many non-Muslims, especially Serbs, left for a variety of reasons, including psychological pressure, discrimination and forced recruitment in the army.[38] By the end of 1995, ethnic cleansing was almost complete, as can be seen from table 3.2. Only 13,000 Muslims remained in Northern Bosnia, according to UNHCR estimates, out of an original population totalling around 350,000, and only 4000 Muslims and Croats remained in East Bosnia and South Herzegovina, out of an original population totalling 300,000. Many Serbs and Croats had also left Tuzla and Zenica.

The worst atrocities, certainly in the early stages of the war, seem to have been committed by paramilitary groups. According to the UN Commission: 'There is a . . . strong correlation between reports of para-military activity and reports of rape and sexual assault, detention facilities and mass graves. These types of activity (i.e. para-military activity and grave breaches

Table 3.2 *Ethnic cleansing in Bosnia–Herzegovina*

	1991 census				Estimates November 1995[a]			
	Serbs	Croats	Muslims	Total	Serbs	Croats	Muslims	Total
Bihac	29,398	6,470	202,310	238,178	1,000	5,000	174,000	180,000
Northern Bosnia–Herzegovina	624,840	180,593	355,956	1,161,389	719,000	9,000	13,000 [38,000 in Dec 94]	741,000
Zenica	79,355	169,657	328,644	577,656	16,000	115,000	439,000	570,000
Tuzla	82,235	38,789	316,000	437,024	15,000	19,000	659,000 [629,000]	693,000
Sarajevo	157,526	35,867	259,085	432,478	n/a	n/a	n/a	455,000
Enclaves	20,000		80,000	100,000			50,000 [115,000]	50,000
West Herzegovina/West-Central Bosnia	43,595	245,586	111,128	400,309	5,000	320,000	160,000	485,000
East Bosnia/South Herzegovina	304,017	40,638	261,003	605,658	450,000	4,000[b]	see previous column	454,000
Total	1,340,966	717,600	1,655,300	3,972,692	1,206,000 (−Sarajevo)	470,000	1,497,000	3,628,000

Notes: Figures in square brackets show numbers in November 1994.

[a] These figures are almost certainly overestimates, since more than a million Bosnian refugees left the country.

[b] This figure refers to both Croat and Muslim communities.

n/a Not available.

Source: UNHCR, Information Notes on Former Yugoslavia 11/95, Zagreb, 1995.

of the Geneva Conventions) tended to occur in the same counties and evidence the localised nature of the activity.'[39] On the
Serbian side, the activities of Arkan and Šešelj are well known;
the UN Commission suggests that these were coordinated with
the activities of the JNA (BSA), whereas, on the Croatian and
Bosnian sides, the paramilitary groups acted more independently of regular forces. On the Croatian side, Paraga is said to
have organized the detention camps at Capljina and Dretelj,
while Juka was reported to have killed some 700 Muslims in
Mostar and was responsible for the detention camp at the heli-
port.[40] On the Bosnian side, the worst atrocities seem to have
been committed by the *Mujahidiin*.

The motivation of the paramilitary groups seems to have
been largely economic, although there were clearly nationalist
fanatics among them. According to Vasić, around 80 per cent
of the paramilitaries were common criminals and 20 per
cent were fanatical nationalists: 'The latter did not last long
(fanaticism is bad for business).'[41] Arkan, reportedly, had lists
of rich Muslims in possession of gold and money. The 'right
to be the first to loot' was viewed as a form of payment.[42]
Many former criminal groups were able to expand their pre-
war rackets; most of the paramilitary groups were involved
in black-market activities and, indeed, cooperated with each
other across supposed confrontation lines in order to profit
from the situation in besieged enclaves. Effectively, paramilitary groups were 'hired' to do the dirty work necessary to
instil the 'fear and hate' which was not yet endemic in Bosnian
society. Thus, the mafia economy was built into the conduct
of warfare, creating a self-sustaining logic to the war both
to maintain lucrative sources of income and to protect criminals from legal processes which might come into effect in
peacetime.

The situation was better in a few places where the local state
apparatus survived. One example was Tuzla, where the non-
nationalists had won the 1990 elections. Tuzla was defended
by the local police and local volunteers, who later became a
local brigade of the Bosnian army, and an ideology of multicultural civic values was vigorously promoted. Throughout the
war, the city maintained local energy sources and some local
production, including mining. At the height of the war,
when the town was completely cut off, the people lived off

humanitarian assistance and rent in kind from UNPROFOR. By the end of the war, taxes raised in Tuzla accounted for 60 per cent of the total tax revenue of the Bosnian government. Nevertheless, it has proved very difficult for these islands of relative civility to survive in what Bougarel calls the communitarianized predatory economy.[43]

Towards the end of the war, the local militia and paramilitary groups were absorbed into the regular armies. The former became local brigades and the latter became 'Special Units'. The capture of Srebrenica, a classic ethnic-cleansing operation, in July 1995 was entirely carried out by the BSA. On the third day, the Special Units were sent in to undertake the most gruesome task – the massacre of 8000 men and boys. On all sides, there were failed attempts to create a mobilization economy. In particular, after Serbia imposed a blockade on the Bosnian Serbs in August 1994, the BSA was reduced to self-finance. The Bosnian Serb government tried to centralize finance and take control of key sectors, but this was rejected by the so-called Serb parliament, whose members were linked in to the criminal economy. On all sides, but especially the Serb side, morale was very low at the end of the war. Vasić suggests that the BSA had only 30,000 effective troops. Many people, especially young people, had left; poverty, criminality and indiscipline were rife.

How far was the strategy of ethnic cleansing planned in advance? Or was it chanced upon by Serb forces in Croatia? The UN Commission says that the JNA's Department of Psychological Operations was reported to 'have had several plans for local provocation by special forces controlled by the Ministry of the Interior and "ethnic cleansing"'.[44] It quotes an article in the Slovenian newspaper *Delo* which claimed that, along with the plan 'RAM' (to arm the Serbs in Croatia and Bosnia–Herzegovina), the JNA had an additional plan for mass killings of Muslims and mass rapes as a weapon of psychological warfare: 'Analysis of the Muslims' behaviour showed their morale, desire for battle, and will could be crushed most easily by raping women, especially minors and even children, and by killing members of the Muslim nationality inside their religious facilities.'[45]

It is sometimes suggested that the JNA drew on its history as a partisan movement. It is certainly true that the localized and decentralized nature of the war has many parallels with guerrilla warfare. The organization of TOs meant that many trained reservists could be drawn into the war at a local level and that small arms in local weapons caches were easily available. However, in many ways, ethnic cleansing is the exact opposite of guerrilla warfare, which depended on the support of the local population; the guerrilla was supposed to be the 'fish in the sea', to use Mao's words. The aim of ethnic cleansing was the wholesale destruction of communities, the manufacture of 'fear and hate'. One speculation is that JNA thinking was perhaps influenced by counter-insurgency doctrines, as developed by the Americans in Vietnam and tried out in the low-intensity conflicts of the 1980s. Alex de Waal has suggested that African military strategists were influenced by these doctrines, and this may, in part, explain the similarities of the Bosnian War to the wars in Africa.[46] Undoubtedly, JNA staff would have studied these wars. The last Yugoslav minister of defence, General Kadijević, had spent six months at West Point Military Academy, although counter-insurgency was only a minor part of the curriculum there, and other JNA officers had also studied in the United States. It is probably more convincing to argue that the strategy of ethnic cleansing was developed on the ground, although prior discussions and experience must have had some relevance.

It was not only members of other ethnic groups who were targeted in the strategy of ethnic cleansing. It was moderates as well, those who refused to hate. This was first learned in Croatia when Babić and Martić, the leaders of the Krajina Serbs, seized control of the town of Pakrac and removed Serbs as well as people of other nationalities in positions of authority. Throughout the war, there were people on all sides who refused to be drawn into the mire of 'fear and hate'. The reports of the Special Rapporteur for the UN Commission on Human Rights consistently notes the actions of brave Serbs who tried to protect their Muslim and Croat neighbours. *The Guardian* newspaper reported a Serb 'Schindler' living in Prijedor who organized his friends and neighbours to protect Muslims. The Jewish community in Mostar organized itself to help Muslims escape. Even though their ranks have been greatly depleted by death and flight, non-nationalist groups and parties still exist in different parts of Bosnia–Herzegovina.

The Nature of International Involvement

From the beginning, international involvement in the war in Bosnia–Herzegovina, and indeed in all the conflicts on the territory of former Yugoslavia, was extensive. This involvement took place both at an official level and at the level of civil society. The war became the focus of media attention and of peace, humanitarian and human rights groups, as well as of civic institutions such as churches or universities. Within the former Yugoslavia, great hopes were vested in the role of the international community. For many people, the term 'Europe' had an almost mystical significance; it was considered synonymous with civilized behaviour and emblematic of an alternative 'civic' outlook to which those who opposed nationalism aspired. What actually happened was deeply disappointing, giving rise to cynicism and despair.

In fact, there were two quite distinct forms of international involvement. One was the high-level political talks and missions. The other was, in effect, a new form of humanitarian intervention. The latter, I would argue, did in fact represent a considerable innovation in international action both in its goals and in its scale and in the way it fostered cooperation between international institutions and civil society. But it was fatally thwarted by the contradictions between what was happening at a humanitarian level and what was happening at the level of high politics, and, connectedly, by misconceptions about the political and military nature of the war.

There have been many explanations for the failure of the international community to prevent or stop the wars in the former Yugoslavia – lack of cohesion in the EU, unwillingness of governments to provide adequate resources, the short-termism of politicians. All these explanations have something in them. But the fundamental problem was conceptual, the failure to understand why or how the war was fought and the character of the new nationalist political formations that emerged after the collapse of Yugoslavia. Both politically and militarily, the war was perceived as a conflict between competing nationalisms of a traditional essentialist type, and this was true both of the Europeans who, like the Serbs, argued that the nationalisms were all equally to blame, and of the Americans, who tended to see the Serbs as bad 'totalitarian' nationalists and the Croats and Muslims as good 'democratic' nationalists. While Serbian and Croatian nationalism was definitely bad nationalism and Muslim nationalism was not quite so bad, such an analysis missed the point that this was a conflict between a new form of ethnic nationalism and civilized values. The nationalists had a shared interest in eliminating an internationalist humanitarian outlook, both within the former Yugoslavia and globally. Both politically and militarily, their war was not against each other but, to repeat the argument of Bougarel, against the civilian population and against civil society.

The so-called international community fell into the nationalist trap by taking on board and legitimizing the perception of the conflict that the nationalists wished to propagate. In political terms, the nationalists had a common totalitarian goal: to re-establish the kind of political control the Communist Party had once enjoyed on the basis of ethnic communities. To this end, they had to partition society along ethnic lines. By assuming that 'fear and hate' were endemic to Bosnian society and that the nationalists represented the whole of society, the international negotiators could see no other solution but the kind of compromise which the nationalists themselves aimed to achieve. By failing to understand that 'fear and hate' were not endemic but were being manufactured during the war, they actually contributed to the nationalist goals and helped to weaken the internationalist humanitarian outlook.

In military terms, it was assumed that the main violence was between the so-called warring parties and that civilians were, so to speak, caught in the crossfire. While the evidence of ethnic cleansing was plain to see, this was treated as a side-effect of the fighting, not as the goal of the war. The UN troops that were sent to Bosnia–Herzegovina to protect the civilian population were hamstrung because their masters were so fearful of being dragged into a conventional war. A sharp distinction was drawn between peacekeeping and war-fighting. Peacekeeping meant that the troops operated on the basis of consent between the warring parties. War-fighting would have meant taking sides. Throughout the war, the fear that any use of force would mean taking sides and would escalate the international military involvement prevented UN troops from effectively carrying out the humanitarian tasks they were sent to perform. What was not understood was that there was rather little fighting between the sides in the conventional sense and that the main problem was the continuing violence against civilians. The UN troops were supposed to be peace-keeping troops; they operated on the basis of consent. The consequence was that they were unable to protect aid convoys or safe havens; instead, they stood by, as one Sarajevan wag put it, 'like eunuchs at the orgy'.

The predominant approach in the high-level talks was an approach 'from above', a *realpolitik* approach, in which it was assumed that the leaders of political parties spoke for the people they represented. The problem of how to deal with the debris of Yugoslavia was thus understood as a problem of reaching a compromise with those leaders. Essentially, it was conceived as a problem of borders and territory, not as a problem of political and social organization. Since ethnic cleansing was seen as a side-effect of the war, the main concern was to stop the fighting by finding a political compromise acceptable to the warring parties. If the political leaders in the former Yugoslavia insisted that they could not live together, then some new set of territorial arrangements had to be found for the post-Yugoslav political space. Hence, the answer was partition. But partition was a cause of war as much as a solution. It was self-perpetuating since, as everyone knew, there was no way to create ethnically pure territories without population displace-ment. Since ethnic cleansing was the goal of the war, the only possible solution was one which accepted the results of ethnic cleansing. Thus, the very principle of partition legitimized nationalist claims.

The first partition was that of Yugoslavia, when Slovenia and Croatia, and later Bosnia–Herzegovina, were recognized.[47] At the same time, Croatia was partitioned after the ceasefire nego-tiated by Cyrus Vance, the UN envoy, in December 1991. The recognition of Bosnia–Herzegovina took place on the day that war broke out. In the efforts to halt the fighting, a series of doomed plans to partition Bosnia–Herzegovina were put forward, culminating in the Dayton Agreement. The first plan was the Carrington–Cuteleiro Plan of the spring of 1992, which proposed to divide the country into three parts. After the failure of this plan, Lord Carrington resigned as EU negotiator and was replaced by David Owen, who became joint chairman with Cyrus Vance of the International Conference on Former Yugoslavia (ICFY), established after the London Conference in August 1992. The Vance–Owen Plan was considered to be an improvement on the Carrington–Cuteleiro Plan because it divided Bosnia–Herzegovina into ten cantons, nine of which were based on the domination of one or other of the ethnic groups. The plan was eventually rejected by the Bosnian Serb Assembly in May 1993, but not before it had provided the legitimation for the Croats to ethnically cleanse the regions they were awarded under the plan: this marked the beginning of the Croat–Muslim conflict. (It was said that HVO stands for 'Hvala Vance Owen' – 'Thank you Vance Owen'.) Under pressure from the Americans, a Muslim–Croat ceasefire was negotiated in the spring of 1994; essentially, the Washington Agreement, as the ceasefire agreement was known, established a Bosnian–Croat federation partitioned into even smaller ethnically dominated cantons. Meanwhile, the Vance–Owen Plan was replaced by the Owen–Stoltenberg Plan (Cyrus Vance having been replaced by Thorvald Stoltenberg), which was in turn supplanted by the Contact Group Plan – the Contact Group being a new negotiating forum involving the major outside players (the USA, Russia, Britain, France and Germany). Both these plans and the Dayton Agreement that eventually succeeded in halting the fighting were very similar to the original Carrington–Cuteleiro Plan.

The Dayton Agreement finally succeeded in bringing about a ceasefire, partly because of military pressure (NATO finally undertook air strikes and an Anglo-French Rapid Reaction Force was sent to Bosnia), partly because of the collapse of Bosnian Serb morale, and perhaps most importantly because the military situation on the ground had been 'rationalized', with the Serb capture of two of the Eastern enclaves and the Croatian capture of the Krajina.[48] In other words, ethnic cleansing was virtually complete. Such was the ease of the military endgame that it has been suggested that there may have been some tacit understanding between Serbia and Croatia, perhaps even encouraged by outside players.[49] Certainly, the eventual partition was close to what Milošević and Tudjman had discussed way back in March 1991, at a famous meeting in Karadjordjevo.[50]

The negotiators were strongly criticized for even talking to the warring parties. How could they be seen to shake hands with people named as war criminals? How could they treat Izetbegović, the president of a recognized country, on a par with the Bosnian Serbs and the Bosnian Croats?[51] Those engaged in the negotiations make the point that those who make the war are the only ones who can stop it and therefore there are no alternatives to talks between the warring parties. There is something in this argument, but these talks should not have been given the priority they received in the overall policy. There were ways in which the non-nationalist political and civic parts of Bosnian society could have been given access to governments and international institutions, in which their ideas and proposals, including proposals for alternatives to partition, could have been heard and taken seriously and in which they were publicly seen to have the respect of the international community. They represented the hope for international values; they should have been seen as the main partners in the search for peace. There was an utter failure to understand that the nationalists did not and could not, because of the nature of their goals and the way in which they were pursued, appeal to 'hearts and minds', and that it was of vital importance to foster a political alternative.

In parallel with the high-level talks was the humanitarian intervention. At an early stage in the conflict, Mrs Ogata, the High Commissioner for Refugees, put forward a seven-point humanitarian response plan which was accepted by governments and international agencies in July 1992. The seven points were: 'respect for human rights and humanitarian law, preventive protection, humanitarian access to those in need, measures to meet special humanitarian needs, temporary protection measures, material assistance, and repair and rehabilitation'.[52] UNHCR took the lead role in a massive humanitarian effort providing aid to around two-thirds of the population of Bosnia–Herzegovina, and it coordinated the activities of a range of international humanitarian agencies and NGOs. Many courageous individuals contributed to this effort as aid workers, medical personnel, convoy drivers, etc. In addition to the aid effort, a series of measures were adopted by the UN aimed at protecting the civilian population and upholding international humanitarian law. These included the decision to protect humanitarian convoys, by force, if necessary (Security Council Resolution (SCR) 770 (1992)); the declaration of safe areas (SCR 836 (1993)); the appointment of a Special Rapporteur for Human Rights by the Commission on Human Rights (August 1992); the appointment of a Commission to investigate war crimes (October 1992) and, in particular, rape (December 1992); and the establishment of 'an international tribunal for the prosecution of persons responsible for serious violations of international humanitarian law' (SCR 808 (1993)). The International Committee of the Red Cross (ICRC) was charged with gaining access to detention camps and organizing prisoner releases. And in the Washington Agreement, an EU administration was established to administer Mostar with the aim of reuniting the city.

These measures, at least in theory, represented a very significant innovation in international practice. Adopted under pressure from the international media, which exposed the reality of the war, and from campaigning groups, they constituted a potential new form of international humanitarianism. Although elements of the package had been introduced in previous conflicts – the safe haven/area concept in Iraq, the protection of humanitarian convoys in Somalia – this was the most ambitious deployment of UN peacekeeping troops designed to assist and protect the civilian population and to uphold humanitarian law. Moreover, the wording of the relevant Security Council resolutions was strong. Both SCR 770 (1992), which called for protection for humanitarian convoys and unimpeded access for the ICRC and other humanitarian organizations to 'camps, prisons and detention centres', and SCR 836 (1993), which established safe areas, were under Chapter VII of the UN Charter, which authorizes the use of force.[53] Some 23,000 UNPROFOR troops were sent to Bosnia–Herzegovina.

In addition to the UNPROFOR troops, NATO and the Western European Union (WEU) maintained naval forces in the Adriatic monitoring the arms embargo, and NATO was responsible for enforcing the No Fly Zone over Bosnian air space, which was also authorized under Chapter VII (SCR 816 (1993)).

However, almost none of these measures was effectively implemented. Humanitarian aid was constantly obstructed and 'taxed' by the warring parties. The safe areas became vast insecure refugee camps constantly subjected to shelling; humanitarian supplies were controlled sadistically by the Bosnian Serbs. War crimes continued to be committed, despite the efforts of Mazowiecki, the UN Commission of Experts and the Tribunal, the ICRC and other humanitarian organizations – indeed some of the worst instances of ethnic cleansing occurred in the last few months of the war. The No Fly Zone was violated on countless occasions and the arms embargo was never strictly maintained. Despite the EU administration, Mostar continued to be divided, freedom of movement was still restricted and numerous violations of human rights were recorded. Many UN personnel themselves engaged in black-market activities, and allegations of crimes committed by UN personnel, especially rape, were never properly investigated. The nadir for the UN came in July 1995, when the so-called safe areas of Srebrenica and Zepa were overrun by Bosnian Serb forces.

Was any other approach possible once the war had begun? In political terms, David Owen argues that the first priority was to stop the fighting. But even now, after Dayton, it can be asked whether an agreement would ever have been reached before the parties were ready for it and whether the role of the international negotiators was anything more than a way of facilitating and legitimizing an agreement which, at least, the Serbs and the Croats wanted to reach. The consequence is that it is now extremely hard, as has already become clear, to dislodge the nationalists and war criminals from power, making long-term peace or normality a distant prospect.

Had the war been understood as, first and foremost, a war of genocide, then the first priority would have been the protection of the civilian population. Negotiations and political pressure could have focused on concrete goals on the ground to ease the humanitarian situation – such as the opening of Tuzla airport or the Mount Igman route to Sarajevo, or the release of prisoners – rather than on partition. The inclusion of non-nationalist parties and groups in the negotiation process could have assisted this task and made possible other 'take it or leave it' overall solutions not based on partition, such as an international protectorate.[54] At the very least, such an approach would have strengthened the alternatives to nationalism, thus obstructing the manufacture of 'fear and hate', and would have left the legitimacy of international organizations more intact. On several occasions, Mazowiecki complained about the lack of cooperation with ICFY: 'The Special Rapporteur requested that human rights concerns should have priority in the peace process, and pointed out that peace negotiations should not have been conducted without ensuring the cessation of massive and gross human rights violations.'[55]

Militarily, a different perception might have led to a tougher, more 'robust' approach to peacekeeping. The belief that this was a war with 'sides' led to an extreme timidity about the use of force for fear that this would escalate and drag the international community into the war on one side or another. General Michael Rose was obsessive about crossing what he called the 'Mogadishu line', in reference to the failure of the UN mission in Somalia. It can, with equal justice, be argued that a tougher approach would have made the task easier and UN forces and personnel much less vulnerable than they were to hostage-taking or sporadic attacks. When in 1993 British soldiers, escorting a relief convoy to Tuzla from Kladanj, started to shoot back at Serbs firing from the hills, harassment was dramatically reduced. Yet General Morillon, the then Commander of UNPROFOR troops in Bosnia–Herzegovina, was reprimanded by the UN Secretary-General for 'exceeding his mandate'. A similar story can be recounted when a Danish officer in Tuzla ordered a tank to fire on the Serbs in retaliation for shelling.

For those on the ground, the frustration was immense, both for the UNPROFOR personnel themselves who were being ordered to appear to be cowards and for the personnel of humanitarian organizations who found their task as difficult as it had been before the arrival of the UN troops. Since humanitarian passage had to be negotiated anyway, this could as easily be done by the sheer willpower of people such as UNHCR's Larry Hollingsworth or Gerry Hulme than by a toothless UNPROFOR. As Larry Hollingsworth pointed out when leaving Bosnia:

> If you send in an army but don't allow it to be aggressive, why send in firepower and tanks? I'm left sadly with the conclusion that the troops were sent in not to be tough but to look tough ... We should have been much tougher from the

beginning. The UN missed the chance to seize the initiative and be forceful, and we have seen a gradual chipping away of authority ever since.[56]

Owen himself argues that tougher peacekeeping was impossible because there were insufficient troops. He points out that it is not feasible, for example, to defend the 55-mile route from Sarajevo to Goradze, which crosses two mountain ranges, forty-four bridges and two narrow ravines: 'Calls for "robust" or "muscular" action from politicians, retired generals and commentators in television studios were greeted with hollow laughs from the men on the ground.'[57] But the argument can be put the other way round. The troops were equally, if not more, vulnerable if they were not prepared to use force, and this was clearly understood by the warring parties; hence, the temptation to expose this and to humiliate the international community by, for example, hostage-taking. Tougher action would have required regrouping and refusal to undertake certain tasks, for example monitoring as opposed to destroying heavy weaponry.

For similar reasons, Owen is very dismissive of the safe haven/area concept. It is true that UNPROFOR originally asked for 30,000 troops to defend the safe areas and argued that, at a pinch, they could make do with 10,000. In the end the Security Council authorized 7500 troops, but money was appropriated only for 3500 troops. The problem was that this argument was used to explain why nothing could be done, instead of intensifying the pressure for more troops. Towards the end of the war, increasing pressure from individuals such as General Morillon or Mazowiecki as well as public opinion did lead eventually to the deployment of the Rapid Reaction Force on Mount Igman and the toughening of the rules of engagement for the Implementation Force (IFOR).

In the end, the main use of force was air strikes, which had always been advocated by the Americans because they are a way of using force without risking casualties. Operation Deliberate Force lasted from 29 August to 14 September 1995; in all, 3515 sorties were flown and more than 1000 bombs were dropped.[58] Air strikes did help to put pressure on the Bosnian Serbs as a prelude to the Dayton Agreement and, supposedly, they deterred an attack on the last eastern enclave, Goradze.

But air strikes are a cumbersome instrument for protecting civilians on the ground, and it was the protection of civilians that was needed above all else. Many people argue that the deployment of the Rapid Reaction Force was more effective.

What was needed, in effect, was not peacekeeping but humanitarian law-enforcement. This does represent a considerable challenge. It requires new strategic thinking about how to counter strategies of population control through ethnic cleansing – how to develop support and promote alternative sources of legitimacy among the local population, new rules of engagement and norms of behaviour, appropriate equipment, forms of organization and command structures.

After Dayton

The longest and most destructive war in Europe since 1945 ended after three and a half years. The international operation mounted to implement the agreement involved an array of institutions – the UN, the EU, the Council of Europe, the OSCE, NATO and the WEU. For NATO, IFOR and its successor, the stabilization force (SFOR), was the largest operation ever undertaken by the alliance. Moreover, NATO was joined by Partnership for Peace countries, formerly members of the Warsaw Pact. Since December 2004, the EU has taken over NATO's role; even though this is not the first autonomous EU military mission, it marks a significant step forward in the development of a common European security policy. The process of implementation has been an important learning experience for the international community, exposing many of the same contradictions that dogged international involvement from the start of the war.

Indeed, the Dayton Agreement could be viewed as a product of those contradictions. It was primarily an agreement born of the *realpolitik* approach of high-level negotiators who perceived the world as divided into primordial nations. It was an agreement which partitioned Bosnia–Herzegovina into three statelets[59] and in which the parties to the agreement – i.e. the nationalists – were primarily responsible for its implementation. Nevertheless, the agreement also contained clauses which commit the parties, including the international community, to a humanitarian approach – clauses about human rights, the prosecution of war criminals, the return of refugees, freedom of movement, economic and social reconstruction. The agreement granted considerable power to the NATO commander and to the high representative responsible for civilian implementation.

Initially, the military side was much more effective than the civilian side. But the tasks that the military undertook – maintaining the ceasefire, separating the warring parties, controlling weapons stores – conformed to the logic of partition. The lack of capacity for public security as well as lack of will permitted the displacement of large numbers of Serbs from Sarajevo in the immediate aftermath of Dayton and continued low-level ethnic cleansing for months after the agreement was signed. Gradually, however, the civilian side has become stronger under successive high representatives. Various measures have been taken to integrate the three communities and to build a common state. These include the integration of the three armies and police reform; the common currency, flag, and licence plate; property laws, which facilitate refugee return; dismissal of extremist politicians and support for moderate democratic or civic politicians; and freedom of movement. Moreover, during this period, military forces deployed in Bosnia have begun to develop a capacity for humanitarian law-enforcement. From 1997, they began, together with local forces, to arrest war criminals, to redeploy forces in such a way as to protect returning refugees, and to act in support of the police in controlling criminality, ensuring freedom of movement, and preventing the worst manifestations of nationalist defiance. For example, in 1997, SFOR seized the transmitter of SRT (the Serb radio and television station which had been broadcasting anti-SFOR propaganda) and, in April 2001, OHR and SFOR seized control of the Herzogovacka Banka in Mostar and in other towns, which was the main source of HDZ finances.

Despite all these efforts, nationalist politicians remain popular and democratic structures are very weak. Essentially, in today's Bosnia, the choice is between imperialist humanitarianism and extreme nationalism. The recent high representative, Paddy Ashdown, was accused of acting like a 'European Raj'.[60] Yet the alternative to a strong international protectorate is nationalist partition and perhaps renewed warfare. The casualty of the war was democratic politics. The nationalist politicians who were responsible for starting the war succeeded in creating a genuine grass-roots nationalism that had hardly existed before the war. The trauma of the war left a trail of fear and insecurity, guilt and mistrust – emotions that cannot easily be allayed but which seek reassurance in the apparent certainties of ethnic identification. Moreover, the economy has never recovered from the impact of the war and the disintegration of Yugoslavia. Unemployment remains at 40 per cent, and many people are still dependent on a variety of illegal or informal activities which, up to now, have received 'protection' from the nationalist parties.

In other words, the nationalists won the war. The top-down realist approach of the international community during the war, unwittingly perhaps, legitimized their position. The humanitarian approach, which was exemplified by the efforts to establish safe havens and international administrations, was never strong enough to protect cosmopolitan politics. By the time the international community had learned from its mistakes, many of their potential partners in Bosnian civil society and politics had been killed or terrorized or had left the country. Moreover, even now, the emphasis is on the construction of institutions rather than cooperation with civil society and helping to foster democratic or cosmopolitan politics. The courageous strategy of Paddy Ashdown, high representative from 2002 to 2006, might have saved multiculturalism in the immediate aftermath of Dayton. Unfortunately, it simply came too late.

The big question is whether the practical experience of humanitarian law-enforcement and state-building, as well as the weakness of economic reconstruction efforts, can influence the philosophy and organization of international interventions in the future, particularly those involving the European Union, or whether international interventions have become discredited. Was the experience of the Bosnian War a brief moment between the Cold War and the War on Terror when a humanitarian international approach seemed possible? Or will the intervention have left a lasting legacy that will enable the European Union to pursue a new approach towards security?

4

The Politics of New Wars

During the war in Bosnia–Herzegovina, Sarajevo was divided territorially between a Serb-controlled part and a Bosnian (mainly Muslim) part. But wartime Sarajevo could also be described in terms of a non-territorial divide. There was a group of people who could be described as the globalists – UN peace-keepers, humanitarian agencies, journalists and Sarajevans who spoke English and were employed as assistants, interpreters and drivers. Protected by armoured cars, flak jackets and blue cards, they were able to move freely in and out of the city and across the territorial divide. At the same time, there were also the local territorially tied inhabitants of the city. On one (the Bosnian) side, they were under siege for the duration of the war, living off humanitarian aid or the black market (if they were lucky enough to have Deutschmarks), prey to sniper fire and occasional shelling. On the other (Serb) side, material conditions were somewhat better, although the climate of fear was worse. On both sides, they were vulnerable to the press gang and the various militias and mafia-types who roamed the streets and claimed legitimacy in terms of the national struggle.

The political goals of the new wars are about the claim to power on the basis of seemingly traditional identities – nation, tribe, religion. Yet the upsurge in the politics of particularistic identities cannot be understood in traditional terms. It has to be explained in the context of a growing cultural dissonance between those who participate in transnational networks, which communicate through e-mail, faxes, telephone and air travel, and those who are excluded from global processes and are tied to localities, even though their lives may be profoundly shaped by those same processes.

It would be a mistake to assume that this cultural divide can be expressed in simple political terms, that those who support particularistic identity politics are reacting against the processes of globalization, while those who favour a more tolerant, multicultural universalistic approach are part of the new global class. On the contrary, among the globalists are to be found diaspora nationalists and fundamentalists, 'realists' and neo-liberals who believe that compromise with nationalism offers the best hope for stability, as well as transnational criminal groups who profit from the new wars. And while there are many among the territorially tied who are likely to cling to traditional identities, there are also courageous individuals and citizens' groups who refuse particularisms and exclusiveness.

The point is rather that the processes known as globalization are breaking up the cultural and socio-economic divisions that defined the patterns of politics which characterized the modern period. The new type of warfare has to be understood in terms of this global dislocation. New forms of power struggle may take the guise of traditional nationalism, tribalism or religious fundamentalism, but they are, nevertheless, contemporary phenomena arising from contemporary causes and displaying new characteristics. Moreover, they are paralleled by a growing global consciousness and sense of global responsibility among an array of governmental and non-governmental institutions as well as individuals.

In this chapter, I describe some of the key characteristics of the process known as globalization and how they give rise to new forms of identity politics. In the last section, I shall try to outline the emerging political cleavage between the politics of particularistic identity and the politics of cosmopolitan or humanist values.

The Characteristics of Globalization

In his book *Nations and Nationalism* Ernest Gellner analyses the association between nationalism and industrialization.[1] He describes the emergence of vertically organized secular national cultures based on vernacular languages which enabled people to cope with the demands of modernity – everyday encounters with industry and government. As varied rural occupations were replaced with factory production, and as the state intruded into more and more aspects of daily life, people needed to be able to communicate both verbally and in writing in a common administrative language, and they needed to acquire certain standardized skills. Earlier societies were characterized by horizontal high cultures, e.g. Latin, Persian, Sanskrit, etc., which were based on religion and were not necessarily linked to the state. These were combined with a great variety of vertical low folk cultures. Whereas earlier high cultures were reproduced in religious institutions and low cultures were passed on through oral traditions, the new vertical national cultures were generated by a new class of intellectuals – writers, journalists, schoolteachers – which emerged along with the establishment of printing, the publication of secular literature such as newspapers and novels, and the expansion of primary education.

The process of globalization, it can be argued, has begun to break up these vertically organized cultures. What appear to be emerging are new horizontal cultures arising out of the new transnational networks, often based on the use of the English language, including the culture of mass consumerism associated with globally known names such as Coca-Cola or McDonald's, combined with a medley of national, local and regional cultures as a result of a new assertion of local particularities.

The term globalization conceals a complex process which actually involves both globalization and localization, integration and fragmentation, homogenization and differentiation, etc. On the one hand, the process creates inclusive transnational networks of people. On the other hand, it excludes and atomizes large numbers of people – indeed, the vast majority. On the one hand, people's lives are profoundly shaped by events taking place far away from where they live over which they have no control. On the other hand, there are new possibilities for enhancing the role of local and regional politics through being linked in to global processes.

As a process, globalization has a long history. Indeed, some argue that there is nothing new about the present phase of globalization; from its inception, capitalism was always a global phenomenon.[2] What is new, however, in the last two decades, is the astonishing revolution in information and communications technology. I would argue that these technological changes impart a qualitative deepening to the process of globalization which is, as yet, by no means determined. The current contours of the process are shaped by the post-war institutional framework and, in particular, the deregulatory policies pursued by governments during the 1980s and 1990s. Its future will depend on the evolution of political and social values, actions and forms of organization. Here, I outline some key trends relevant to an understanding of that evolution.

In the economic sphere, globalization is associated with a set of changes variously described as post-Fordism, flexible specialization, or the New Economy. These changes generally refer to a transformation in what is known as the technico-economic paradigm, the prevailing way in which the supply of products and services is organized to meet the prevailing pattern of demand.[3] The relevant features of these changes are the dramatic decline in the importance of territorially based mass production, the globalization of finance and technology and the increased specialization and diversity of markets. Improved information means that physical production is less important as a share of the overall economy, both because of the increased importance of services and because an increasing proportion of the value of individual products consists of know-how – design, marketing, legal and financial advice. Likewise, the standardization of products, which is linked to territorially based economies of scale, can be supplanted by greater differentiation according to local or specialist demand. Hence, national levels of economic organization have declined in importance along with the relative decline of territorially based production. On the other hand, global levels of economic organization have greatly expanded because of the global character of finance and technology, while local levels of economic organization have also become more significant because of the increasing differentiation of markets.

Globalization also involves the transnationalization and regionalization of governance. There has been, since the war, an explosive growth in international organizations, regimes and regulatory agencies. More and more activities of government are regulated through international agreement or integrated into transnational institutions; more and more departments and ministries are engaged in formal and informal forms of cooperation with their equivalents in other countries; more and more policy decisions are coopted upwards to often unaccountable international forums. At the same time, recent decades have witnessed a reassertion of local and regional politics, especially, but not only, for development purposes. This reassertion has taken a variety of forms, ranging from science- and business-led initiatives, as in the case of 'technopoles' such as Silicon Valley or Cambridge, England; to a rediscovery of municipal traditions, as in Northern Italy; and peace- or Green-led initiatives such as nuclear-free zones or waste-recycling projects; as well as new or renewed forms of local clientelism and patronage.[4]

Parallel to the changing nature of governance has been a striking growth in informal non-governmental transnational networks.[5] These include NGOs – both those which undertake functions formerly undertaken by government, e.g. humanitarian assistance, and those which campaign on global issues, e.g. human rights, ecology, peace, etc. These NGOs are most active at local and transnational levels, partly because these are the sites of the problems with which they are concerned and partly because access to national politics is blocked by nationally organized political parties. Thus, organizations such as Greenpeace or Amnesty International are known all over the world; their effectiveness comes from operating at several different levels – local and global as well as national – and in many different places at the same time. In addition, other kinds of transnational network have flourished: links between a variety of cultural and sporting activities; transnational religious and ethnic groups; transnational crime. Tertiary education is increasingly globalized both because of student and faculty exchanges, and because of the privileged use of the Internet.

These economic and political changes also involve far-reaching changes in organizational forms. Most societies are characterized by what Bukharin called a 'monism of architecture'.[6] In the modern era, nation-states, enterprises and military organizations had very similar vertical forms of hierarchical organization – the influence of modern war, particularly the experience of World War II on organizational forms, was pervasive. Robert Reich, in his book *The Work of Nations*, describes how enterprises have been transformed from national vertical organizations, where power is concentrated in the hands of owners at the top of a pyramid-shaped chain of command, into global phenomena whose organizations most resemble a spider's web, with power in the hands of those who possess technical or financial know-how and who are spread around the points of the web:

> Their dignified headquarters, expansive factories, warehouses, laboratories, and fleets of trucks and corporate jets are leased. Their production workers, janitors, and bookkeepers are under temporary contract; their key researchers, design engineers and marketeers are sharing in the profits. And their distinguished executives, rather than possessing great power and authority over this domain, have little direct control over much of anything. Instead of imposing their will over a corporate empire, they guide ideas through the new webs of enterprise.[7]

Something similar is happening to governmental and non-governmental organizations. Government departments, at all levels, are developing horizontal transnational links; government activity is increasingly contracted out through various forms of privatization and semi-privatization arrangements. The decentralized and horizontal forms of organization typical of NGOs or new social movements are often contrasted to the traditional, vertical forms of organization typical of political parties.[8] Political leaders, like corporate executives, are, at most, facilitators and opinion-shapers and, at least, images or symbols – public representations of interconnected webs of activity over which they have little control.

Globalization has profoundly affected social structures. In advanced industrial countries, the traditional working classes have either declined or are declining along with the drop in territorially based mass production. Because of improvements in productivity and because production work is less skilled, manufacturing production employs fewer and lower-paid workers, especially women and immigrants, or else it is relocated to low-wage countries.

What has grown in number has been those people whom Alain Touraine calls information workers[9] and Robert Reich calls symbolic analysts, those people who possess and use know-how, who, to quote Reich, identify, solve and broker problems through 'manipulations of symbols – data, words, oral and visual representations'.[10] These are the people who work in technology or finance, in expanded higher education, or in the growing myriad of transnational organizations. The majority of people fit neither of these two categories. They either work in services, as waiters and waitresses, salespersons, taxi-drivers, cashiers, etc., or they join the increasing ranks of unemployed made redundant by the productivity increases associated with globalization. This emerging social structure is reflected in growing income disparities both between those in work and those not in work and among those in work depending on skill.

Income disparities are also associated with geographical disparities, both within and across continents, countries and regions. There is the growing disparity between those areas, mainly the advanced industrial regions, that can capitalize on their technological capabilities and the rest. Some areas may thrive, at least temporarily, through attracting volume production, i.e. Southeast Asia, Southern Europe and, potentially, Central Europe. The remainder are caught up in the global economy as traditional sources of livelihood are eroded, but can participate neither in production nor in consumption. Maps drawn by global enterprises of the segmentation of their markets generally leave out the larger part of the world. But even within countries, continents or, indeed, cities, these widening geographical disparities can be found – and this is true of both the advanced industrial world and the rest. Everywhere, boundaries are being drawn between protected and prosperous global enclaves and the anarchic, chaotic, poverty-stricken areas beyond.

The trends outlined above are simultaneously haphazard and constructed. There is no inevitability, for example, about the growth of social, economic and geographical disparities; in part, they are the consequence of disorganization or of organization evolving out of past inertia. What can, however, be accepted as a given is the historic shift away from vertical cultures characteristic of the era of the nation-state which gave rise to a sense of national identity and a sense of security. The abstract symbols, such as money and law, which form the basis of social relations in societies no longer dominated by face-to-face interactions were a constitutive part of these national cultures.[11] It is now commonplace to talk about a 'crisis of identity' – a sense of alienation and disorientation that accompanies the decomposition of cultural communities.

It is also possible, however, to point to certain emerging forms of cultural classification. On the one hand, there are those who see themselves as part of a global community of like-minded people, mainly well-educated information workers or symbolic analysts, who spend a lot of time on aeroplanes, tele-conferencing, etc., and who may work for a global corporation, an NGO, or some other international organization, or who may be part of a network of scholars or sports clubs or musicians and artists, etc. On the other hand, there are those who are excluded and who may or may not see themselves as part of a local or particularistic (religious or national) community.

As yet, the emerging global groupings are not politicized, or, at least, are hardly politicized. That is to say, they do not form the basis of political communities on which new forms of power could be based. One reason is the individualism and anomie that characterizes the current period: the sense that political action is futile given the enormity of current problems, the difficulty of controlling or influencing the web-like structure of power, the cultural fragmentation of both horizontal networks and particularistic loyalties. Both what Reich calls the laissez-faire cosmopolitan, who has 'seceded' from the nation-state and who pursues his or her individualistic consumerist interests, and the restless young criminals, the new adventurers, to be found in all the excluded zones, reflect this political vacuum.

Nevertheless, there are seeds of politicization in both groupings. Cosmopolitan politicization can be located, both within the new transnational NGOs or social movements and within international institutions, as well as among individuals, around a commitment to human values (universal social and political rights, ecological responsibility, peace and democracy, etc.) and to the notion of transnational civil society – the idea that self-organized groups, operating across borders, can solve problems and lobby political institutions. The new politics of particularistic identities can also be interpreted as a response to these global processes, as a form of political mobilization in the face of the growing impotence of the modern state.

Identity Politics

I use the term 'identity politics' to mean movements which mobilize around ethnic, racial or religious identity for the purpose of claiming state power.[12] And I use the term 'identity' narrowly to mean a form of labelling. Whether we are talking about tribal conflict in Africa, religious conflict in the Middle East or South Asia, or nationalist conflict in Europe, the common feature is the way in which labels are used as a basis for political claims. Such conflicts are often described as ethnic conflicts. The term ethnos has a racial connotation even though a number of writers insist that 'ethnie' refers to a cultural community rather than a blood-based community. Although it is clear that there is no racial basis to ethnic claims, the point is that these labels tend to be treated as something one is born with and cannot change; they cannot be acquired through conversion or assimilation. You are German if your grandmother was German, even if you cannot speak the language and have never been to Germany; but you are not German if your parents were Turkish, even if you live and work in Germany. A Catholic born in West Belfast is doomed to remain a Catholic even if he or she converts to Protestantism. A Croat cannot become a Serb by adopting the Orthodox religion and writing in a Cyrillic script. To the extent that these labels are considered birthrights, conflicts based on identity politics can also be termed ethnic conflicts. In many cases, these identities are both religious and nationalist.[13] To claim the political identity of a Muslim in Bosnia, a Catholic in Northern Ireland, or a Hindu in India is, at one at the same time, to claim a national identity. There are, of course, forms of identity politics where labels are not birthrights but can be voluntarily or forcibly imposed. And indeed, in areas of endemic conflict, identity politics often becomes more extreme and morphs into fundamentalism, that is to say, rigid adherence to doctrine. Certain sects of militant Islam, for example, aim to create pure Islamic states through the conversion of non-Muslims as opposed to exclusion.[14]

The term 'politics' refers to the claim to state power. In many parts of the world there are religious revivals, or renewed interest in the survival of local cultures and languages, and this, in part, is a response to the stresses of globalization. Political campaigns to protect or promote religion or culture may often lead to demands for power. Nevertheless, this is not what is meant by identity politics. Such political campaigns are demands for cultural and religious rights. These are quite different from the demand for political rights based on identity. The latter is a form of communitarianism that is distinct from and may conflict with individual political rights.

The politics of identity can be contrasted with the politics of ideas. The politics of ideas is about forward-looking projects. Thus, religious struggles in Western Europe in the seventeenth century were about freeing the individual from the oppressive hold of the established Church. Early nationalist struggles in nineteenth-century Europe or in colonial Africa were about democracy and state-building. They were conceived as ways of welding together diverse groups of people under the rubric of nation for the purpose of modernization. More recently, politics has been dominated by abstract secular ideas such as socialism or environmentalism which offer a vision for the future. This type of politics tends to be integrative, embracing all those who support the idea, even though, as recent experience has demonstrated, the universalistic character of such ideas can serve as a justification for totalitarian and authoritarian practices.

In contrast, identity politics tends to be fragmentative, backward-looking and exclusive. Political groupings based on exclusive identity tend to be movements of nostalgia, based on the reconstruction of an heroic past, the memory of injustices, real or imagined, and of famous battles, won or lost. They acquire meaning through insecurity, through rekindled fear of historic enemies, or through a sense of being threatened by those with different labels. Labels can always be divided and subdivided. There is no such thing as cultural purity or homogeneity. Every exclusive identity-based polity necessarily generates a minority. At best, identity politics involves psychological discrimination against those labelled differently. At worst, it leads to population expulsion and genocide.

The new identity politics arises out of the disintegration or erosion of modern state structures, especially centralized, authoritarian states. The collapse of communist states after 1989, the loss of legitimacy of post-colonial states in Africa or South Asia, or even the decline of welfare states in more advanced industrial countries provide the environment in which the new forms of identity politics are nurtured.

The new identity politics has two main sources, both of which are linked to globalization. On the one hand, it can be viewed as a reaction to the growing impotence and declining legitimacy of the established political classes. From this perspective, it is a politics fostered from above which plays to and inculcates popular prejudices. It is a form of political mobilization, a survival tactic, for politicians active in national politics either at the level of the state or at the level of nationally defined regions, as in the case of the republics of the former Yugoslavia or the former Soviet Union or in places such as Kashmir or Eritrea before independence. On the other hand, it emerges out of the insecurity associated with the process of globalization and, in particular, the advent of what can be described as the parallel economy – new forms of legal and illegal ways of making a living that have sprung up among the excluded parts of society – and constitutes a way of legitimizing these new shadowy forms of activity. Particularly in Eastern Europe, the events of 1989 compressed the impact of globalization both in undermining the nation-state and in releasing new forms of economic activity into a short 'transitional' space of time, so that this form of nationalism from below merged with nationalism from above in an explosive combination.[15]

In Eastern Europe, the use of nationalism as a form of political mobilization pre-dated 1989. Particularly in the former communist multinational states, national consciousness was deliberately cultivated in a context in which ideological differences had been disallowed and when societies had, in theory, been socially homogenized and 'socially cleansed'.[16] Nationality, or certain officially recognized nationalities, became the main legitimate umbrella for pursuing various forms of political, economic and cultural interests. This was particularly important in the former Yugoslavia and Soviet Union, where national difference was 'constitutionally enshrined'.[17]

These tendencies were reinforced by the functioning of economies of shortage. In theory, planned economies are supposed to eliminate competition. Such planning does of course eliminate competition for markets. But it gives rise to another form of competition – competition for resources. In theory, the plan is drawn up by rational planners and transmitted downwards through a vertical chain of command. In practice, it is 'built up' through a myriad of bureaucratic pressures and subsequently 'broken down'. In effect, the plan operates as an expression of bureaucratic compromise, and, because of the 'soft budget' constraint, individual enterprises always spend more than is anticipated. The consequence is a vicious circle in which shortage intensifies the competition for resources and the tendency among ministries and enterprises for hoarding and autarchy, which further intensifies shortage. In this context, nationality becomes a tool which can be used to further the competition for resources.[18]

Already in the early 1970s there were writers who were warning of a nationalist explosion in the former Soviet Union as a result of the way in which nationality policy was used to prop up the decaying socialist project.[19] In a classic article, published in 1974, Teresa Rakowska-Harmstone used the term the 'new nationalism' to describe 'a new phenomenon which is present even among people who, at the time of the revolution, had only an inchoate sense of a common culture'.[20] Soviet policy created a hierarchy of nationalities based on an elaborate administrative structure in which the status of nationalities was linked to the status of territorially based administrative units – republics, autonomous regions and autonomous provinces. Within these administrative arrangements the indigenous language and culture of the so-called titular nationality was promoted, and members of the titular nationality were given priority in local administration and education.[21] The system gave rise to what Zaslavsky has described as an 'explosive division of labour' in which an indigenous administrative and intellectual elite presided over an imported Russian urban working class and an indigenous rural population.[22] The local elite used the development of national consciousness to promote administrative autonomy, especially in the economic sphere.

As I argued in the previous chapter, a similar process took place in the former Yugoslavia, especially after the 1974 constitution entrenched the nations and republics that made up the federation and restricted the powers of the federal government. What held these multinational states together was the monopoly of the Communist Party. In the aftermath of 1989, when the socialist project was discredited and the monopoly of the party was finally broken, and when democratic elections

were held for the first time, nationalism erupted into the open.
In a situation where there is little to choose between parties,
where there has been no history of political debate, where
the new politicians are hardly known, nationalism becomes a
mechanism for political differentiation. In societies where
people assume that they are expected to vote in certain ways,
where they are not habituated to political choice and may be
wary of taking it for granted, voting along national lines became
the most obvious option.

Nationalism represents both a continuity with the past and
a way of denying or 'forgetting' a complicity with the past. It
represents a continuity partly because of the ways in which it
was nurtured in the preceding era, not only in multinational
states, and partly because its form is very similar to the preceding Cold War ideologies. Communism, in particular, thrived
on an us–them, good–bad war mentality and elevated the
notion of an homogeneous collective community. At the same
time, it is a way of denying the past because communist regimes
overtly condemned nationalism. As in the case of rabid attach-
ment to the market, nationalism is a form of negation of what
went before. Communism can be treated as an 'outsider' or
'foreigner', particularly in countries occupied by Soviet troops,
thus exculpating those who accepted, tolerated or collaborated
with the regime. National identity is somehow pure and
untainted in comparison with other professional or ideological
identities that were determined by the previous context.

Similar tendencies can be observed in other places. Already
by the 1970s and 1980s the fragility of post-colonial administrative structures was becoming apparent. States in Africa
and Asia were having to cope with the disillusion of post-
independence hopes, the failure of the development project to
overcome poverty and inequality, the insecurity of rapid urbanization and the break-up of traditional rural communities, as
well as the impact of structural adjustment and policies of
stabilization, liberalization and deregularization. Moreover, as
in the case of ex-Yugoslavia, the loss of an international identity
based on membership of the non-aligned movement in the
aftermath of the Cold War had domestic repercussions as well.
Both ruling politicians and aspiring opposition leaders began
to play upon particularistic identities in different ways – to
justify authoritarian policies, to create scapegoats, to mobilize

support around fear and insecurity. In many post-colonial
states, the ruling parties saw themselves as left parties occupy-
ing the space for emancipatory movements. As in post-
communist states, the absence of a legitimate emancipatory
movement opened politics up to claims based on tribe or clan,
or religious or linguistic group.

In the pre-colonial period, most societies had only a loose
sense of ethnic identity. The Europeans, with their passion for
classification, with censuses and identity papers, imposed more
rigid ethnic categories, which then evolved along with the
growth of communication, roads and railways, and the emergence, in some countries, of a vernacular press. In some cases,
the categories were quite artificial: the Hutu–Tutsi distinction
in Rwanda and Burundi was a rough, largely social distinction
before the Belgian administration introduced identity cards;
likewise, the Ngala, the tribe former President Mobutu of Zaire
(now the Democratic Republic of Congo) claimed to come
from, was largely a Belgian invention. In the post-independence
period, most ruling parties espoused a secular national identity
that embraced the often numerous ethnic groups within the
artificially defined territory of the new nations. As post-
independence hopes faded, many politicians began to appeal to
particularistic tendencies. In general, the weaker the administrative structures the earlier this took place. In some countries,
such as Sudan, Nigeria or Zaire, what have been called 'predatory' regimes developed in which access to power and personal
wealth depended on religion or tribe.[23] In India, where democracy was sustained for almost all of the post-independence
period, the Congress Party's use of Hindu rituals and symbols
in the 1970s paved the way for new forms of political mobilization based on identity, particularly religion.[24]

Many of these states were strongly interventionist. As foreign
assistance began to be replaced by commercial borrowing in
the 1970s, as foreign debt mounted and 'structural adjustment'
programmes were introduced, state revenues declined and, as
in the former communist countries, political competition for
control over resources intensified. The end of the Cold War
meant the reduction of foreign assistance to countries such as
Zaire or Somalia which had been considered strategically
important. At the same time, pressure for democratization led
to increasingly desperate bids to remain in power, often through

fomenting ethnic tension and other forms of identity politics. In the Middle East, the growth of Islamic movements was associated with the disillusion with secular nationalist post-colonial regimes.

Even in advanced industrial countries, the erosion of legitimacy associated with the declining autonomy of the nation-state and the corrosion of traditional, often industrially based sources of social cohesion became much more transparent in the aftermath of 1989. A specifically Western identity defined in relation to the Soviet threat was undermined because it was more difficult to defend democracy with reference to its absence elsewhere. Indeed the rhetoric of the 'War on Terror' can be viewed as a way of reinventing that distinctive Western identity. Of equal significance is the growing consensus of major political parties as the space for substantive political difference on economic and social issues narrows in the context of globalization and a prevailing ideology that emphasizes budgetary discipline and control of inflation. Nationalism or seeds of nationalism, such as asylum laws or anti-immigrationism, are exploited as party political forms of differentiation. In recent years, extreme right-wing parties have managed to capture significant shares of the vote in places such as France, the Netherlands, Belgium and elsewhere. In the United States, the Republican Party has deliberately built up its constituency among fundamentalist Christian churches. In Australia, the Conservative Party captured power on an explicit anti-asylum platform. Particularly in the aftermath of 9/11, xenophobic ideas have capitalized on a growing sense of insecurity.

Western countries do not of course share the experience of collectivist authoritarianism, although regions such as Northern Ireland where particularist politics are strong tend to be those where democracy has been weak. An active civil society tends to counterbalance the distrust of politicians, the alienation from political institutions, the sense of apathy and futility that provide a potential basis for populist tendencies. Nevertheless, the 'secession' of the new cosmopolitan classes and the fragmentation and dependence of those excluded from the benefits of globalization are characteristic of advanced industrial countries as well.

The other main source of the new identity politics is the insecurity associated with globalization, particularly rapid urbanization and the parallel economy. This is, to a large extent, the product of neo-liberal policies pursued in the 1980s and the 1990s – macro-economic stabilization, deregulation and privatization – which effectively represented a speeding up of the process of globalization. These policies increased the level of unemployment, resource depletion and disparities in income, rapid urbanization, and increased migration both from countryside to town and across borders. These changes, in turn, provided an environment for growing criminalization and the creation of networks of corruption, black marketeers, arms and drug traffickers, etc. In societies where the state controlled large parts of the economy and where self-organized market institutions do not exist, policies of 'structural adjustment' or 'transition' effectively mean the absence of any kind of regulation. The market does not, by and large, mean new autonomous productive enterprises. It means corruption, speculation and crime. New groups of shady 'businessmen', often linked in to the decaying institutional apparatuses through various forms of bribery and 'insider' dealing, are engaged in a kind of primitive accumulation – a grab for land and capital. They use the language of identity politics to build alliances and to legitimize their activities. Often these networks are linked to wars, e.g. in Afghanistan, Pakistan and large parts of Africa, and to the disintegration of the military-industrial complex in the aftermath of the Cold War. Often, they are transnational, linking up to international circuits of illegal goods sometimes through diaspora connections.

In addition, religious institutions or humanitarian organizations linked to nationalist or religious parties often provide the only social safety net available to newly arrived immigrants from the countryside or from other countries. Likewise, religious schools and community organizations have been growing in the context of economic policies, which involve cuts in social spending, including education.

A typical phenomenon consists of the new bands of young men, the new adventurers, who make a living through violence or through threats of violence, who obtain surplus weapons through the black market or through looting military stores, and who either base their power on particularistic networks or seek respectability through particularistic claims. These networks can include hostage-takers in the Transcaucasus who take prisoners in order to exchange them for food, weapons, money, other hostages and even dead bodies; mafia-rings in Russia; the new Cossacks who don the Cossack uniform in order to 'protect' Russian diaspora groups in the near abroad; nationalist militia groups of unemployed youths in Western Ukraine or Western Herzegovina. All these groups feed, like vultures, on the remnants of the disintegrating state and on the frustrations and resentments of the poor and unemployed. A similar breed of restless political adventurer is to be found in conflict areas in Africa and South Asia.[25]

The new identity politics combines these two sources of particularism in varying degrees. Former administrative or intellectual elites ally with a motley collection of adventurers on the margins of society to mobilize the excluded and abandoned, the alienated and insecure, for the purposes of capturing and sustaining power. The greater the sense of insecurity, the greater the polarization of society, the less is the space for alternative integrative political values. In conditions of war, such alliances are cemented by shared complicity in war crimes and a mutual dependence on the continued functioning of the war economy. In Rwanda, the plan for mass genocide has been explained as the way in which the extremist Hutus could retain their grip on power in the context of economic crisis and international pressure for democratization. According to the NGO Africa Rights: 'The extremists' aim was for the entire Hutu populace to participate in the killings. That way, the blood of genocide would stain everybody. There could be no going back.'[26] The intensification of the war in Kashmir, including the involvement of Afghan *Mujahidiin* has created a polarization between Hindu and Muslim identities which has increasingly supplanted syncretic traditions and the common bonds based on Kashmiri identity – the *kashmiriyat*.[27] One of the explanations for the ferocity of nationalist sentiment in the former Yugoslavia is the fact that all the various sources of the new identity politics are concentrated there: the former Yugoslavia had the most Westernized, indeed cosmopolitan, elite of any East European country, thus exacerbating the resentments of those excluded; it experienced nationalistic bureaucratic competition typical of the centralized state in decline; and, because it was exposed to the transition to the market earlier than other East European countries, its parallel economy was more developed. Even so, a vicious war was required to create the hatred on which exclusive identities could be reconstructed.

The new form of identity politics is often treated as a throwback to the past, a return to pre-modern identities temporarily displaced or suppressed by modernizing ideologies. It is of course the case that the new politics draws on memory and history and that certain societies where cultural traditions are more entrenched are more susceptible to the new politics. But, as I have argued, what really matters is the recent past and, in particular, the impact of globalization on the political survival of states. Moreover, the new politics has entirely new contemporary attributes.

First of all, it is horizontal as well as vertical, transnational as well as national. In nearly all the new nationalisms, the diasporas play a much more important role than formerly because of the speed of communication. There were always expatriate nationalist groups plotting their country's liberation in cafés in Paris or London. But such groups have become much larger and more significant because of the scale of emigration, the ease of travel and the spread of telephones, faxes and electronic mail. There are two types of diaspora. On the one hand, there are minorities living in the near abroad, fearful of their vulnerability to local nationalisms and often more extreme than those living on home territory. These include Serbians living in Croatia and Bosnia–Herzegovina, Russian minorities in all the new ex-Soviet republics, the Hungarian minority in Vojvodina, Romania, Ukraine and Slovakia, Tutsis living in Zaire or Uganda. On the other hand, there are disaffected groups living far away, often in the new melting-pot nations, who find solace in fantasies about their origins which are often far removed from reality. The idea of a Sikh homeland, Khalistan, the notion of uniting Macedonia and Bulgaria, the call for an independent Ruthenia – all originated from diaspora communities in Canada. Irish-American support for the Irish Republican Army (IRA), violent conflict between the Greek and Macedonian communities in Australia and the pressure from Croatian groups in Germany for recognition of Croatia are all further examples of diaspora influence.

Among Kosovo Albanians, the diaspora played a critical role, especially in Germany and Switzerland. Many of those who had taken part in protests and student demonstrations in the early 1980s left the country. During the 1990s, a 3 per cent income tax was collected from half a million Kosovar Albanians who lived and worked abroad. Moreover, an Albanian-language television service was run from Switzerland and could be received by those Kosovar Albanians who had satellite dishes. After 1997, the increasingly influential role of the KLA (the Kosovo Liberation Army) was made possible because many in the diaspora switched support from the non-violent nationalist movement to the KLA.

Diaspora groups provide ideas, money, arms and know-how, often with disproportionate effects. Among the individuals who make up the new nationalist compacts are romantic expatriates, foreign mercenaries, dealers and investors, Canadian pizza-parlour owners, etc. Radha Kumar has described the support given by Indians living in the United States to Hindu fundamentalists: 'Separated from their countries of origin, often living as aliens in a foreign land, simultaneously feeling stripped of their culture and guilty for having escaped the troubles "back home", expatriates turn to diaspora nationalism without understanding the violence that their actions might inadvertently trigger.'[28] The same kind of transnational networks are to be found among religious groupings. Islamic connections are well known, but such links also apply to other religious groupings. I visited the office of the so-called foreign minister of South Ossetia, a breakaway region of Georgia, and he had a picture of the Bosnian Serb leader Karadžić on his wall. He explained that he had been given it by the delegation from Republika Srpska when he attended a meeting of Eastern Orthodox Christians.

Second, the capacity for political mobilization is greatly extended both as a result of the improved education and the expansion of educated classes and as a consequence of new technologies. Many explanations for the growth of political Islam focus on the emergence of newly literate urban classes, who are often excluded from power, the increase in Islamic schools and the expansion of newspaper readership.[29] Growing literacy in the vernacular languages, together with the spread of tabloid-type communitarian newspapers, new global television channels such as Al-Jazeera or Al-Arabiya in the Middle East, or Star television in South Asia, as well as access to websites and forums through the Internet, or the circulation of videos, create new 'imagined communities'. These new forms of electronic communication provide rapid and effective ways of disseminating a particularistic message. Specifically, the electronic media has an authority that newspapers cannot match; in parts of Africa, the radio is 'magic'. The circulation of cassettes with sermons by militant Islamic preachers, the use of 'hate' radio to incite people to genocide in Rwanda, the control of television by nationalist leaders in Eastern Europe – all provide mechanisms for speeding up the pace of political mobilization.

Cosmopolitanism versus Particularism

A. D. Smith, in his book *Nations and Nationalism in a Global Era*, takes issue with the view that nation-states are an anachronism.[30] He argues that the new global classes still need to feel a sense of community and identity based on what he calls ethnies to overcome the alienation of their technical scientific universalizing discourse. And he criticizes what he calls the modernist fallacy that nation-states are artificial and temporary polities, staging-posts in the evolution towards global society. He sees the new nationalism as evidence of the persistence of ethnies, and he offers a positive perspective on cultural separatism, which he sees as a way of grounding nation-states more firmly round a dominant ethnie while, at the same time, enabling them to embrace civic ideals.

It may well be that the new particularistic identities are here to stay, that they are the expression of a new post-modern cultural relativism. But it is difficult to argue that they offer a basis for humanistic civic values precisely because they are unable to present a forward-looking project relevant to the new global context. The main implication of globalization is that territorial sovereignty is no longer viable. The effort to reclaim power within a particular spatial domain will merely further undermine the ability to influence events. This does not mean that the new form of particularistic identity politics will go away. Rather, it is a recipe for new closed-in chaotic statelets with permanently contested borders dependent on continuing violence for survival.

The particularists cannot do without those people who are
labelled differently. Globalization, as its name implies, is global.
Everywhere, in varying proportions, those who benefit from
globalization have to share territory with those excluded from
its benefits but who are nevertheless deeply affected by it.
Both losers and gainers need each other. No patch of territory,
however small or large, can any longer insulate itself from the
outside world.

Of course, it is possible to envisage, and it is already happening, a new assertion of regional and local politics, a claim
for greater democratic accountability at regional and local
levels. But if such claims are to succeed, they would have to
be situated in a global context; they would have to involve
greater access and openness towards global levels of governance, and they would have to be based on greater democratic
accountability for all inhabitants of the territory in question,
not just for those with a particular label. This type of politics
would thus need to be embedded in what might be described
as a cosmopolitan political consciousness.

By cosmopolitanism, I do not mean a denial of identity.
Rather, I mean a celebration of the diversity of global identities,
acceptance and, indeed, enthusiasm for multiple overlapping
identities, and, at the same time, a commitment to the equality
of all human beings and to respect for human dignity. The term
originates in the Kantian notion of cosmopolitan right that
is combined with recognition of separate sovereignties; thus
it brings together both universalism and diversity. Anthony
Appiah talks about the 'cosmopolitan patriot' or the 'rooted
cosmopolitan, attached to a home of one's own, with its own
cultural particularities, but taking pleasure from the presence
of other different people'. He distinguishes cosmopolitanism
from humanism 'because cosmopolitanism is not just the
feeling that everybody matters. For the cosmopolitan also cel-
ebrates the fact that there are *different* local human ways of
being; humanism, by contrast, is consistent with the desire for
global homogeneity.'[31]

Two possible sources of a cosmopolitan political consciousness can be identified. One, which could be described as cosmopolitanism from above, is to be found in the growing myriad
of international organizations, a few of which, most notably the
EU, are developing supra-national powers. These institutions

develop their own logics and internal structures. They enable activities to be carried out rather than undertaking them through their own resources. They function through complex partnerships, cooperation agreements, negotiation, and mediation with other organizations, states, and private or semi-private groups. They are restricted both by lack of resources and, relatedly, by the inter-governmental arrangements which make it extremely difficult for them to act, except on the basis of time-consuming and often unsatisfactory compromises. In many of these institutions there are committed idealistic officials. They have an interest in seeking alternative sources of legitimacy to their frustrating national masters.

The other source is what could be described as cosmopolitanism from below, the new social movements of the 1980s and what came to be called NGOs in the 1990s. This new form of activism has developed since the early 1980s primarily in response to new global problems. These movements differ from earlier social movements. They do not easily fit a traditional left–right divide; they are concerned with new issues – peace, ecology, human rights, gender, development. They tend to be horizontal rather than vertical in organization, operating most effectively at local and transnational levels. In the 1990s, they tended to function in individualistic ways. They are often sceptical about politics. They express their individual commitments through vegetarianism or through driving convoys of aid to war zones. And their actions tend to be symbolic or spectacular – as, for example, the activities of the Greenpeace ship *Rainbow Warrior*. Terms such as 'anti-politics', 'self-organization' and 'civil society' express their disaffection with conventional political forms. With the growth of networks organized around particular campaigns such as debt relief or climate change, and with the emergence of new forms of organization such as the social forums, they are becoming more institutionalized. The eleven million people who demonstrated all over the world on 15 February 2003 against the war in Iraq testified to their growing organization. Of course, not everyone who participates in these activities is a cosmopolitan. Many are anti-globalization, yearning for a return to the nation-state, who sometimes make common cause with groups associated with identity politics, nationalists or Islamists in the Middle East, for example.

At present, cosmopolitanism and particularism coexist side by side in the same geographical space. Cosmopolitanism tends to be more widespread in the West and less widespread in the East and South. Nevertheless, throughout the world, in remote villages and towns, both sorts of people are to be found. The new particularistic conflicts throw up courageous groups of people who try to oppose war and exclusivism – both local people, often women, and those who volunteer to come from abroad to provide humanitarian assistance, to help mediate, etc. Local groups gather strength in so far as they can gain access to or support and protection from transnational networks.

It is in wars that the space for cosmopolitanism is narrowed. Particularisms need each other to sustain their exclusive identities; hence the paradoxical combination of conflict and cooperation. It is cosmopolitanism that undermines the appeal of particularism and it is the representatives of humane civic values that are often targeted in wars. Indeed, war itself can be understood as a form of political mobilization, constructing an environment of insecurity, in which particularist groups thrive. Areas of conflict become 'black holes' – havens for fanatics and criminals, breeding the new terrorism. More and more no-go areas come into being, such as Somalia or Afghanistan and now Iraq, where isolated humanitarian agencies gingerly negotiate and bribe their way through to help those in need. Some argue that such situations are the harbingers of the future for much of the world.[32] Nothing is more polarizing than violence and more likely to induce a retreat from utopian inclusive projects. 'Sarajevo is Europe's future. This is the end of history', Sarajevo's disenchanted cosmopolitans used to say. But politics is never determined. Whether another future can be envisaged is, in the end, a matter of choice.

5

The Globalized
War Economy

The term 'war economy' usually refers to a system which is centralized, totalizing and autarchic, as was the case in the total wars of the twentieth century. Administration is centralized to increase the efficiency of the war and to maximize revenue to pay for the war. As many people as possible are mobilized to participate in the war effort either as soldiers or in the production of arms and necessities. By and large, the war effort is self-sufficient, although in World War II Britain and the Soviet Union received lend-lease assistance from the United States. The main aim of the war effort is to maximize the use of force so as to engage and defeat the enemy in battle.

The new type of war economy is almost totally the opposite. The new wars are 'globalized' wars. They involve the fragmentation and decentralization of the state. Participation is low relative to the population both because of lack of pay and because of lack of legitimacy on the part of the warring parties. There is very little domestic production, so the war effort is heavily dependent on local predation and external support. Battles are rare, most violence is directed against civilians, and cooperation between warring factions is common.

Those who conceive of war in traditional Clausewitzean terms, based on definable geo-political goals, fail to understand the underlying vested interests, both political and economic, in the continuation of war. They tend to assume that political solutions can be found without any need to address the

underlying economic logic. At the same time, however, those
who recognize the irrelevance of traditional perceptions of war,
and observe the complexity of the political, social and economic relationships expressed in these wars, tend to conclude
that this type of violence can be equated with anarchy. In these
circumstances, the most that can be done is to treat the symptoms through, for example, humanitarian assistance.

In this chapter, I argue that it is possible to analyse the
typical political economy of new wars so as to draw conclusions
about possible alternative approaches. Indeed, the implication
of such an analysis is that many of the well-meaning efforts of
various international actors, based on inherited assumptions
about the character of war, may turn out to be counterproductive. Conflict resolution from above may merely enhance
the legitimacy of the warring parties and allow time for
replenishment; humanitarian assistance may contribute to the
functioning of the war economy; peacekeeping troops may lose
legitimacy either by standing aside when terrible crimes are
committed or by siding with groups who commit terrible
crimes.

In the first section, I describe the various fighting units
typical of contemporary wars and how they have emerged out
of the disintegration of the state's formal security capacities.
Then, I analyse patterns of violence and the character of military strategy and the way these have evolved out of the conflicts that developed during and after World War II as a way
of reacting against or coping with modern conventional war –
guerrilla warfare, counter-insurgency, and the 'low-intensity'
conflicts of the 1980s. Next, I consider how the fighting units
acquire resources with which to fight the new wars and the
interaction between the new pattern of violence and the social
relations that are generated in the context of war. In the final
section, I describe how the new wars, or rather the social conditions of the new wars, tend to spread.

The Privatization of Military Forces

Madeleine Albright, the former US secretary of state, used
the term 'failed states' to describe countries with weak or
non-existent central authority – the classic examples are

Somalia or Afghanistan. Jeffrey Herbst argues that many African states never enjoyed state sovereignty in the modern sense – that is, 'unquestioned physical control over the defined territory, but also an administrative presence throughout the country and the allegiance of the population to the idea of the state'.[1] One of the key characteristics of failing states is the loss of control over and fragmentation of the instruments of physical coercion. A disintegrative cycle sets in, which is almost the exact opposite of the integrative cycle through which modern states were established. The failure to sustain physical control over the territory and to command popular allegiance reduces the ability to collect taxes and greatly weakens the revenue base of the state. In addition, corruption and personalistic rule represent an added drain on state revenue. Often, the government can no longer afford reliable forms of tax collection; private agencies are sometimes employed who keep part of the takings, much as happened in Europe in the eighteenth century. Tax evasion is widespread both because of the loss of state legitimacy and because of the emergence of new forces who claim 'protection money'. This leads to outside pressure to cut government spending, which further reduces the capacity to maintain control and encourages the fragmentation of military units. Moreover, outside assistance is predicated on economic and political reforms which many of these states are constitutionally incapable of implementing. A downward spiral of loss of revenue and legitimacy, growing disorder, and military fragmentation creates the context in which the new wars take place. Effectively, the 'failure' of the state is accompanied by a growing privatization of violence.

Typically, the new wars are characterized by a multiplicity of types of fighting units, both public and private, state and non-state, or some kind of mixture. For the purpose of simplicity, I identify five main types: regular armed forces or remnants thereof; paramilitary groups; self-defence units; foreign mercenaries; and, finally, regular foreign troops, generally under international auspices.

Regular armed forces are in decay, particularly in areas of conflict. Cuts in military spending, declining prestige, shortages of equipment, spare parts, fuel and ammunition, and inadequate training all contribute to a profound loss of morale.

In many African and post-Soviet states, soldiers no longer receive training or regular pay. They may have to seek out their own sources of funding, which contributes to indiscipline and breakdown of the military hierarchy. Often this leads to fragmentation, situations in which local army commanders act as local warlords, as in Tadjikistan. Or soldiers may engage in criminal behaviour as, for example, in Zaire (now DRC), where unpaid soldiers were encouraged to loot or pillage. In other words, regular armed forces lose their character as the legitimate bearers of arms and become increasingly difficult to distinguish from private paramilitary groups. This is compounded in situations where the security forces were already fragmented as a result of deliberate policy; often there were border guards, a presidential guard and a gendarmerie, not to mention various types of internal security forces. By the end, President Mobutu of what was then Zaire could rely only on his personal guard to protect him. Saddam Hussein engaged in a similar proliferation of security agencies, and, as with Mobutu, it was only the motley group known as Firqat Fedayeen Saddam, Saddam's Martyrs, that offered sporadic resistance to the initial American invasion.

The most common fighting units are paramilitary groups, that is to say, autonomous groups of armed men generally centred around an individual leader. Often these groups are established by governments in order to distance themselves from the more extreme manifestations of violence. This was probably the case for Arkan's Tigers in Bosnia, or so Arkan himself insisted. Likewise, the pre-1994 Rwandan government recruited unemployed young men to a newly formed militia linked to the ruling party; they were given training by the Rwandan army and granted a small salary.[2] In a similar vein, the South African government secretly supplied arms and training to the Inkatha Freedom Party (IFP), which had been promoting the violent activities of groups of Zulu workers during the transition to democracy. Often, paramilitary groups are associated with particular extremist parties or political factions. In Georgia, after independence, each political party, except the Greens, had its own militia; after his recall to power, Eduard Shevardnadze tried to re-establish a monopoly over the means of violence by welding together these militias into a regular army. It was this ragbag of armed bands that was defeated by a combination of the Abkhazian National Guard and Russian military units in Abkhazia. One of the most notorious paramilitary groups in Kosovo was known as 'Frenki's Boys'. According to intelligence sources, Franko Simatović was the link between Milošević and freelance paramilitary groups.

The paramilitary groups are composed mostly of redundant soldiers, or even whole units of redundant or breakaway soldiers which sometimes include common criminals, as in the former Yugoslavia, where many were deliberately released from prison for the purpose, and unemployed young men in search of a living, a cause or an adventure. They rarely wear uniforms, which makes them difficult to distinguish from non-combatants, although they often sport distinctive clothing or signs. Symbols of global material culture often serve as important quasi-uniforms; for example, Ray-Ban sunglasses, Adidas shoes, jogging suits and caps. Reportedly, Frenki's Boys had their headquarters at the back of a dress shop in Djakovica. They wore cowboy hats over ski masks, and painted Indian stripes on their faces. Their trademark was the sign of the Serbian Chetniks and a silhouette of a destroyed city with the words 'City Breakers' in English.[3]

The use of child soldiers is not uncommon in Africa; there have also been reports of fourteen-year-old boys operating in Serbian units. In Charles Taylor's National Patriotic Front of Liberia, for example, which invaded Sierra Leone on Christmas Eve 1989, some 30 per cent of the soldiers were said to be under the age of seventeen; Taylor even created a 'Boys' Own Unit'. He supported an invasion of Sierra Leone by a rather small number of rebels, after which the Sierra Leone government recruited large numbers of citizens into its army, including boys some of whom were as young as eight years old: 'Many of the boys recruited into the government army were street-children from Freetown, involved in petty theft before their recruitment. Now they were given an AK47 and a chance to engage in theft on a larger scale.'[4] RENAMO (Resistência Nacional Moçambiçana – the movement founded by Portuguese special forces after the independence of Mozambique and supported by South Africa) also recruited children, some of whom were forced to return to their own villages and attack their families.

Self-defence units are composed of volunteers who try to defend their localities. These would include local brigades in Bosnia–Herzegovina who tried to defend all the citizens of their locality, for example in Tuzla; self-defence units of both Hutus and Tutsis who tried to stop the massacres in 1994; or the self-defence units in South Africa set up by the African National Congress (ANC) to defend localities from Inkatha. Such units are very difficult to sustain mainly because of inadequate resources. Where they are not defeated, they often end up by cooperating with other armed groups and getting sucked into the conflict.

Foreign mercenaries include both individuals on contract to particular fighting units and mercenary bands. Among the former are former Russian officers working on contract with the new post-Soviet armies, and British and French soldiers made redundant by the post-Cold War cuts, who used to train, advise and even command armed groups during the wars in Bosnia and Croatia and still do so in various African countries. The most well-known mercenary bands are the *Mujahidiin*, veterans from the Afghan war, generally to be found in all conflicts involving Islam, funded by the Islamic states, most notably Iran and Saudi Arabia. A new and growing phenomenon is private security companies, often recruited from retired soldiers from Britain or the United States, who are hired both by governments and by multinational companies and are often interconnected. During the 1990s, a notorious example was the South African mercenary company Executive Outcomes and its partner, the British company Sandline International. Sandline International became famous as a result of the scandal concerning arms sales to Sierra Leone in early 1998. Executive Outcomes has been credited with considerable military success in defending diamond mines in Sierra Leone and Angola. In February 1997 the government of Papua New Guinea hired Sandline International to launch a military assault against the secessionist Bourgainville Revolutionary Army (BRA) and to reopen the Bourgainville copper mine; Sandline International subcontracted the work to Executive Outcomes.[5] American private security companies have become a characteristic feature of American interventions, especially in Iraq and Afghanistan. Particularly well-known names include MPRI (Military Professional Resources Inc), which trained the Croatian army towards the end of the war in Bosnia and was also involved in Angola and Sierra Leone, and is now in a range of countries, and DymCorps, which tends to undertake policing duties.

The final category is regular foreign troops, usually operating under the umbrella of international organizations, mainly the UN but also NATO in Bosnia, Kosovo and Afghanistan, ECOMOG (Economic Community of West African States Ceasefire Monitoring Group) in Liberia, the African Union (AU) in Darfur, the EU in eastern Congo, Macedonia and now Bosnia, and the CIS (Commonwealth of Independent States) or OSCE, which have both provided umbrellas for different Russian peacekeeping operations. In general, these troops are not directly involved in the war, although their presence is very significant and I will discuss their role in chapter 6. In some cases, these troops have become involved by fighting, as in the case of ECOMOG in Liberia and Sierra Leone or Russian peacekeepers in Tadjikistan, and, in such instances, they have taken on some of the characteristics of the other fighting units. In the war in DRC, several neighbouring countries (Uganda, Angola, Rwanda, Burundi) sent troops to participate on different sides. And, of course, as I discuss in chapter 7, the United States and Britain and some other countries have troops in Iraq.

While the small-scale character of the fighting units has much in common with those involved in guerrilla warfare, they lack the hierarchy, order and vertical command systems that have been typical of guerrilla forces and that were borrowed from modern warfare as well as the structure of Leninist or Maoist political parties. These various groups operate both autonomously and in cooperation. What appear to be armies are actually horizontal coalitions of breakaway units from the regular armed forces, local militia or self-defence units, criminal gangs, groups of fanatics, and hangers-on, who have negotiated partnerships, common projects, divisions of labour or spoils. Robert Reich's concept of the 'spider's web' to characterize the new global corporate structure, which I referred to in the previous chapter (see p. 77), is probably also applicable to the new warfare.

Because of cost, logistics and inadequate infrastructure and skills, these 'armies' rarely use heavy weapons, although where they are used they may well make a considerable difference. The Serbian monopoly of heavy artillery was important in Bosnia, as was the intervention of Russian units with aircraft and artillery in Abkhazia. One of the reasons given for the success of Executive Outcomes has been their ability 'to carry out sophisticated operations such as flying helicopter gun ships and light ground-attack fixed-wing aircraft'.[6]

For the most part, light weapons are used – rifles, machine-guns, hand-grenades, landmines and, at the upper end of the scale, low-calibre artillery and short-range rockets. Although these weapons are often described as 'low-tech', they are the product of a long and sophisticated technological evolution. Compared with the weapons used in World War II, they are much lighter, easier to use and transport, more accurate and more difficult to detect. In contrast to heavy weapons, they can be used to great effect by unskilled soldiers, including children. Modern communications are also very important to enable the fighting groups to cooperate, especially radios and mobile telephones. US forces in Somalia were unable to eavesdrop the commercially bought cellular phones used by Somali militiamen.

The end of the Cold War and of related conflicts such as those in Afghanistan or South Africa greatly increased the availability of surplus weapons. In some cases, wars are fought with weapons raided from Cold War stockpiles; such is largely the case in Bosnia–Herzegovina. In other cases, redundant soldiers sell their weapons on the black market, or small-scale producers (as in Pakistan) copy their designs. In addition, arms enterprises which have lost state markets seek new sources of demand. Certain conflicts, for example in Kashmir, took on a new character as a result of the influx of arms, in this case a spill-over from the conflict in Afghanistan. An important factor in the escalation of the conflict in Kosovo was the sudden availability of arms after the Albanian state collapsed in the summer of 1997; arms caches were opened and hundreds of thousands of Kalashnikovs were available for sale at a few dollars each and could easily be brought across the border into Kosovo. The new wars could be viewed as a form of military waste-disposal – a way of using up unwanted surplus arms generated by the Cold War, the biggest military build-up in history.

Patterns of Violence

The techniques of the new fighting units owe much to the types of warfare that developed during and after World War II as a reaction to modern war. Revolutionary warfare, as articulated by Mao Tse-tung and Che Guevara, developed tactics that were designed to find a way round large-scale concentrations of conventional forces and that were almost counter to conventional strategic theory.

The central objective of revolutionary warfare is the control of territory through gaining support of the local population rather than through capturing territory from enemy forces. The zones under revolutionary control are usually in remote parts of the country which cannot easily be reached by the central administration. They provide bases from which the military forces can engage in tactics which sap the morale and efficiency of enemy forces. Revolutionary warfare has some similarities with manoeuvre theory. It involves decentralized dispersed military activity, with a great emphasis on surprise and mobility. But a key feature of revolutionary warfare is the avoidance of head-on collisions which guerrilla units are likely to lose because of inferior numbers and equipment. Strategic retreats are frequent. According to Mao Tse-tung: 'The ability to run away is precisely one of the characteristics of guerrillas. Running away is the chief means of getting out of passivity and regaining the initiative.'[7] Great stress is placed by all revolutionary writers on winning 'hearts and minds', not just in the territory under revolutionary control but in enemy territory as well, so that the guerrilla can operate, according to Mao's well-known dictum, 'like a fish in the sea', although, of course, terroristic methods were also used.

Counter-insurgency, which has been an almost universal failure,[8] was designed to counter this type of warfare using conventional military forces. The main strategy has been to destroy the environment in which the revolutionaries operate, to poison the sea for the fish. Techniques like forcible resettlement developed by the French in Algeria, or area destruction through scattering mines or herbicides or napalm developed by the Americans in Vietnam, have also been used by, for example, the Indonesians in East Timor or the Turkish government against the Kurds.

The new warfare borrows from both revolutionary warfare and counter-insurgency. It borrows from revolutionary warfare the strategy of controlling territory through political means rather than through capturing territory from enemy forces. This is somewhat easier than it was for revolutionary forces, since in most cases the central authority is very weak and the main contenders for the control of territory are not governments with conventional modern forces but rather similar types of fighting units, even if they bear the name of regular armies. Nevertheless, as in the case of revolutionary warfare, the various factions continue to avoid battle mainly in order to conserve men and equipment. Strategic retreats are typical and ground is conceded to what appears to be the stronger party. Often, the various factions cooperate in dividing up territory between them.

An important difference between revolutionaries and the new warriors, however, is the method of political control. For the revolutionaries, ideology was very important; even though fear was a significant element, popular support and allegiance to the revolutionary idea was the central aim. Hence, the revolutionaries tried to build model societies in the areas under their control. In contrast, the new warriors establish political control through allegiance to a label rather than an idea. In the brave new democratized world, where political mobilization is based on labels and where elections and referenda are often forms of census-taking, this means that the majority of people living in the territory under control must admit to the right label. Anyone else has to be eliminated. Indeed, even in non-democratized areas, fear of opposition, dissidence or insurgency reinforces this demand for homogeneity of population based on identity.

This is why the main method of territorial control is not popular support, as in the case of revolutionary warfare, but population displacement – getting rid of all possible opponents. To achieve this, the new warfare borrows from counter-insurgency techniques for poisoning the sea – techniques which were refined by guerrilla movements created or promoted by Western governments with experience of counter-insurgency to topple left-wing governments in the 'low-intensity' conflicts of the 1980s such as RENAMO in Mozambique, the *Mujahidiin* in Afghanistan, or the Contras in Nicaragua.

Indeed, this approach was a reaction to the failure of counter-insurgency in Vietnam and Southern Africa and the implicit realization that a conventional modern war is no longer a viable option.

Instead of a favourable environment for the guerrilla, the new warfare aims to create an unfavourable environment for all those people it cannot control. Control of one's own side depends not on positive benefits, since in the impoverished, disorderly conditions of the new warfare there is not much that can be offered. Rather, it depends on continuing fear and insecurity and on the perpetuation of hatred of the other. Hence the importance of extreme and conspicuous atrocity and of involving as many people as possible in these crimes so as to establish a shared complicity, to sanction violence against a hated 'other' and to deepen divisions.

The techniques of population displacement include:

1 Systematic murder of those with different labels, as in Rwanda. The killing of Tutsis in 1994 was directed by government officials and the army. According to Human Rights Watch: 'In such places as the commune of Nyakizu in Southern Rwanda, local officials and other killers came to "work" every morning. After they had put in a full day's "work" killing Tutsi, they went home "singing" at quitting time . . . The "workers" returned each day until the job had been finished – that is, until all the Tutsi had been killed.'[9]

2 Ethnic cleansing, that is to say, forcible population expulsion, as in Bosnia–Herzegovina (see chapter 3) or the Transcaucasus. In Abkhazia, another example, the Abkhaz inhabitants accounted for only 17 per cent of the population. In order to control the territory, the secessionist forces had to expel most of the remaining population, mainly Georgian. Even after the expulsion of the Georgians, the Abkhaz remain a minority.

3 Rendering an area uninhabitable. This can be done physically, through scattering anti-personnel landmines or through the use of shells and rockets against civilian targets, especially homes, hospitals or crowded places such as markets or water sources. It can be done economically through forced famines or sieges. By depriving the people

of their livelihood, they either die of hunger, as in Southern Sudan, or they are forced to migrate. And it can be done psychologically by instilling unbearable memories of what was once home, by desecrating whatever has social meaning. One method is the destruction of history and culture by removing the physical landmarks that define the social environment for particular groups of people. The destruction of religious buildings and historic monuments is supposed to erase all traces of cultural claim to a particular area. In Banja Luka, at the height of the war, the Serbs destroyed all seventeen mosques and all but one of the Catholic churches. In particular, they flattened two very beautiful sixteenth-century mosques; they were demolished on a Friday, and on Monday the ground was razed and turfed over. The wanton destruction of the ancient Buddhist statues in Afghanistan by the Taliban was presumably supposed to achieve something similar. Another method is defilement through systematic rape and sexual abuse, which is characteristic of several wars, or by other public and very visible acts of brutality. Psychological methods have the advantage of differentiating between people with different labels.

All of these techniques fall within the definition of genocide contained in the 1948 Geneva Convention. Article 2 reads:

> In the present Convention, genocide means any of the following acts committed with intent to destroy, in whole or in part, a national, racial, or religious group as such: a) Killing members of the group; b) Causing serious bodily or mental harm to members of the group; c) Deliberately inflicting on the group conditions of life calculated to bring about its physical destruction in whole or in part; d) Imposing measures intended to prevent births within the group; e) Forcibly transferring the children of the group to another group.[10]

Essentially, what were considered to be undesirable and illegitimate side-effects of old war have become central to the mode of fighting in the new wars. It is sometimes said that the new wars are a reversion to primitivism. But primitive wars were highly ritualistic and hedged in by social constraints. These wars are rational in the sense that they apply rational thinking to the aims of war and refuse normative constraints.

The pattern of violence in the new type of warfare is confirmed by the statistics of the new wars. The tendency to avoid battle and to direct most violence against civilians is evidenced by the dramatic increase in the ratio of civilian to military casualties. At the beginning of the twentieth century, 85 to 90 per cent of casualties in war were military. In World War II, approximately half of all war deaths were civilian. By the late 1990s, the proportions of a hundred years ago have been almost exactly reversed, so that nowadays approximately 80 per cent of all casualties in wars are civilian.[11]

The importance of population displacement is evidenced by the figures on refugees and displaced persons. According to UNHCR, the global refugee population rose from 2.4 million people in 1975 to 10.5 million people in 1985 and 14.4 million people in 1995, and subsequently declined to 9.6 million in 2004, primarily as a consequence of increased repatriation. This figure includes only refugees who cross international boundaries. According to the same figures, the number of internally displaced people increased from 5.4 million in 1995 to 7.6 million in 2004.[12] Figures provided by the US Committee on Refugees are much higher, increasing from 22 million in 1980 to 38 million in 1995, of whom approximately half were internally displaced persons, and declining to 32.8 million in 2004, of whom two-thirds were internally displaced.[13] Using the latter figures, Myron Weiner has calculated that the number of refugees and internally displaced persons per conflict increased from 327,000 per conflict in 1969 to 1,316,000 in 1992. (1992 was, of course, a peak year for conflict.)[14] Using the Uppsala University database, it can be estimated, nevertheless, that the number of refugees and displaced persons per conflict in 2004 was 1,093,300.[15]

Financing the War Effort

The new wars take place in a context which could be represented as an extreme version of globalization. Territorially based production more or less collapses either as a result of liberalization and the withdrawal of state support; or through physical destruction (pillage, shelling, etc.); or because markets are cut off as a result of the disintegration of states, fighting, or deliberate blockades imposed by outside powers, or, more likely, by fighting units on the ground; or because spare parts, raw materials and fuel are impossible to acquire. In some cases, a few valuable commodities continue to be produced – e.g. diamonds in Angola and Sierra Leone, lapis lazuli and emeralds in Afghanistan, oil in Angola or Chechnya or Iraq, drugs in Colombia and Tadjikistan – and they provide a source of income for whoever can offer 'protection'. Unemployment is very high and, as long as governments continue to spend, inflation is rampant. In extreme cases, the currency collapses to be replaced by barter, the use of valuable commodities as currency or the circulation of foreign currencies, dollars or euros.

Given the erosion of the tax base both because of the collapse of production and because of the difficulties of collection, governments, like privatized military groups, need to seek alternative sources of funding in order to sustain their violent activities. Given the collapse of productive activity, the main sources of funding are either what Mark Duffield calls 'asset transfer',[16] i.e. the redistribution of existing assets so as to favour the fighting units, or external assistance. The simplest form of asset transfer is loot, robbery, extortion, pillage and hostage-taking. This is widespread in all contemporary wars. Rich people are killed and their gold and valuables stolen; property is transferred in the aftermath of ethnic cleansing; cattle and livestock are raided by militiamen;[17] shops and factories are looted when towns are taken. Hostages are captured and exchanged for food, weapons or other hostages, prisoners of war or dead bodies.

A second form of asset transfer is market pressure. A typical characteristic of the new wars is the numerous checkpoints which control the supply of food and necessities. Sieges and blockades, the division of territory between different paramilitary groups, allow the fighting units to control market prices. Thus a typical pattern, observed in Sudan, former Yugoslavia and other places, is that urban dwellers or even farmers will be forced to sell their assets – cars, fridges, televisions or cows – at ridiculously low prices in exchange for highly priced necessities simply in order to survive.

More sophisticated income-generating activities include 'war taxes' or 'protection' money from the production of primary commodities and various forms of illegal trading. The production and sale of drugs is a key source of income in Colombia, Peru and Tadjikistan. It is estimated that income from drugs accounts for 70 per cent of the opposition revenue in Tadjikistan, while the income of the Colombian guerrillas is said to amount to some $US800 million a year, which compares with government defence expenditure of $US1.4 billion.[18] Chechen warlords sell oil from backyard oil wells to Russian commanders; revenue from oil and natural gas fuelled the fighting in Angola, parts of Colombia, and Aceh in Indonesia; smuggling in oil products helps to sustain Nagorno Karabakh.[19] Sanctions busting and trading in drugs, arms or laundered money are all examples of revenue-raising criminal activities in which the various military groups are engaged.

However, given the collapse of domestic production, external assistance is crucial, since arms, ammunition and food, not to mention Mercedes cars or Ray-Ban sunglasses, have to be imported. External assistance can take the following forms:

1 Remittances from abroad to individual families, for example, Sudanese or Palestinian workers in the oil-rich countries of the Middle East, Bosnian and Croatian workers in Germany or Austria. These remittances can be converted into military resources through the various forms of asset transfer described above.
2 Direct assistance from the diaspora living abroad. This includes material assistance, arms and money, for example from Irish Americans to the IRA, from Armenians all over the world to Nagorno-Karabakh, from Canadian Croatians to the ruling Croatian party, and so on.
3 Assistance from foreign governments. During the Cold War period, both regular forces and guerrillas relied on their superpower patrons. This source of assistance has largely dried up although the USA still provides support to a number of governments. Neighbouring states often fund particular factions, to assist minorities or because of the presence of large numbers of refugees or because of involvement in various types of (illegal) trading arrangements. Thus Serbia and Croatia have provided support to

their client statelets in Bosnia–Herzegovina; Armenia aids
Nagorno-Karabakh; Russia has backed a variety of secessionist movements on its borders, whether as a way of re-
establishing control over post-Soviet space, or because of
mafia or military vested interests, is a matter for speculation; Rwanda encouraged the opposition in Zaire as a way
of preventing Hutu militiamen from operating from refugee
camps there; and Uganda supported the Rwandan Patriotic
Front which took over after the massacres of 1994 and
continues to abet the SPLA in Southern Sudan (and, in
return, the Sudanese government supports the Lord's
Resistance Army in Uganda). Other foreign governments
that offer a source of finance include former colonial powers
concerned about 'stability', for example France and Belgium
in Central Africa, or Islamic states.

4   Humanitarian assistance. There are various ways in which
both governments and warring factions divert humanitarian assistance for their own use. Indeed, donors regard a 5
per cent diversion of humanitarian aid as acceptable in view
of the needs of the most vulnerable parts of the population.
The most common method is 'customs duties'. The Bosnian
Croats demanded 27 per cent for humanitarian assistance
transported through so-called Herzeg–Bosne, which, at the
height of the war, was the only way to reach certain areas
in Central Bosnia. But there are also other ways, including
robbery and ambush. By insisting on the use of an overval-
ued official exchange rate, both the Sudanese and Ethio-
pian governments were able to profit from the provision of
humanitarian aid.

Essentially, the fragmentation and informalization of war is
paralleled by the informalization of the economy. In place of
the national formal economy, with its emphasis on industrial
production and state regulation, a new type of globalized
informal economy is established in which external flows,
especially humanitarian assistance and remittances from
abroad, are integrated into a local and regional economy based
on asset transfer and extra-legal trading. Figure 5.1 illustrates
the typical resource flows of a new war. It is assumed that
there is no production and no taxation. Instead, external
support to ordinary people, in the form of remittances and

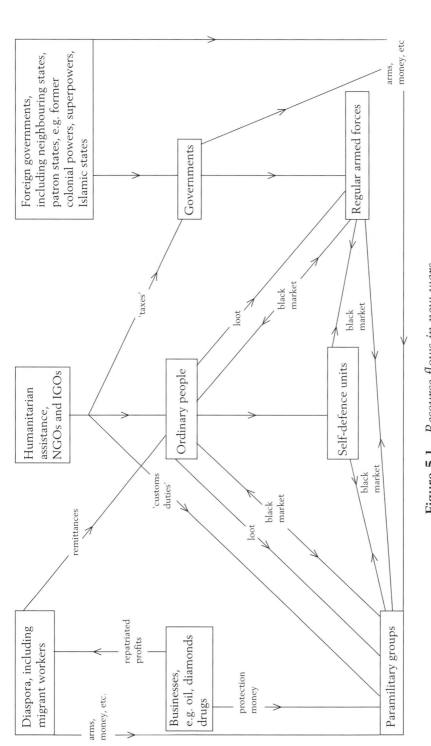

Figure 5.1 *Resource flows in new wars*

humanitarian assistance, is recycled via various forms of asset transfer and black-market trading into military resources. Direct assistance from foreign governments, protection money from producers of commodities, and assistance from the diaspora enhance the capacity of the various fighting units to extract further resources from ordinary people and thus sustain their military efforts.

Mark Duffield describes how this functioned in the Sudanese case where an illegal dollar trade involving Sudan, Zaire and Uganda was operated, making use of relief convoys both for transport and to control prices:

> In the case of Sudan, the parallel economy consists of a number of interconnecting levels or systems. Local asset transfer is linked to national level extra-legal mercantile activity. In turn, this articulates with higher-level political and state relations together with regional and international parallel networks which trade in commodities and hard currency. It is this level that provides the initial site for the integration of international aid and relief assistance with the parallel economy. As assets flow upwards and outwards, culminating in capital flight, international assistance flows downwards through the same or related systems of power.[20]

Just as it is possible to find examples of military cooperation between fighting units so as to divide up territory or to foster mutual hatred among the respective populations, so it is possible to find examples of economic cooperation. David Keen describes what is known as the 'sell-game' in Sierra Leone, through which government forces sell arms and ammunition to the rebels:

> [Government forces] withdraw from a town, leaving arms and ammunition for the rebels behind them. The rebels pick up the arms and extract the loot, mostly in the form of cash, from the townspeople and then they themselves retreat. At this point, the government forces reoccupy the town and engage in their own looting, usually of property (which the rebels find hard to dispose of) as well as engaging in illegal mining.[21]

John Simpson describes how Peruvian government soldiers set free captured Shining Path guerrillas 'apparently in order to perpetuate insecurity in areas where officers can benefit from illegal trading – in this case, principally the trade in cocaine.'[22]

There are similar examples in the Bosnian War, which I have described in chapter 3.

Some writers argue that economic motivation explains the new type of warfare. David Keen suggests that a 'war where one avoids battles but picks on unarmed civilians and perhaps eventually acquires a Mercedes may make more sense . . . [than] risking death in the name of the nation-state with little or no prospect of significant financial gain.'[23] But economic motivation alone is insufficient to explain the scale, brutality and sheer viciousness of new wars.[24] No doubt some join the fighting as a way of legitimizing criminal activities, providing a political justification for what they do and socially sanctioning otherwise illegal methods of financial gain. No doubt there are others – rational power-seekers, extreme fanatics or victims intent on revenge – who engage in criminal activities to sustain their political military goals. Yet others are press-ganged into the fighting, propelled by fear and hunger.

The point is rather that the modern distinctions between the political and the economic, the public and the private, the military and the civil are breaking down. Political control is required to embed the new coercive forms of economic exchange, which in turn are required to provide a viable financial basis for the new gangsters/powerholders in the context of state disintegration and economic marginalization. A new retrograde set of social relationships is being established in which economics and violence are deeply intertwined within the shared framework of identity politics.

The Spread of Violence

The new type of warfare is a predatory social condition.[25] While it may be possible to contain particular groups or individuals, it is very difficult to contain the social condition either in space or in time. Neighbouring countries are the most immediately affected. The cost of the war in terms of lost trade, especially where sanctions or communications blockades are introduced or where borders are closed, either deliberately or because of fighting; the burden of refugees, since generally it is the neighbouring states who accept the largest numbers; the spread of illegal circuits of trade; and the spill-over of identity politics – all these factors reproduce the conditions that nurture the new forms of violence.

The NGO Saferworld has enumerated the cost of conflict to neighbouring countries in several cases. One example is the war in Mozambique, which was an important trade route for land-locked countries such as Zambia, Zimbabwe, Malawi, Botswana and Swaziland. Malawi lost all its trade with Mozambique, and the additional costs of transport during the height of the war were estimated at 11 per cent of annual export earnings; likewise, trade with Zimbabwe fell dramatically and the cost of rerouting goods through South Africa was estimated at $US825 million at 1988 prices.[26] In the Balkans, the decline in GDP following the wars in Croatia and Bosnia–Herzegovina, as a result of the loss of trade following the closure of borders and sanctions and the increased cost of transportation, was more or less inversely proportionate to distance from the epicentre of violence. The decline in GDP in Bosnia–Herzegovina was most dramatic, falling from $US2719 per head before the war broke out to just $US250 per head when the war ended. Surrounding Bosnia–Herzegovina is an inner ring of countries – Serbia/Montenegro, Croatia, and Macedonia – whose GDPs fell to 49 per cent, 65 per cent and 55 per cent of their 1989 levels, respectively. By 1996, Serbia/Montenegro and Macedonia had just managed to arrest the decline, while Croatia was able to achieve a very small growth rate. Surrounding these three countries is an outer ring of further affected countries – Albania, Bulgaria, Romania and Slovenia – whose GDPs fell to 81 per cent, 88 per cent, 73 per cent and 90 per cent of their 1989 levels. Finally, the outermost ring – Hungary, Greece and Turkey – all also reported economic losses as a consequence of the war.[27]

As well as direct economic costs, the neighbouring countries bear the main burden of refugees. Most refugees are based in neighbouring countries. According to UNHCR figures, out of the 14.5 million refugees recorded for 1995, the majority (6.7 million and 5.0 million, respectively) were based in Africa and Asia. Countries hosting more than 500,000 refugees included Guinea (from Liberia and Sierra Leone), Sudan (mainly from Ethiopia, Eritrea and Chad), Tanzania (mainly from Rwanda and Burundi), Zaire (which had, as of 1995, received 1.7 million refugees, of whom 1.2 million came from Rwanda and the remainder mainly from Angola, Burundi and Sudan), Iran (from Afghanistan and Iraq), Pakistan (also from Afghanistan and Iraq), Germany (mainly from the former Yugoslavia) and the United States. In Europe, after Germany, the biggest recipients of refugees have been Croatia and Serbia/Montenegro. In 2004, the pattern had changed somewhat. Out of the 9.6 million refugees, some 60 per cent were based in Africa, the Middle East and Central Asia. The biggest recipients of refugees were Iran and Pakistan (from Afghanistan), Germany and Tanzania. Not only are these huge concentrations of refugees an immense economic burden on countries that are already poor, but they represent a permanent source of tension between the refugees and the host populations – for economic reasons, since they are competing for resources; for political reasons, since they constitute a permanent pressure on host governments to take action in order that they can return; and for security reasons, because the camps are often used as bases for various radical factions. The most long-standing example of both economic and political burdens are the Palestinian refugees squashed into the West Bank and Gaza or based in Jordan and the Lebanon. As in the case of the Palestinian refugees, up to a million or so Azeri refugees from Nagorno-Karabakh in Azerbaijan, or the Georgian IDPs (internally displaced persons) from Abkhazia in Georgia or the refugees and IDPs in the former Yugoslav republics all constitute a permanent source of political pressure for radical action. In Zaire, the Hutu refugee camps served as a base for Hutu militiamen and contributed to the mobilization of Zairian Tutsis against the Mobutu regime.

Illegal circuits of trade are another conduit for the spread of the new type of war economy. Trade routes necessarily cross borders. The instability in Albania in the mid-1990s was mainly the consequence of the growth of mafia groups well connected to the ruling circles involved in sanctions-busting to Serbia/ Montenegro and gun-running to Bosnia–Herzegovina. The pyramid schemes that collapsed so dramatically were used to finance these activities – a classic case of asset transfer. The huge transfer of arms by the United States to Afghan guerrilla groups in the 1980s (much of which was largely diverted) transformed itself into networks of arms and drug trade covering Afghanistan, Pakistan, Kashmir and Tadjikistan.[28] Mark Duffield shows how the illegal dollar trade linked to the war in Sudan involved 'Zairois with gold wanting imported goods, food and fuel; Sudanese with dollars wanting food, clothing and coffee; and Ugandans with imported goods wanting gold and dollars for Kampala's parallel markets.'[29]

Finally, the politics of identity, itself, has a tendency to spread. All identity-based groups, whether defined in terms of language, religion or some other form of differentiation, spill over borders; after all, it is precisely the heterogeneity of identities that offers the opportunity for various forms of exclusivism. Majorities in one country are minorities in another: Tutsis in Rwanda, Burundi and Zaire; Russians in most post-Soviet states, especially so-called Cossacks on the borders of Russia; Islamic groups in Central Asia – these are among the many vectors through which identity politics passes.

It is possible to identify spreading regional clusters characterized by this predatory social condition of the new war economies. Myron Weiner calls them 'Bad Neighbourhoods'. The clearest examples are the Balkan region surrounding Bosnia–Herzegovina; the Caucasus stretching south from Chechnya as far as Western Turkey and Northern Iran; the Horn of Africa, including Ethiopia, Eritrea, Somalia and Sudan; Central Africa, especially Rwanda, Burundi and Zaire; the West African countries surrounding Liberia and Sierra Leone; and Central Asia, from Tadjikistan to India. The countries hosting Palestinian refugees might be treated as another cluster; since Israel made peace with the neighbouring states, the conflict is no longer expressed in terms of inter-state war and has begun to exhibit many of the characteristics of the new types of conflict.

Conclusion

The new wars have political goals. The aim is political mobilization on the basis of identity. The military strategy for achieving this aim is population displacement and destabilization so as to get rid of those whose identity is different and to foment hatred and fear. Nevertheless, this divisive and exclusive form of politics cannot be disentangled from its economic basis. The various political/military factions plunder the assets of ordinary people as well as the remnants of the state, and cream off external assistance destined for the victims, in a way that is only possible in conditions of war or near war. In other words, war provides a legitimation for various criminal forms of private aggrandizement while at the same time these are necessary sources of revenue in order to sustain the war. The warring parties need more or less permanent conflict both to reproduce their positions of power and for access to resources.

While this predatory set of social relationships is most prevalent in the war zones, it also characterizes the surrounding regions. Because participation in the war is relatively low (in Bosnia, only 6.5 per cent of the population took part directly in the prosecution of the war) the differences between zones of war and apparent zones of peace are not nearly as marked as in earlier periods. Just as it is difficult to distinguish between the political and the economic, public and private, military and civil, so it is increasingly difficult to distinguish between war and peace. The new war economy could be represented as a continuum, starting with the combination of criminality and racism to be found in the inner cities of Europe and North America and reaching its most acute manifestation in the areas where the scale of violence is greatest.

If violence and predation are to be found in what are considered zones of peace, so it is possible to find islands of civility in nearly all the war zones. They are known about far less than violence and criminality, because it is these and not normality that is generally reported. But there are regions where local state apparatuses continue to function, where taxes are raised, services are provided and some production is maintained. There are groups who defend humanistic values and refuse the politics of particularism. The town of Tuzla in Bosnia–Herzegovina represents one celebrated example. The self-defence units created in Southern Rwanda are another example. In isolation, these islands of civility are difficult to preserve, squeezed by the polarization of violence, but the very fragmentary and decentralized character of the new type of warfare makes such examples possible.

Precisely because the new wars are a social condition that arises as the formal political economy withers, they are very difficult to end. Diplomatic negotiations from above fail to take into account the underlying social relations; they treat the various factions as though they were proto-states. Temporary ceasefires or truces may merely legitimize new agreements or partnerships that, for the moment, suit the various factions.

Peacekeeping troops sent in to monitor ceasefires which reflect the status quo may help to maintain a division of territory and to prevent the return of refugees. Economic reconstruction channelled through existing 'political authorities' may merely provide new sources of revenue as local assets dry up. As long as the power relations remain the same, sooner or later the violence will start again.

Fear, hatred and predation are not recipes for long-term viable polities; indeed, this type of war economy is perennially on the edge of exhaustion. This does not mean, however, that they will disappear of their own accord. There has to be some alternative. In the next chapter, I will consider the possibilities for such an alternative; in particular, how islands of civility might offer a counterlogic to the new warfare.

6

Towards a Cosmopolitan Approach

At the beginning of the 1990s, there was a lot of optimism about the possibilities for solving global problems, particularly wars. In the *Agenda for Peace*, the UN Secretary-General Boutros Boutros-Ghali talked about the 'second chance' for the UN now its activities were no longer blocked by the Cold War. The term 'international community', implying a cohesive group of governments acting through international organizations, entered into everyday usage. Conflicts in a number of countries seemed close to resolution – Cambodia, Namibia, Angola, South Africa, Nicaragua, Afghanistan. And in those conflicts which were not resolved, the idea, enunciated by the French minister and former director of Médecins Sans Frontières Bernard Kouchner, of a right/duty to intervene for humanitarian purposes seemed to be gaining widespread acceptance.

The number of UN peacekeeping operations increased dramatically in the 1990s, as did the range of tasks they were asked to perform, including the delivery of humanitarian aid, the protection of people in safe havens, disarmament and demobilization, creating a secure environment for elections and reporting violations of international humanitarian law, in addition to the traditional tasks of monitoring and maintaining ceasefires. Mandates were also strengthened; in both Somalia and Bosnia, peacekeeping troops were authorized to act under Chapter VII of the UN Charter, which allows the use of force. Moreover, the UN was not the only umbrella for multilateral peacekeeping operations; regional organizations such as NATO, the EU, the CIS, the AU or the Economic Community of West African States (ECOWAS) were also responsible for organizing peacekeeping missions.

Yet despite the hopes and good intentions, the experience so far of what has come to be known as humanitarian intervention has been frustrating, to say the least. At best, people have been fed and fragile ceasefires have been agreed, although it is not clear whether this can be attributed to the presence of peacekeeping troops. At worst, the UN has been shamed and humiliated, as, for example, when it failed to prevent genocide in Rwanda, when the so-called safe haven of Srebrenica was overrun by Bosnian Serbs, or when the hunt for the Somali warlord Aideed ended in a mixture of farce and tragedy. Moreover, the term humanitarian intervention has been used to justify wars, as in Kosovo, and now Iraq and Afghanistan, giving rise to scepticism about the whole concept; hence the phrase 'military humanism' coined by Noam Chomsky.[1]

There have been many explanations for the failures – the short-termism of politicians, the role of the media, which raises public consciousness at particular times and particular places, the lack of coordination of governments and international agencies, inadequate resources – and all of these have some merit. But the most important explanation is misperception, the persistence of inherited ways of thinking about organized violence, the inability to understand the character and logic of the new warfare. One response to the new wars has been to treat them as Clausewitzean wars in which the warring parties are states or, if not states, groups with a claim to statehood. Many of the terms used, such as 'intervention', 'peacekeeping', 'peace-enforcement', 'sovereignty', 'civil war', are drawn from conceptions of the nation-state and of modern war that are not only difficult to apply in the current context, but may actually pose an obstacle to appropriate action. The other response is fatalistic. Because the wars cannot be understood in traditional terms, they are thought to represent a reversion to primitivism or anarchy, and the most that can be done, therefore, is to ameliorate the symptoms. In other words, wars are treated as natural disasters; hence the use of terms such as 'complex emergencies', which are emptied of political meaning. Indeed the very term 'humanitarian' acquired a non-political meaning in the 1990s. It came to be associated with the provision of humanitarian relief assistance in wars, or help to non-combatants or the wounded, rather than with respect for human rights which was implied in the classic usage of the term 'humanitarian intervention'.[2]

The analysis in the previous chapters implies a different approach towards trying to solve these conflicts. What is needed is a much more political response to the new wars. A strategy of capturing 'hearts and minds' needs to be counterposed to the strategy of sowing 'fear and hate'. A politics of inclusion needs to be counterposed against the politics of exclusion; respect for international principles and legal norms needs to be counterposed against the criminality of the warlords. In short, what is needed is a new form of cosmopolitan political mobilization, which embraces both the so-called international community and local populations, and which is capable of countering the submission to various types of particularism. A sceptic might argue that a form of cosmopolitan politics is already on the international agenda; certainly, respect for human rights, abhorrence of genocide and ethnic cleansing are increasingly part of the accepted rhetoric of political leaders. But political mobilization involves more than this; it has to override other considerations – geo-politics or short-term domestic concerns; it has to constitute the primary guide to policy and action which has not been the case up to now.

In this chapter, I develop this argument, first with some general considerations about the construction of legitimacy and the terminology of humanitarian intervention; second, I will explore what a cosmopolitan approach might mean in political, military and economic terms.

The Reconstruction of Legitimacy

The key to the control of violence is the reconstruction of legitimacy. I agree with Hannah Arendt when she says that power rests on legitimacy and not on violence. By legitimacy, I mean both consent and even support for political institutions, as well as the notion that these institutions acquire their authority on the basis of operating within an agreed set of rules – the rule of law. Arendt claims that:

> No government exclusively based on the means of violence has ever existed . . . Single men without others to support them never have enough power to use violence successfully. Hence, in domestic affairs, violence functions as the last resort of power against criminals or rebels – that is, against single individuals who, as it were, refuse to be overpowered by the consensus of the majority. And as for actual warfare . . . an enormous superiority in the means of violence can become helpless if confronted with an ill-equipped but well-organized opponent who is much more powerful.[3]

The same point is made by Giddens. The internal pacification of modern states was achieved not by violence, but by the extension of the rule of law and, concomitantly, the administrative reach of the state, including the extension of surveillance. The monopoly of legitimate organized violence implied the control of violence and much less reliance on the use of physical coercion, except, of course, in the international arena. Pre-modern states were much more violent in domestic affairs than the modern state, but also much less powerful. In so far as external violence contributed to internal pacification, it was an indirect contribution, arising from the increased legitimacy of the state associated with the defence of territory from external enemies and the augmentation of administrative capacities.

In the new wars, the monopoly of legitimate violence has broken down. And what is crucial is not the privatization of violence, as such, but the breakdown of legitimacy. As I have argued in the previous chapter, the goals of the new warfare are particularistic. The strategy is political control on the basis of exclusion – in particular, population displacement – and the tactics for achieving this goal are terror and destabilization. For this reason, it is virtually impossible for any of the warring parties to re-establish legitimacy. Violence may be controlled sporadically through uneasy truces and ceasefires, but in situations in which the moral, administrative and practical constraints against private violence have broken down, they rarely last long. At the same time, however, isolated citizens' groups or political parties which try to re-establish legitimacy on the basis of inclusive politics are relatively powerless in conditions of continuing violence.

'Cosmopolitanism', used in a Kantian sense, implies the existence of a human community with certain shared rights and obligations. In 'Perpetual Peace' Kant envisaged a world federation of democratic states in which cosmopolitan right is confined to the right of 'hospitality' – strangers and foreigners should be welcomed and treated with respect.[4] I use the term more extensively to refer both to a positive political vision, embracing tolerance, multiculturalism, civility and democracy, and to a more legalistic respect for certain overriding universal principles which should guide political communities at various levels, including the global level.

These principles are already contained in various treaties and conventions that comprise the body of international law. In chapter 2, I referred to the various rules of engagement and laws of war which deal with the abuses of armed power. Laws and customs of war which date back to early modern times were codified in the nineteenth and twentieth centuries; particularly important were the Geneva Conventions sponsored by the ICRC and the Hague Conferences of 1899 and 1907. The Nuremberg trials after World War II marked the first enforcement of 'war crimes' or, even more significantly, 'crimes against humanity'. To what was known as international humanitarian law, human rights norms were added in the post-war period. The difference between humanitarian and human rights law has to do largely with whether violation of the law takes place in war or peacetime. The former is confined to abuses of power in wartime situations. The assumption tends to be that war is usually modern inter-state war and that such abuses are inflicted by a foreign power – in other words, aggression. The latter is equally concerned with abuses of power in peacetime, in particular those inflicted by a government against its citizens – in other words, repression.[5]

The violations of international norms with which both bodies of law are concerned are, in fact, those which form the core of the new mode of warfare. As I have argued, in the new wars the classic distinctions between internal and external, war and peace, aggression and repression are breaking down. A war crime is at one and the same time a massive violation of human rights. A number of writers have suggested that humanitarian law should be combined with human rights law to form 'humane' or 'cosmopolitan' law.[6] Elements of a cosmopolitan regime do already exist. NGOs and the media draw attention to violations of human rights or to war crimes, and to some extent governments and international institutions respond through methods ranging from persuasion and pressure to, as yet tentative, enforcement. Particularly important in the latter respect has been the establishment of international tribunals with respect to violations of international humanitarian law for Rwanda and former Yugoslavia, and the creation of an International Criminal Court (ICC) to deal with 'core crimes' – war crimes, crimes against humanity and genocide. War crimes tribunals were established in 1993 and 1994, and the ICC in 1998.

These tentative steps towards a cosmopolitan regime, however, conflict with many of the more traditional geopolitical approaches adopted by the so-called international community which continue to emphasize the importance of state sovereignty as the basis of international relations. This is especially true since 9/11 and the promulgation of the 'War on Terror'. The prevalence of geo-politics is reflected in the terminology used to describe the response of the international community to post-Cold War conflicts. The literature is replete with discussions about intervention and non-intervention.[7] Intervention is taken to mean an infringement of sovereignty and, in its strong version, a military infringement. The prohibitions against intervention, expressed in particular in Article 2(1) of the UN Charter, which refers to the 'principle of sovereign equality', is considered important as a way of restricting the use of force, respecting pluralism and acting 'as a brake on the crusading, territorial and imperial ambitions of states'.[8]

But what does intervention and non-intervention mean nowadays? The new types of war are both global and local. There is already extensive international involvement, both private through diaspora connections, NGOs, etc., and public through patron states or international agencies providing aid or loans or other kinds of assistance. Indeed, as I argued in the previous chapter, the various parties to the conflict are totally dependent on outside support. Likewise, these are wars usually characterized by the erosion or disintegration of state power. In such a situation, what does it mean to talk about infringements of sovereignty?

An illustration of the artificiality of these terms was the debate about whether the war in Bosnia was an international or a civil war. Those who argued that this was an international war favoured intervention to support the Bosnian state. They argued that the Bosnian state had been internationally recognized and that the war was the result of an act of aggression by Serbia. Hence, intervention was justified under Chapter VII of the UN Charter, since Serbian aggression was a 'threat to international peace and security'. Those who argued that this was a civil war were against intervention. They claimed that this was a nationalist war between Serbs, Croats and Bosnians to control the remnants of the Yugoslav state – intervention would have a been a violation of sovereignty. Both positions missed the point. This was a war of ethnic cleansing and genocide. What did it matter whether the crime was committed by Serbs from Belgrade or by Serbs from Bosnia? What did it matter, in practical terms, whether Yugoslavia or Bosnia was the internationally recognized state? Something had to be done to protect the victims and to uphold respect for international humanitarian norms. In effect, the debate about whether the conflict was an international or a civil war treated it as an old war between the fighting sides, in which violence against civilians is merely a side-effect of the war.

Moreover, because outside involvement in various forms is already so extensive in this type of conflict, there is no such thing as non-intervention. The failure to protect the victims is a kind of tacit intervention on the side of those who are inflicting humanitarian or human rights abuses.

It is sometimes argued that intervention refers only to military intervention. Military means are often contrasted with political means as a way of solving conflicts. Behind this distinction is an assumption that these wars are comparable to modern wars. Military intervention implies military support for one side in the conflict. A political approach, on the other hand, implies negotiation between the sides. Hence, the debate about whether the war in Bosnia was an international or a civil war was sometimes presented as a debate about military versus political means. Again, this debate missed the point. The question was not whether to use military or political means, but what kind of politics would guide the use of military force. Both the argument for intervention on the side of the Bosnian state and the argument for negotiation which might lead to the use of troops in a peacekeeping role presuppose a traditional geo-political view of the conflict in which both sides were proto-states and in which a political solution would emerge either as a result of the victory of one side or as a result of a compromise. The solution had to do with the division of territory.

An alternative cosmopolitan approach starts from the assumption that no solution is workable based on the political goals of the warring parties and that legitimacy can only be restored on the basis of an alternative politics which operates within cosmopolitan principles. Once the values of inclusion, tolerance and mutual respect are established, the territorial solutions will easily follow. What this means in practical terms is the subject of the rest of this chapter.

From Top-down Diplomacy to Cosmopolitan Politics

In recent wars, the dominant approach of the international community has been to attempt a negotiated solution between the warring parties. This approach has several drawbacks.

First, the talks raise the profile of the warring parties and confer a sort of public legitimacy on individuals who may be criminals. Many people remarked on the paradox that international negotiators were seen on television shaking hands with Karadžić and Mladić, both of whom had earlier been named by the International Tribunal and by leading Western politicians as war criminals. The same contradiction applied to the involvement of the Khmer Rouge in the Paris talks which led to the agreements to end the war in Cambodia, to the high-profile talks between Mohammed Aideed and Ali Mahdi about the division of Mogadishu shortly after the arrival of US troops in Somalia in December 1992, or to the involvement of Afghan warlords in the post-Taliban Afghan government.

Second, because of the particularistic nature of the political goals of the warring parties, it is extremely difficult to find a workable solution. One option is territorial partition – a kind of identity-based apartheid. The other option is power-sharing on the basis of identity. The record of such agreements is dismal. Partitions do not provide a basis for stability; refugees, displaced persons or newly created minorities constitute a long-term source of tension, as the history of partitions in Cyprus, India and Pakistan, Ireland or Palestine testifies.[9] Nor do power-sharing agreements fare any better. The constitutions of both Cyprus and Lebanon offer examples of unworkable compromises which exacerbated ethnic and/or religious competition and mutual suspicion. Today, the Washington Agreement between Croats and Muslims, the Dayton Agreement, the Oslo Agreement between Israel and the Palestinians, or the Paris Agreements on Cambodia are all displaying the strains of trying to combine incompatible forms of exclusivism.

A third drawback is that such agreements tend to be based on exaggerated assumptions about the power of the warring parties to implement agreements. Since the power of the warring parties depends largely on fear and/or self-interest and not on consent, they need an insecure environment to sustain themselves both politically and economically. Politically, identity is based on fear and hatred of the other; economically, revenues depend on outside assistance for the war effort and on various forms of asset transfer based on loot and extortion or on price distortions resulting from restrictions on freedom of movement. In peacetime, these sources of sustenance are eroded.

It is often argued that, despite these drawbacks, there is no alternative. These are the only people who can end the violence. It is true that those responsible for the violence have to end it, but it does not follow that these are the people who can make peace. Negotiations with warlords may sometimes be necessary, but they need to take place in a context where alternative non-exclusive political constituencies can be fostered. The aim is to establish conditions for an alternative political mobilization. This means that the mediators have to be very clear about international principles and standards and refuse compromises that violate those principles, otherwise the credibility of the institutions will suffer and any kind of implementation could be very difficult. The point of the talks is to control violence so that space can be created for the emergence or re-emergence of civil society. The more 'normal' the situation, the greater the possibilities for developing political alternatives. There is, as it were, another potential source of power that has to be represented at the talks, involved or consulted in any compromise and, generally, made more visible. Precisely because these are not total wars, participation is low, loyalties change, sources of revenue dry up; it is always possible to identify local advocates of cosmopolitanism, people and places that refuse to accept the politics of war – islands of civility.

In chapter 3, I described the example of Tuzla in Bosnia–Herzegovina (see p. 57). Northwest Somaliland represents another example where local elders have succeeded in establishing relative peace through a process of negotiation. In Armenia and Azerbaijan, the local branches of the Helsinki Citizens' Assembly have succeeded in negotiating with local authorities on each side of the border, Kazakh and Echevan, and establishing a peace corridor; the corridor provides a place where hostages and prisoners of war can be released and where dialogue between women's groups, young people and even security forces can be organized. In Sierra Leone, the women's movement played a critical role in pressing for democracy and paving the way for peace.[10]

In South Africa, there have been many cases of locally negotiated peace accords during the violence between Inkatha and the ANC. Davin Bremmer has described how the Wilgespruit Fellowship Centre was able to establish a zone of peace in the Meadowlands Hostel in Soweto, which had been a flashpoint of violence between the IFP and the ANC.[11] In the Mpumalanga community in KwaZulu-Natal, two local leaders representing the two main political factions joined with other residents to form the Peace and Hope Foundation Trust, which provided mediation and other conflict resolution services at a local level, such as a 'rumour control system'.[12] In the Philippines, a peace zones strategy was adopted after a town in the north, Hungduan, convinced guerrillas to withdraw from the town and then acted to prevent the military from moving in; the peace zones strategy is said to have been an important factor in ending the war.[13]

Many other examples from Northern Ireland, Central America, Vojvodina or West Africa can be enumerated. In nearly all these cases, women's groups play an important role. They are rarely reported because they are not news. They may involve local negotiations and conflict resolution between local factions or pressure on the warring parties to keep out of the area. They are often difficult to sustain because of the pressures of the war economy – influxes of refugees seeking safety, unemployment, and propaganda, especially television, radio and video cassettes controlled by the warring parties. But they need to be taken seriously and given credibility by outside support.

These groups represent a potential solution. To the extent that they are capable of mobilizing support, they weaken the power of the warring parties. To the extent that the areas they control can be extended, so the zones of war are diminished. They also represent a repository of knowledge and information about the local situation; they can advise and guide a cosmopolitan strategy.

In many places, there is a growing emphasis by governments and international organizations on the role of local NGOs and grass-roots initiatives, and they provide funding and other forms of support. In some cases, support for NGOs is seen as a substitute for action. They are supposed to undertake the tasks that the international community is unable to fulfil. But what is not understood is that, in a context of war, the survival of such groups is always precarious. Civil society needs a state. If the local state does not provide the conditions in which alternative politics can develop, there has to be support from international organizations. However courageous those engaged in NGOs, they cannot operate without law and order. The peace movement in Bosnia–Herzegovina was destroyed when the Serbs began to shoot demonstrators. What happened in Rwanda is a classic illustration of what happens to local advocates of cosmopolitanism without outside support. According to Alex de Waal:

> Rwanda had an exemplary 'human rights community'. Seven indigenous human rights NGOs collaborated closely with their foreign friends and patrons, providing unrivaled documentation of the ongoing massacres and assassinations . . . They predicted massive atrocities unless named perpetrators were called to account. But there was no 'primary movement' that could underpin the activists' agenda, no political establishment ready to listen to their critique and act on it, and no international organizations ready to take measures and risks necessary to protect them . . . On April 6 1994, the Hutu extremists called the bluff of the human rights community and launched their final solution. As well as eradicating all Tutsis, they embarked

upon the systematic assassination of all critics. The UN ran away, while the US government thought up nice excuses for inaction.[14]

Just as the warring factions depend on outside support, so there needs to be a conscious strategy of building on local cosmopolitan initiatives. What form support takes, whether or not it involves sending troops, depends on each situation and what the local groups consider necessary. But there is still a reluctance to engage in a serious dialogue on a par with the dialogue with the warring parties, to see these groups as partners in a shared cosmopolitan project and to work out jointly a mutual strategy for developing a peace constituency. There is a tendency on the part of Western political leaders to dismiss such initiatives as worthy but insignificant; 'citizens can't make peace', said David Owen when negotiator in the former Yugoslavia. This attitude can perhaps be explained by the horizontal character of top-level communication, the fact that leaders generally talk only to leaders. It also has to do with the colonial mentality that seems to grip representatives of international institutions when on missions in faraway countries – there are widespread complaints, whether in Somalia, Bosnia or the Transcaucasus, about the seemingly systematic failure to consult local experts or NGOs.

A Somali driver in Mogadishu commented on the negotiations between Mohammed Aideed and Ali Mahdi in the following terms:

> Everyone agrees that these men have caused so much unnecessary suffering in this country. We understand that the US Embassy had to deal with these men. But did the embrace have to be so fast so public? They are all war criminals in my view. What the outside world should be doing is giving them the message that, yes, other leaders should be allowed to emerge. Why didn't the US embassy also invite religious leaders, elders, women, professionals, when Aideed and Ali Mahdi met, to let these men know that these are the people they have stolen power from? It is a great pity they did not think of it. It sent all the wrong signals.[15]

In fact, this had been the strategy of Mohamed Sahnoun, who was appointed UN Special Representative to Somalia in

April 1992 and resigned in October because of frustration over UN policy. Sahnoun's role has become 'mythologized', to use Alex de Waal's word, in Somalia. He explicitly pursued what he called a 'civil society' strategy, including elders, women and neutral clans in a variety of talks: 'His strategy was not so much one of marginalizing the warlords as of including the non-warlords in political discussions.'[16]

The failure to take seriously alternative sources of power displays a myopia about the character of power and the relationship between power and violence. An effective response to the new wars has to be based on an alliance between international organizations and local advocates of cosmopolitanism in order to reconstruct legitimacy. A strategy of winning 'hearts and minds' needs to identify with individuals and groups respected for their integrity. They have to be supported, and their advice, proposals and recommendations need to be taken seriously. There is no standard formula for a cosmopolitan response; the point is rather that, in each local situation, there has to be a process involving these individuals and groups through which a strategy is developed. The various components of international involvement – the use of troops, the role of negotiation, funds for reconstruction – need to be worked out jointly.

It is often argued that it is difficult to identify local cosmopolitans. Are they just marginal groups of intellectuals? Are there moderate religious and nationalist groups who count as cosmopolitan? There has to be, of course, widespread consultation. But through such a consultation it is possible to situate those who are concerned about the future of the whole society and not just sectarian interest. Women's groups usually play a key role in a more inclusive approach. Even if the cosmopolitans are a small minority, they are often the best source of ideas and proposals.

This argument also has implications for the way in which political pressure from the international community is exerted on political and military leaders to reach agreement or to consent to peacekeeping forces. Typical methods include the threat of air strikes or economic sanctions, which have the consequence of identifying the leaders with the population instead of isolating them, treating them as representative of 'sides', as legitimate leaders of states or proto-states. Such methods can easily be counterproductive, alienating the local population and narrowing the possibilities of pressure below. There may be circumstances in which these methods are an appropriate strategy and others where more targeted approaches may be more effective – arraigning the leaders as war criminals so that they cannot travel, exempting cultural communication so as to support civil society, for example. The point is that local cosmopolitans can provide the best advice on what is the best approach; they need to be consulted and treated as partners.

From Peacekeeping and/or Peace-enforcement to Cosmopolitan Law-enforcement

In the literature about peacekeeping, a rigid division tends to be drawn between peacekeeping and peace-enforcement.[17] Both terms are based on traditional assumptions about the character of war. Peacekeeping is based on the assumption that an agreement has been reached between the two sides in a war; the task of the peacekeeper is to supervise and monitor implementation of the agreement. The principles of peacekeeping as developed in the post-war period are consent, impartiality and the non-use of force. Peace-enforcement, on the other hand, which is authorized under Chapter VII of the UN Charter, is basically war-fighting; it means intervening in a war on one side. The distinction is considered important because war-fighting is assumed to involve the use of maximum force, since Clausewitzean wars tend to extremes. General Rose's preoccupation with 'crossing the Mogadishu line' is about maintaining this distinction and not sliding from peacekeeping to peace-enforcement.

The analysis of new wars suggests that what is needed is not peacekeeping but enforcement of cosmopolitan norms, i.e. enforcement of international humanitarian and human rights law. Precisely because these wars are directed mainly against civilians, they do not have the same extremist logic as modern wars. Therefore, it ought to be possible to devise strategies for the protection of civilians and the capture of war criminals. The political aim is to provide secure areas in which alternative forms of inclusive politics can emerge. Many of the tactics that have been developed in recent wars are relevant – for example, the use of safety zones, humanitarian corridors, or no-fly zones

– but their implementation up to now has been hampered by inflexible mandates and/or rigid adherence to what are viewed as the principles of peacekeeping. A number of authors have proposed new definitions for what is needed that fall between the perception of peacekeeping and peace-enforcement – such as 'second generation peacekeeping', 'robust peacekeeping', or the official British term 'wider peacekeeping' (which the British insist is still peacekeeping and not an in-between term) – but all of them tend to remain within the traditional framework of thinking about wars.[18]

Cosmopolitan law-enforcement is somewhere between soldiering and policing. Some of the tasks that international troops may be asked to perform fall within traditional ambits, for example, separating belligerents and maintaining ceasefires, controlling airspace. Others are essentially new tasks, e.g. the protection of safety zones or relief corridors. And yet others are close to traditional policing tasks – ensuring freedom of movement, guaranteeing the safety of individuals, especially returned refugees or displaced persons, and the capture of war criminals. Policing has been the great lacuna of peacekeeping. Back in the 1960s, when peacekeeping forces were sent to Cyprus, they were unable to prevent communal conflict because policing was not part of their mandate. Military forces have been notoriously unwilling to undertake police tasks, but, at the same time, it has proved difficult to recruit policemen because they are needed in their own societies. However one judges their record, the British forces in Northern Ireland did undertake policing tasks. Given the unlikelihood of another old war, military forces will eventually have to be reoriented to combine military and policing tasks.

Such tasks require enforcement and therefore necessarily involve the use of force, but in terms of the principles governing their application, the tasks of cosmopolitan law-enforcement are closer to peacekeeping. It is worth spelling out those principles and showing how they would need to be reformulated.

Consent

In the scenarios that were developed when preparing the official British peacekeeping manual, it was concluded that 'forcible pacification' is impracticable:

Without the broader co-operation and consent of the majority of the local population and the leadership of the principal ruling authorities, be they parties to the dispute or government agencies, success is simply not a reasonable or realistic expectation. The risks entailed and force levels required of an approach that dispensed with a broad consensual framework is simply not a reasonable or realistic expectation. Put simply, consent (in its broadest form) is necessary for any prospect of success.[19]

According to this argument, consent is required at both the operational and the tactical level. At an operational level, consent is required before the mission is established. At a tactical level, commanders need to negotiate local consent.

The argument that 'forcible pacification' is impossible is clearly correct. The implication of the argument in this book is that international military forces have to be seen to be legitimate – that is to say, they have to operate on the basis of some sort of consent and even support, and to be acting within an agreed set of rules. Otherwise, there is a risk that they will become just another party to the conflict, as seems to have happened to some extent to the ECOMOG peacekeeping force in Liberia, where lack of pay, equipment and training meant that soldiers became engaged in the black market and/or theft from humanitarian supplies, and where the troops veered from neutrality to support for particular factions.[20]

However, unqualified consent is impossible; otherwise there would be no need for peacekeeping forces. If, for example, protection of humanitarian convoys is based on consent, then this can be negotiated as easily and perhaps more effectively by unarmed UN agencies or NGOs. The need for troops is based on the fact that not everyone consents and that those who prevent the convoys may have to be dealt with forcefully. For similar reasons, it may be impossible to obtain consent from *both* the local population and the warring parties. If an agreement has to be negotiated with a war criminal, then the credibility of the operation in the eyes of the local population may be damaged.

In general, international troops can expect considerable initial goodwill. In former Yugoslavia, the standing of the UN was very high; many local people had served in UN contingents. But the failure to react forcefully against those who interrupted aid convoys, to protect effectively safe havens, to capture war criminals or even to maintain the No Fly Zone greatly undermined the legitimacy of the entire organization. The same was true in Somalia, where many local people hoped that the American troops who arrived in large numbers would disarm the warring parties. There was great disappointment when the Americans announced they would not disarm the factions and opened negotiations with the warlords. As a former Somali banker put it:

> You mean they have come all this way, with all this equipment and all these weapons just to move food from Baidoa to Berdara? (Laughter) Sooner rather than later, the fighting that continues in many parts of the country will displace people and create hunger and havoc in a few months. Then what? You can be sure there will not be more troops: Somalia, they will say, had its chance.[21]

What *is* important is widespread consent from the victims, the local population, whether or not formal consent has been obtained from the parties at an operational level. If consent at the operational level can be obtained, without sacrificing the goals of the mission, it is clearly an advantage. Retaining and building on the consent of the local population at a tactical level may well mean acting without the consent of one or other of the parties.

Impartiality

Impartiality tends to be interpreted as not taking sides. The ICRC makes a useful distinction between impartiality and neutrality. The principle of impartiality, it stated, means that, it 'makes no discrimination as to nationality, race, religious beliefs, class, or political opinions. It endeavours to relieve the suffering of individuals, being guided solely by their needs, and to give priority to the most urgent cases of distress.' The principle of neutrality means that, in 'order to continue to enjoy the confidence of all, the Red Cross may not take sides in hostilities or engage at any time in controversies of a political, racial, religious or ideological character'.[22]

In practice, impartiality and neutrality have been confused. The distinction is important for cosmopolitan law-enforcement. The law has to be enforced impartially, that is to say, without any discrimination on the basis of race, religion, etc. Since it is almost inevitable that one side violates the law more frequently than another, it is impossible to act according to both impartiality and neutrality. Neutrality may be important for an organization such as the Red Cross which depends on consent for its activities, although the insistence on neutrality has frequently raised questions, particularly during World War II. It could also be important for the traditional concept of peacekeeping or for a purely humanitarian conception of the role of peacekeepers, i.e. the delivery of food. But if the task of the troops is to protect people and to stop violations of human rights, then insistence on neutrality is, at best, confusing and, at worst, undermines legitimacy.

In the aftermath of the bombing of the United Nations headquarters in Iraq in the summer of 2003, many NGOs and humanitarian agencies have been calling for a return to the Red Cross principles and a renewed separation of the military and those who undertake humanitarian tasks so as to preserve humanitarian space. The problem is that, in the new wars, humanitarian space has been squeezed. It is no longer possible to separate military and humanitarian activities. Rather, the military have to operate differently so as to protect humanitarian space. In Iraq, US forces were warfighting forces and the international agencies were identified with the United States. There was no force capable of or responsible for cosmopolitan law-enforcement.

According to Mackinlay: 'A UN soldier has the same approach as a policeman enforcing the law. He will uphold it regardless of which party is challenging him. But legitimacy must be intact at all levels.' However, Mackinlay seems to think that, if the UN soldier enforces the rules impartially, it is possible to retain the respect of both sides.[23] The same point is made by Dobbie, one of the authors of the British peacekeeping manual, when he compares the role of the peacekeeper to the role of the referee at a football match. But these wars are not football matches; the various parties do not accept the rules. On the contrary, the nature of these wars is rule-breaking. The point is rather to persuade ordinary people of the advantages of rules so as to isolate and marginalize those who break them.

Use of Force

Traditional peacekeeping insisted on the non-use of force. The new British peacekeeping manual uses the term 'minimum necessary force', defined in the manual as 'the measured application of violence or coercion, sufficient only to achieve a specific end, demonstrably reasonable, proportionate and appropriate; and confined in effect to the specific and legitimate target intended.'[24]

The British contrast this position with what is known as the Weinberger–Powell doctrine of overwhelming force. The UN intervention in Somalia is often cited as an example of the perils of using force. It was largely an American intervention authorized under Chapter VII of the UN Charter. After an attack by his forces on Pakistani peacekeepers, the Americans began a manhunt for Mohammed Aideed. Bombardments in Southern Mogadishu resulted in many deaths and the manhunt for Aideed failed. (Owing to the refusal of the Americans to share intelligence information with the UN, a careful raid on what was supposed to be Aideed's hideout failed because it turned out to be a UN office.) The nadir for the Americans was reached when Aideed succeeded in shooting down two US helicopters, killing eighteen soldiers, whose mutilated bodies were publicly paraded in front of television cameras, and wounding seventy-five others.

The problem, as various commentators have pointed out, was not the use of force as such, but the assumption of overwhelming force and the failure to take into account the local political situation and the need to act in such a way as to lend support to legitimacy and credibility. Ioan Lewis and James Mayall describe the American reaction to the initial killing of Pakistani peacekeepers:

> Instead of holding an independent legal enquiry and seeking to marginalize Aideed politically, Admiral Howe's forces reacted with injudicious force causing considerable Somali casualties – not necessarily all supporters of Aideed . . . Admiral Howe, behaving as if he were the Sheriff of Mogadishu, proclaimed

Aideed an outlaw, offering a reward of $20,000 for his capture.[25]

Much the same dilemma is faced by American forces in Iraq and Afghanistan.

Modern armies are uneasy about using minimum force because they are organized along Clausewitzean lines and have been trained to confront other similarly organized armies. As was shown in the case of Somalia, when confronted with the challenge of new wars, they find it extremely difficult to identify a middle way between the application of massive firepower and doing nothing. Unlike war-fighting, in which the aim is to minimize casualties on your own side whatever the cost in casualties on the other side, and peacekeeping, which does not use force, cosmopolitan law-enforcement has to minimize casualties on all sides. The significance of Nuremberg was that individuals and not collectivities were held responsible for war crimes. It is the arrest of individuals who may have committed war crimes or violations of human rights that is required for cosmopolitan law-enforcement, not the defeat of sides.

Cosmopolitan law-enforcement may mean risking the lives of peacekeepers in order to save the lives of victims. This is perhaps the most difficult presupposition to change. International personnel are always a privileged class in the new wars. The lives of UN or national personnel are valued over the lives of local people, despite the UN claim to be founded on the principles of humanity. The argument about humanitarian intervention revolves around whether it is acceptable to sacrifice national lives for the sake of people far away. The preference of Western powers, especially the United States, for air strikes, despite the physical and psychological damage caused even with highly accurate munitions, arises from this privileging of nationals or Westerners. This type of national or statist thinking has not yet come to terms with the concept of a common human community.

In effect, the proposal for cosmopolitan law-enforcement is an ambitious proposal to create a new kind of soldier-cum-policeman which will require considerable rethinking about tactics, equipment and, above all, command and training. The kind of equipment required is generally cheaper than that which national armed forces order for imagined Clausewitzean wars in the future. Transportation, especially air and sealift, is very important, as are efficient communications. Much of this equipment can be bought or rented from civilian sources, although military equipment tends to be more easily available and flexible. The American provision of airlift facilities has often been critical. In Bosnia and in Iraq, very sophisticated airborne equipment has been used in air strikes. While tactical air support and, indeed, air superiority may prove to be the decisive advantage of multinational peacekeeping forces in controlling violence, the utility of large-scale sophisticated air strikes is limited in relation to its disadvantages – collateral civilian damage, difficulty of hitting hidden targets, lack of control on the ground. Weapons that are heavier than those possessed by the warring parties may also prove important, although lack of manoeuvrability on difficult terrain may rule out many of the heavier types of equipment.

More importantly, the new cosmopolitan troops will have to be professionalized. Since they are likely to comprise multilateral forces, integrated command systems, joint exercises and standard rates of pay and conditions would need to be introduced. The new cosmopolitan troops have to become the legitimate bearers of arms. They have to know and respect the laws of war and follow a strict code of conduct. Reports of corruption or violations of human rights have to be properly investigated.[26] Above all, the motivations of these new forces have to be incorporated into a wider concept of cosmopolitan right. Whereas the soldier, as the legitimate bearer of arms, had to be prepared to die for his or her country, the international soldier/police officer risks his or her life for humanity.

The Example of Kosovo

The war over Kosovo illustrates the problem of using warfighting techniques for humanitarian ends. The intervention was hailed as the first war for human rights. The British prime minister, Tony Blair, used the occasion of NATO's fiftieth anniversary, which took place during the air strikes, to enunciate a new 'Doctrine of International Community'. 'We are all internationalists now whether we like it or not', he told an audience in Chicago. 'We cannot refuse to participate in global markets if we want to prosper. We cannot ignore new political ideas in other countries if we want to innovate. We cannot turn our backs on conflicts and the violation of human rights in other countries if we still want to be secure.'[27]

But the actual record of the war is much more ambiguous. The proclaimed goal did represent an innovation and an important precedent in international behaviour; it is to be hoped that, after Kosovo, it will be much more difficult for the international community to stand aside when tragedies such as the genocide in Rwanda take place. However, the methods were much more in keeping with a traditional conception of war and had little connection with the proclaimed goal. Because of the concern about casualties, the tactic chosen to achieve this goal was air strikes over Yugoslavia.

In practice, however, the utility of the air strikes was highly questionable. Altogether, some 36,000 sorties were flown, of which 12,000 were strike sorties. Some 20,000 'smart' bombs and 5000 conventional bombs were dropped. But it appears that not much damage was done to the Yugoslav military machine. For fifty years, the Yugoslav army had been trained to withstand a superior enemy. A vast underground network had been built, including stores, airports and barracks. Tactics had been developed which involved constructing decoys, hiding tanks and artillery, conserving air defences and avoiding troop concentrations. NATO did not succeed, in the initial stages, in knocking out the Yugoslav air-defence system: this is why NATO aircraft continued to fly at 15,000 feet. Nor did they succeed in doing much damage to Serb forces on the ground. NATO claims that the air strikes did constrain Serb forces and prevented them from bringing equipment into the open, but, nevertheless, the air strikes evidently did not prevent operations against Kosovar Albanian civilians. In particular, NATO appears to have had a poor record in hitting armour. Despite higher claims, only twenty-six 'tank carcasses' were found in Kosovo after the Serbs withdrew.[28] Moreover, some 40,000 Yugoslav troops left Kosovo, suggesting that rather few had been lost.

There was more success in hitting civilian targets – roads, bridges, power stations, oil depots and factories. Because of the insistence that aircraft fly above 15,000 feet, pilots could not see what was happening on the ground and were dependent on intelligence from numerous, often badly coordinated, sources.

Consequently, repeated mistakes were made, as became embarrassingly clear for the duration of the air strikes. Low points included the bombing of the Chinese Embassy and of refugees inside Kosovo. Some 1400 people were killed in so-called collateral damage. Environmentalists are only now assessing the consequences of damage to industrial facilities. Historic sites were destroyed, in Novi Sad for example. A TV transmitter was blown up, killing journalists inside. And targets were hit in Montenegro, whose government had refused to participate in the war in Kosovo.

Far from halting the exodus of Kosovar Albanians, the Serb forces accelerated the process under the cover of the bombing. In the period up to 24 March 1999, when the bombing began, KLA activities were used as an excuse for ethnic cleansing, mainly by regular Yugoslav forces and Serb police – some 400,000 people left the country. After 24 March, some 10,000 people were killed in the cleansing operation, including children, and more than a million were forced to leave the country. When NATO forces entered in June, only 600,000 people were left in Kosovo and, of these, 400,000 were internally displaced.[29]

Moreover, the process of reverse ethnic cleansing began soon after the entry of NATO troops, and some 160,000 Serbs left the country. Today, the Serbs that remain live in protected enclaves, and the tension between Serbs and Albanians remains very high, as evidenced by the divided city of Mitrovica and the riots in March 2004.

It can be argued that the political consequences of this type of bombing were also counterproductive. Despite the insistence of NATO spokesmen that there is a big difference between killing by mistake and killing deliberately, this difference was not obvious to the victims of the bombing. Who determines whether the killing of civilians counts as a 'massacre' or as 'collateral damage'? Likewise, the insistence of Western leaders that the bombing was directed against the regime and not against Serbs was not at all evident to those who experienced its effects. The air strikes mobilized Serbian national sentiment, allowing Milošević to crack down on NGOs and independent media during the war and thus minimize domestic constraints against his activities in Kosovo and permitting the sense of victimhood to overshadow any sense of responsibility for the wars. Together with the influx of refugees, the air strikes polarized opinion in both Macedonia and Montenegro, accentuating domestic tensions and the risk of the further spread of violence. They also polarized international opinion: for many in the East and South, the claim that this was a war for human rights was viewed as a cover for the pursuit of Western imperial interests in the Balkans.

In the end, Milošević capitulated and the refugees returned to Kosovo, allowing NATO to claim a victory and install a United Nations transitional administration. But the trauma of ethnic cleansing on all sides can never be reversed. Indeed, the prospects for a long-term solution seem to be receding. Some argue that the air strikes contributed to the fall of Milošević in October 2000. Undoubtedly, together with economic sanctions, they helped to precipitate economic collapse, but they also helped to entrench embittered anti-Western nationalistic attitudes that persist even after the departure of Milošević and his death in The Hague.

A cosmopolitan approach to the Kosovo crisis would have been aimed directly at protecting people. There should have been a humanitarian intervention on the ground designed to minimize all casualties, even if this meant risking the lives of international troops. Humanitarian intervention is different from air strikes and different from classic 'old war' ground operations; the goal is the prevention of gross violations of human rights, not the defeat of an enemy. Humanitarian intervention is defensive and non-escalatory by definition. Its focus is the individual human being and not another state. Humanitarian intervention also has to involve respect for the rule of law and support for democracy. Effectively, it constitutes cosmopolitan law-enforcement and is thus more like policing than war-fighting.

If possible such an intervention should be based on consent. But instead of high-level negotiations aimed at finding a political compromise between irreconcilable parties, as happened in the period prior to the intervention, negotiations should have focused on the position on the ground. The goal was to establish an international presence in Kosovo, not to resolve the issue of status. Instead of using the threat of air strikes to strengthen the hands of the negotiators, the NATO position on the ground in neighbouring Macedonia should have been strengthened;

the position of the OSCE monitors in Kosovo should also have been expanded (these were withdrawn when the bombing began; the local staff who stayed were killed).

Humanitarian intervention, by protecting people and enforcing law, can create the conditions for a cosmopolitan political response. The aim is to establish a secure environment where people can act freely without fear and where inclusive forms of politics can be nurtured. Ways have to be found to sideline those responsible for ethnic cleansing, not to elevate them through negotiations. The indictment of Milošević and some of his co-conspirators the week before the bombing ended was a constructive step in this direction. Targeted sanctions such as the denial of visas or the freezing of bank accounts could also be applied. An intervention of this kind would have made it more difficult for Milošević to justify his behaviour within Yugoslavia and it would have generated much more international support.

From Humanitarian Assistance to Reconstruction

Mark Duffield writes about a two-tier system of economic assistance in the 1990s. On the one hand, official assistance is predicated on structural adjustment programmes or transition strategies which contribute to the decline of the formal economy. On the other hand, a safety net to cope with the consequences has been developed, largely based on contracting out the provision of assistance to NGOs.[30] A similar point is made by Alvaro de Soto and Graciana del Castillo in their discussion of the lack of coordination between the IMF and the World Bank, on the one hand, and the UN, on the other. The consequences and the cost in political and humanitarian terms of the policies of the former agencies are simply not taken into account. They describe the problems of implementing a peace programme in El Salvador against the backdrop of an IMF stabilization programme. In order to keep within the IMF spending limits, El Salvador was unable to afford to build a national civil police force and to embark on an arms-for-land programme to reintegrate guerrillas as required by the peace agreement: 'The adjustment program and the stabilization plan, on the one hand, and the peace process, on the other, were born and reared as if they were children of different families. They lived under different roofs. They had little in common other than belonging roughly to the same generation.'[31]

During the 1990s, there was a big increase in humanitarian assistance; in 2000 it amounted to over 10 per cent of official development assistance, and it has continued to rise. The establishment of the UN Department of Humanitarian Affairs in 1991 and of the European Community Humanitarian Office (ECHO) in 1992 reflects the growing importance of humanitarian assistance. In chapter 5, I described the way in which the provision of humanitarian assistance is built into the functioning of the war economy. In fact, humanitarian assistance also contributes to the failures of the formal economy. It substitutes for local production. In Somalia, the policy of flooding the country with food in late 1992 in order to ensure that some aid reached those who really needed it led to a dramatic fall in prices, so that it was no longer economical for farmers to produce food.[32] In Tuzla, a centre of salt-mining, several tons of salt were being thrown away every day because it was dangerous to halt mining, yet UNHCR was importing salt from the Netherlands for humanitarian purposes. Providing humanitarian assistance in camps often means that poor farmers abandon their own means of livelihoods.[33] Humanitarian programmes also tend to bypass local specialists and create new hierarchies, in which those who work for international agencies receive salaries and other perks, while well-qualified local people, such as doctors and teachers, live off humanitarian aid.

Humanitarian assistance is essential; otherwise, people would starve. But it needs to be much more carefully targeted, taking the advice of local experts who really know the local situation. And it needs to be accompanied by assistance for reconstruction. By reconstruction, I mean the rebuilding of a formal political economy, based on accepted rules, and the reversal of the negative social and economic relationships I described in chapter 5. The word 'reconstruction' has other connotations drawn from earlier wars. It is usually assumed to be a programme of economic assistance, on the 1947 Marshall Plan model, that is put into effect once an overall political settlement has been reached. Aid agencies often insist that no reconstruction assistance can be provided before a political settlement is reached and, indeed, that the lure of reconstruction assistance represents an incentive to reach a political settlement. But I have argued that a lasting settlement can only be reached in a situation based on alternative politics, the politics of civility – which is very difficult so long as these negative social and economic relations persist. Instead, reconstruction should be viewed as a strategy to achieve peace rather than a strategy to be implemented after peace has been established.

The situation in what might be called near war economies is not so very different from situations of war. Whether we are referring to places where ceasefires have recently been agreed to or to 'bad neighbourhoods' where the negative relationships of war have spread, the symptoms are much the same – unemployment, breakdown of basic infrastructure, pervasive criminality – and these are the symptoms that contribute to the outbreak or renewal of war. In other words, reconstruction is both a pre-war and a post-war strategy, aimed at prevention and at cure.

Reconstruction has to mean, first and foremost, the rebuilding of political authorities, even if only at the local level, and the reconstruction of civil society in the sense both of law and order and of providing the conditions in which alternative political groupings can mobilize. It does not mean reconstruction of what went before. Necessarily, it must entail the restructuring of political and economic arrangements so as not to repeat the conditions that gave rise to war. The adaptation of appropriate forms of governance and the introduction of regulated market relationships take time, and have to be part of a long-term process through which different groups in society can participate.

It is often argued that reconstruction has to encompass transition, in the sense that there is clearly a need to reform the institutions that preceded the war. Unfortunately, the term transition has come to be associated with a standard formula for democratization and transition to the market, which includes the formal aspects of democracy, for example elections, as well as economic liberalization and privatization. In the absence of meaningful political institutions through which genuine debate and participation can take place, and in situations where the rule of law is weak and where trust and confidence is lacking, this standard formula can exacerbate the

underlying problems, providing incentives for exclusivist politics or for criminalization of formerly state-owned enterprises.
Reconstruction has to involve reform, but not necessarily along
the lines of the standard transition formula.

Reconstruction should be focused on zones of civility so that
they can act as models encouraging similar initiatives in other
places. Where legitimate local authorities do not exist, local
trusteeships or protectorates could be proposed. The experience of the EU administration in Mostar has led to scepticism
about the idea of local trusteeships. The problem there, however,
was that the administration did not have adequate policing
capacities and had to share power with the nationalist parties
which controlled the police forces and included notorious criminals. The rhetoric of self-help is used as an argument against
trusteeships or protectorates, but it is very difficult for people
to help themselves when they are at the mercy of gangsters.

The primary requisite is the restoration of law and order in
order to create a situation in which normal life can resume and
refugees and displaced persons can be repatriated. This task
includes disarmament, demobilization, protection of the area,
capture of war criminals, policing and/or establishing and training local police forces, and the restoration of the judiciary.

Despite greatly increased efforts at achieving disarmament
and demobilization, the record is mixed.[34] It is very difficult
for UN forces to achieve more than partial disarmament, and
techniques such as weapons 'buy-back' programmes have
tended to result in the handing back of sub-standard weapons,
while the high-quality weapons remain hidden. Moreover,
there are now so many sources for acquisition, at least of small
arms, because of both the high number of producers and the
availability of surplus weapons, that the task is never-ending.
Creating a secure environment may well turn out to be more
important than disarmament. Effective policing and the capture
of war criminals are essential conditions for security, whether
they are undertaken by international forces, together with
civilian affairs officers, or by local police forces under international supervision, or whether local authorities can take responsibility, perhaps with some outside support, as is the case in
better-established zones of civility.

As well as disarmament and policing, law and order needs
an independent and trustworthy judiciary and an active civil

society, i.e. the creation of a relatively free public space. For this reason, investment in education and a free media are essential to stop the relentless particularistic propaganda and to end not just physical intimidation but also psychological intimidation. These conditions are much more important than the formal procedures of democracy. Outsiders often insist on elections as a way of providing a timetable and terminal point for their involvement. But without the preconditions of security, public space, reconciliation and open dialogue, elections may end up legitimizing the warring parties, as was the case, for example, in Bosnia after Dayton.

To create a self-sustaining zone of civility, so that law and order, education and media can be paid for, soldiers find jobs and education, and taxes are paid, the local economy has to be restored. As well as disarmament, demobilization is also difficult, and not only because of the insecure environment. Indeed, the biggest weakness of DDR (disarmament, demobilization and reintegration) programmes has been reintegration. Many soldiers would like to give up banditry and find settled jobs or, in the case of children and young people, an education. But reintegration programmes have not been very successful because of unemployment and labour shortages and inadequate educational facilities.

The priorities are basic services and local production. Infrastructure – water, power, transport, post and telecommunications – needs to be restored at both local and regional levels. As well as being necessary on grounds of need, infrastructure is vital for the restoration of normal trade links and can be a subject of negotiation even when there is no agreement in other areas. Even at the height of wars, it is sometimes possible to reach agreement on these kinds of concrete issue, especially where there is a mutual interest. Gas supplies to Sarajevo were maintained more or less throughout the war, for example. The other area is support for local production of basic necessities so as to reduce the need for humanitarian assistance, especially food, clothing, building materials, and so on. Along with public services, this is a good way to generate local employment.

In so far as reconstruction is a strategy for peace, it has to provide economic security and hope for the future so as to remove the atmosphere of fear in which people live, and to offer, to young people especially, an alternative livelihood to the army or the mafia. What needs to be done is specific in every situation, but certain principles can be specified.

First, all assistance projects should be based on the principles of openness and integration. It is all too easy, in the interests of restoring services, to accept divisions and partitions established through war and, thereby, legitimize the status quo instead of helping to change it. In Mostar, for example, the EU administration was supposed to reintegrate the town, which was divided into Croat and Muslim halves. Although in a few limited cases, for example water supply, the EU managed to negotiate common projects, for the most part it has turned out to be easier to introduce separate projects in each half of the town, thereby explicitly following a strategy of separate development. Because there was no secure environment and because the EU feared taking sides, everything had to be negotiated between the nationalist leaders. Openness and integration means that anyone should be able to benefit from the projects and that projects are explicitly directed towards bringing people together, through, for example, employing refugees, displaced persons or demobilized soldiers, or involving an element of sharing. Openness and integration need to be fostered not only at a local level, but also at national and regional levels.

Second, assistance needs to be decentralized and to encourage local initiatives. By spreading recipients, more people are involved in the programme, there are greater possibilities to experiment and there is less risk of aid being creamed off or being distorted by political compromises. Where demobilization has taken place, it has been local community-based programmes, often organized by the veterans themselves, that seem to have been the most successful – for example, the Uganda Veterans' Board or the National Demobilization Commission in Somaliland, which developed a programme of demobilization and reintegration together with the veterans' organization SOYAAL. Some veterans explained:

> The boys on the 'technicals' (pick-up vehicles mounted with machine guns or anti-tank guns) are themselves tired. They see no benefit, only death. They climb the technicals out of need. Some of those in secure jobs now include some who were the worst gangsters. They prefer the $200 that comes with a settled job to the millions they get as bandits.[35]

A successful programme in Sierra Leone is the arms for development programme, where local communities disarm themselves with the help of police and, when they are declared 'weapons free', receive a reward of a development project of their choosing.

Third, it is very important to make use of local specialists and to encourage a wide-ranging local debate about how aid should be provided. This is important in order to increase efficiency by using people who have knowledge and experience of the area, to increase transparency, to reduce corruption and to build up civic engagement. One of the worst consequences of international assistance has been the displacement of skilled people as a result of foreign contracts and a distorted pay scale. Highly skilled doctors, engineers, teachers or lawyers often take jobs as drivers and interpreters because the salaries are so much higher. Bosnia, Kosovo and Afghanistan all provide examples of this pattern of skill displacement.

Even in areas that seem the most intractable there are some possibilities for funding assistance based on these principles. The strategy of expanding zones of civility to offset the spread of 'bad neighbourhoods' needs to be able to extend itself directly into the bad neighbourhoods. Poor, uncivil areas become caught in a vicious circle in which assistance is refused because of the behaviour of the local 'authorities'; unemployment and criminality flourish, thereby helping to sustain the position of the particularist warlords. It is all the more important to identify ways to support certain bottom-up projects that cross war divides in order to begin to open up spaces in these areas.

Reconstruction can be thought of as a new approach to development, an alternative to both structural adjustment/transition and humanitarianism. As is the case of cosmopolitan law-enforcement, it is bound to be costly in the short term, to require greater resources than rich countries have so far been willing to commit to peacekeeping and overseas assistance. It would mean abandoning some of the neo-liberal assumptions about levels of public expenditure that have dominated international economic orthodoxy in recent years. Reconstruction means that politics, economics and security issues have to be integrated into a new type of humanistic global policy which should be capable of enhancing the legitimacy of international institutions and mobilizing popular support.

7

The 'New War' in Iraq

'In the images of falling statues', said President Bush on 1 May 2003, as he announced the end of hostilities in Iraq, dressed in fatigues on the deck of USS *Abraham Lincoln*, 'we have witnessed the arrival of a new era.'[1] Like his Defense Secretary, Donald Rumsfeld, President Bush claimed to have discovered a new form of warfare, making use of information technology so that war can be rapid, precise, and low in casualties. In the immediate aftermath of the invasion, military commentators were jubilant. Bush himself described the invasion as 'one of the swiftest advances in history'.[2] Max Boot, writing in *Foreign Affairs*, described the war as 'dazzling'. 'That the United States and its allies won anyway – and won so quickly – must rank as one of the signal achievements of military history.'[3]

The ongoing war in Iraq is, indeed, a new type of war but of the kind described in this book. It is true that all kinds of new technologies, ranging from sophisticated satellite-based systems to mobile phones and the Internet, have been used. But if we are to understand the war in ways that are useful to policy-makers, then its novel character should not be defined in terms of technology. What is new about the war needs to be analysed in terms of the disintegration of states and the changes in social relations under the impact of globalization rather than in terms of technology along the lines developed in previous chapters.

Bush and Rumsfeld's conception of a new war, it can be argued, is more like an updated version of old war, making use of new technology. The failure by the United States to understand the reality on the ground in Iraq and the tendency to impose its own view of what war should be like has been immensely dangerous. It has fomented the real new war and it carries the risk of being self-perpetuating. In a way, the war in Iraq could be treated as a test case of the central argument developed in this book – the danger of not adjusting our conceptions of war to the new global context.

In what follows, I first describe why the American view of the war they were fighting is better described as updated 'old war', then analyse the reality on the ground as a 'new war'. In the final section, I describe the possibilities for an alternative strategy to reduce the risks posed both to the Iraqi population and to the wider international community, first by Saddam Hussein before the war, and later by the 'new war' itself.

'Operation Iraqi Freedom' – Technology-Intensive Old War

Over the last two decades, successive American administrations developed the notion that the United States could use advanced technology to fight long-distance wars in such a way as to retain American military predominance and thus reassure American citizens that the US government can defend them, and preserve American security, without risking, or risking very few, American casualties and without requiring additional taxation.

The origins of this idea can be traced back to the Cold War framework. During the Cold War, deterrence could be understood as imaginary war.[4] Throughout the period of the Cold War, both sides behaved as though they were at war, with military build-ups, technological competition, espionage and counter-espionage, war games and exercises. This activity helped to remind people of World War II and, on the American side, to sustain a belief in the American mission to defend the world against evil through the use of superior technology. Technological developments responded to what planners imagined the Soviet Union might acquire – the so-called worst-case scenario. This introverted planning, as I have argued elsewhere, meant that American and Soviet technological change was better explained as though they were both arming against a phantom German military machine that continued to evolve in the planners' imaginations, rather than against each other.[5]

The advent of information technologies generated a debate about the future direction of military strategy in the 1970s and 1980s. The so-called military reform school argued that the platforms of the World War II era were now as vulnerable as soldiers were in World War I because of the use of precision guided munitions (PGMs) and that the advantage had shifted to the defence. High attrition rates in the Vietnam and Middle East wars as a result of the use of hand-held missiles seemed to confirm that argument. The advocates of traditional American strategy argued that the offensive manoeuvres of World War II were even more important, since the use of area destruction munitions could swamp defensive forces and missiles and unmanned aerial vehicles (now known as UAVs) could replace vulnerable manned aircraft. The consequence was the AirLand Battle strategy of the 1980s, with its centrepiece, 'deep strike', to be carried out by the then new Tomahawk cruise missiles, at that time armed with nuclear warheads.

During the 1990s, this thinking was taken a stage further with the Revolution in Military Affairs (RMA). For RMA enthusiasts, the advent of information technology is as important as was the discovery of the stirrup or the internal combustion engine in revolutionizing warfare. RMA is spectacle war; it is war carried out at long distance using computers and new communications technologies.[6] After the end of the Cold War, US military spending declined by one-third, but this affected mainly personnel. Military Research and Development (R&D) declined by much less than military spending as a whole, and this allowed for the development of both follow-ons to traditional Cold War platforms and the new technologies associated with the RMA. An important aspect of the new technologies is the improvement in virtual war-gaming, which further underscores the imaginary nature of contemporary conceptions of war. Increasingly, the Defense Department has recruited Hollywood producers to help invent future worst-case scenarios, giving rise to what James Der Derian describes as MIME-NET, the military-industrial-entertainment network.[7] One of the most quoted remarks of the Iraq War was that of

General William Wallace, commander of the army's V Corps and in charge of all US Army units in Iraq, that 'the enemy we're fighting is a bit different from the one we war-gamed against.'[8]

For the Bush administration, the term 'defence transformation' has come to supplant RMA as the new jargon. As one enthusiast for defence transformation has put it:

> However jerky the transmission belt, the qualities of the modern American economy – its adventurousness, spontaneity and willingness to share information – eventually reach the American military. Just as the teenager who grew up tinkering with automobile engines helped to make the motorized armies of WWII work, so do the sergeants accustomed to playing video games, surfing web pages, and creating spread sheets make the information-age military of to-day effective.[9]

Donald Rumsfeld claims that defence transformation 'is about more than building new high-tech weapons – although that is certainly part of it. It is also about new ways of thinking and new ways of fighting.'[10]

He talks about 'overmatching' power as opposed to 'overwhelming' power:

> In the 21st century, mass may no longer be the best measure of power in a conflict. After all, when Baghdad fell, there were just over 100,000 American forces on the ground. General Franks overwhelmed the enemy not with the typical three to one advantage in mass but by overmatching the enemy with advanced capabilities in innovative and unexpected ways.[11]

Yet it is hard to escape the conclusion that information technology is being grafted on to traditional assumptions about the ways in which military forces should be used and to traditional institutional defence structures. The methods have not changed much since World War II.[12] Despite the changed names every decade – AirLand Battle, Revolution in Military Affairs, and now Defence Transformation, they involve a combination of aerial bombardment at long distance and rapid offensive manoeuvres. The very use of video gaming feeds in the assumptions of the gamers who have been schooled in the Cold War framework.

The Iraq War is a good example of the way in which information technology was grafted on traditional ways of thinking about war – ways which obscured what was actually happening in Iraq. It was showy and dramatic. With the help of accurately targeted air power, the Coalition forces were able to claim that they had toppled the Iraqi regime 'with a combination of precision, speed, and boldness the enemy did not expect and the world had not seen before.'[13] Much was made of the American information advantage; Coalition forces were able to process information received both from satellite pictures and from reports from the ground so that, at any one moment, the wireless Internet system could show the deployment of troops with enemy forces in red and friendly forces in blue. Known as Force XXI Battle Command, Brigade and Below, it was installed on nearly every vehicle. This allowed red forces to be directly destroyed from the air. Max Boot points out that, at the beginning of World War II, Germany managed to defeat France, the Netherlands and Belgium in forty-four days at a cost of 'only' 27,000 casualties (quotes are his); in comparison, the Americans and the British took twenty-six days to invade Iraq, a country three-quarters the size of France, at a cost of 161 dead (many of them by friendly fire – or 'blue on blue', as the jargon put it).

The war was also portrayed as a powerful moral crusade. There was always an idealist strain in American Cold War thinking. Bush's 'Axis of Evil' echoes Ronald Reagan's 'Evil Empire'. The argument is that America is a cause, not a nation, with a mission to convert the rest of the world to the American dream and to rid the world of enemies. The war in Iraq was represented as one victory in the 'War on Terror' – a global conflict as far-reaching and ambitious as was the Cold War, designed to establish a new world order. 'We will not leave the safety of America and the peace of the planet at the mercy of a few mad terrorists and tyrants', said Bush, speaking at the West Point graduation ceremony on 1 June 2002. 'We will lift this dark threat from our country and the world.'[14] And, in his victory speech on USS *Abraham Lincoln*, he described the 'liberation of Iraq' as a 'crucial advance in the campaign against terror.'[15]

In fact, there was almost no resistance. The Iraqi Army and the Republican Guard melted away. The Americans dropped leaflets in Arabic telling soldiers to take off their uniforms and go home, and most of them obeyed instructions. There was, as one commentator put it, an 'unpleasant short-lived episode of violent irregular combat' in the third week of March, when Firqat Fedayeen Saddam (Saddam's Martyrs), and other small units established to defend the regime, tried to resist.[16] But, otherwise, the Americans entered Iraq with the consent of the Iraqi people, including the armed forces. The situation appeared calm initially not because the Coalition forces controlled the country but because the Iraqi people were ready to give the Coalition forces the benefit of the doubt. When I visited Iraq in November 2003, Iraqis were still referring to the invasion as liberation/occupation. In fact, at the time of writing, the only areas the Coalition forces actually occupy are their own protected bases – elsewhere it is extremely dangerous for members of the Coalition to venture. Likewise, the Americans appear to have toppled the regime, but former members of that regime, even after the capture of Saddam Hussein and the killing of his two sons, still seem to control large parts of the country.

In other words, the invasion of Iraq was not really a war; it was more like an exercise. Nor was it a victory against the Iraqi regime. But it was portrayed as such and, indeed, the American policy-makers continue to see the invasion in these terms, which makes it very difficult for them to deal with the actual situation in Iraq. In particular, the newly established Coalition Provisional Authority behaved as the victorious occupier, taking steps reminiscent of the aftermath of World War II such as the dissolution of the army or sweeping de-Ba'athification, which infuriated and humiliated those very people who had allowed the invasion to take place with minimal resistance.

The New War

As Yahia Said points out, both President Bush, advised by the exiled opposition, and Saddam Hussein had a common interest in portraying the Iraqi regime as a classic totalitarian system, controlling every aspect of society and removable only by force.[17] In fact, at the time of Operation Iraqi Freedom, the regime exhibited characteristics that are typical of the last phases of totalitarianism – a system that is breaking up under the impact of globalization, unable to sustain its closed autarchic tightly controlled character.

In the 1970s and 1980s, the Ba'athist regime had organized society along the lines of a command economy, with centralized administration and planning, large expenditure on security, and an atmosphere of fear combined with a secular populist Arab nationalist ideology, as well as socialist elements deriving from land reform and the establishment of a welfare system. Unlike in communist countries, private business was always permitted, but because of the rentier character of the economy as a result of dependence on oil, these businesses were entirely dependent on the state and had an interest in preserving its secretive patrimonial methods.

In order to maintain control and prevent coups, such as the one that brought the Ba'athists to power, security agencies proliferated – the army, the Republican Guard, the Special Republican Guard, the various intelligence agencies and, more recently, new units expressly designed to protect Saddam Hussein, such as Firqat Fedayeen Saddam or the Presidential Protection Unit, as well as armed tribal units. The senior levels of the security agencies were frequently purged, and clans, kinship networks, ideological indoctrination, and family ties were used to ensure the loyalty of different units. In effect, a complex system of overlapping commands was created. According to Saddam Hussein: 'With our party methods, there is no chance for anyone who disagrees with us jumping into a couple of tanks and overthrowing the government. These methods have gone.'[18]

Oil revenues were insufficient to cover the costs of the devastating war with Iran (1980–8), and during this period Iraq accumulated very high levels of debt. Both the first Gulf War and the imposition of sanctions had ruinous consequences for the economy, resulting in dramatic falls in GDP, increases in infant mortality, and declines in literacy; de-urbanization took place as the proportion of those engaged in agriculture doubled, and a parallel dollar economy arose based on UN Agencies, remittances, income from Iranian pilgrims, smuggling, contraband petrol sales, etc.[19] During this period, many educated middle-class people left the country and state institutions were decaying and fragmenting. Indeed, the state was literally divided with the establishment of Kurdish autonomy in the North after 1991. With his legitimacy declining, Saddam Hussein began to give more emphasis to identity politics, both to generate more political support and as a basis for patronage networks. Just as nationalism was mobilized in the dying days of the former Soviet Union or former Yugoslavia, so Saddam Hussein appealed to both tribalism and Islam to fill the vacuum left by the destruction of civil society, the decline in state institutions and the discrediting of Ba'athist ideology.

Tribalism had been on the decline since the late nineteenth century, but both the British and the Ba'ath Party found it useful to reconstruct tribal identities.[20] A further process of retribalization occurred after the Shi'ite uprising in the South in 1991. In 1992, Saddam Hussein invited the tribal chieftains to his palace. He apologized for agricultural reforms and the chieftains were asked to sign an oath of allegiance to the president, renamed as the 'Chief of Chiefs'. 'Exempted from military service, they were provided with light arms, communication and transport facilities to impose law and order in their districts. . . . Major tribes, mostly Sunnis, were charged with national security tasks, minor tribes took on local duties such as law and order, dispute settlement and tax collection.'[21]

Religion also became more important in the 1990s, even though the role of the clerics and of religious institutions had been rather weak in Iraq compared with other countries. This was partly a consequence of a deliberate emphasis on religion by Saddam Hussein and partly because religious charities and religious rituals offered some sense of meaning in a fragmented, fear-ridden, impoverished society. In 1999, the regime launched the 'Enhancement of Islamic Faith Campaign', which involved restrictions on drinking and gambling, the promotion of religious education and religious programming in the media, and even a circumscribed politicization of both Sunni and Shi'ia clerics.

Finally, ethnic politics became more important as the Kurdish parties in the North established what was effectively an autonomous statelet.

Along with the rise of identity politics came the rise in criminality. With the introduction of the oil-for-food programme in 1996, the opportunities for patronage, smuggling, manipulation, middlemen, and various types of criminal activity were further enhanced, as Charles Duelfer's report to the CIA amply illustrates.[22]

Hence, on the eve of the invasion, Iraq was showing all the signs of incipient state failure – lack of legal revenue sources, decline of state services, loss of legitimacy, erosion and proliferation of military and security agencies, and the rise of sectarian identity politics and of criminality. The invasion simply condensed that process into a short three-week period. In the aftermath, the growing political violence exhibits all the characteristics of what I call a 'new war'.

First of all, this is a war fought by loose networks of state and non-state actors, more like a social movement than the typical vertically organized guerrilla insurgency of earlier wars. No one knows the true size of the insurgency. Until October 2003, American officials insisted that there were no more than 5000 insurgents, consisting primarily of remnants of the former regime. In October 2004, the *New York Times* reported that senior officials believe that the 'hard core resistance' comprises between 8000 and 12,000 fighters, with numbers jumping to 20,000 if 'active sympathizers or covert accomplices' are included. Even now, there are repeated claims by US officials that the insurgency is 'in its last throes'. In hearings before the Senate Armed Services Committee, Senator Carl Levin asked the Deputy Defense Secretary how he reconciled the claim by General George Casey that some 15,000 insurgents had been killed, when estimates of the size of the insurgency were only 6000 to 9000.[23] The insurgency consists of numerous small cells, with varying degrees of coordination; most estimates suggest that there are around seventy cells.[24]

What we can glean about the insurgency from Iraqi media reports, from reports from American think tanks emanating from American intelligence, and from interviews on the ground suggests that the bulk of the insurgency is Iraqi nationalist and Sunni Islamist and arose more or less spontaneously, starting in the summer of 2003. The most important recruits are former military personnel. According to the *New York Times* report quoted above, there are some 100,000 former Iraqi security service personnel without employment, mainly in the Sunni triangle. These former military personnel groups are based largely in Fallujah, which was home to the Special Forces, Mosul, where senior army officers were largely located, and parts of Baghdad. According to Yahia Said:

> In the 1990s Fallujah emerged as a centre of Sunni Islamic scholarship. Many in the military establishment embraced the conservative form of Islam emanating from Fallujah's numerous mosques and seminaries. When the army was dissolved, many of the soldiers and officers returned home to these areas to form the backbone of the insurgency. These insurgents are fighting both to protect their status as well as a conservative Islamic culture from the onslaught of the foreign occupiers and their Westernised Iraqi allies.[25]

These people provide the professional know-how and are able to access some of the former regime's weapons stores.

The names of these nationalist and Sunni Islamist cells are said to include the Iraqi National Islamic Resistance, 'The 1920s Revolution Brigades' (a reference to the Iraqi rebellion against British rule), the National Front for the Liberation of Iraq, the General Command of the Armed Forces and Liberation in Iraq, the Popular Resistance for the Liberation of Iraq, the Patriotic Front and, more recently, the Iraqi Resistance Islamic Front 'JAMI'.[26] There are also some smaller, leftist and secular groups with names such as the Nasserites, the Al Anbar brigades, or the General Secretariat for the Liberation of Democratic Iraq.

These groups are often opposed both to Saddam Hussein and to the occupation. One taped message, released in the spring of 2003, issued the following warning:

> Yesterday, through their media outlets the tyrant and his hench-men announced from the holes in which they are stuck that he is the one behind the resistance and that the men carrying out the resistance are loyal and linked to him. The one behind the mass graves and executions wants to employ the struggle of our people who reject the occupation, hegemony and guardianship to his own benefit and the benefit of his regime.[27]

Likewise a Fallujah-based group called Awakening and Holy War sent a tape to Iranian television in July 2003 saying that Saddam and the United States were two sides of the same coin.[28]

Former Ba'athists, reportedly, constitute a quite separate group. According to reports, their activities consist mainly of financing resistance operations. There are a few fighting factions, the Firqat Fedayeen Saddam, which apparently still exists, the Snake's Head Movement, and Al-Adawh (the Return).[29] According to one report, Ba'athist groups held a major meeting in Al Hawaka in April or May 2004; they include former aides to Saddam Hussein and Saddam Hussein's half brother Ibrahim Sabawi.[30] A subsequent clandestine meeting of Ba'ath supporters in Baghdad reportedly drew nearly 2000 participants.[31]

In addition to the nationalists and Sunni Islamists, there are some Shi'ite resistance groups. The Mehdi Army, led by the populist leader Moqtada al-Sadr, played a critical role in the summer of 2004. Within a very few weeks, al-Sadr had mobilized between 10,000 and 15,000 young, mostly very poor recruits, mainly from al-Sadr City in Baghdad and other southern cities. American attacks on al-Sadr City caused some 3000 casualties. Since then, the role of the Mehdi Army has been much more ambiguous. Supporters of al-Sadr held four ministries in the first post-election Iraqi government, yet the militias continue to be active like other party militias described below, and are occasionally involved in violence against the Coalition forces, especially allied groups in Southern Iraq, and more recently in sectarian violence.

Most of these groups insist that their main target is the occupation, and, according to Iraqi media reports, they oppose abductions, assassinations, and the killing of hostages. However, there are some extreme Islamist groups that seem to specialize in these latter roles. They include groups with such names as the Islamic Anger Brigades, or the Black Banners group, the *Mujahidiin* of the Victorious Sect, or the *Mujahidiin* battalions of the Salafi group of Iraq. Some of these groups are linked to al-Qaeda such as the Jama'at al-Tawi, led by Abu Musab al-Zarqawi, responsible for the deaths of Nicholas Berg and Ken Bigley, or the groups based in Northern Kurdistan before the invasion, such as Ansar al-Sunna or Ansar al-Islam. In October 2004, Zarqawi publicly pledged allegiance to Osama bin Laden and renamed his group al-Qaeda in the Land of the Two Rivers, or al-Qaeda in Mesopotamia, and in December 2004 bin Laden said that Zarqawi was his 'emir' in Iraq. During the spring of 2005, Zarqawi called for a sectarian war in Iraq, and increasing numbers of attacks and executions were directed against Shi'ite targets; there was also an increase in suicide bombing.[32] On 14 September 2005, Zarqawi's organization claimed responsibility for a string of suicide bombs across Baghdad, especially in Shi'ite areas, killing some 150 people. In an audio tape published on the Internet, Zarqawi announced:

> The al-Qaeda organization in the Land of the Two Rivers is declaring an all-out war on the Rafidha [perjorative term for Shi'ia] wherever they are in Iraq. Any religious group that wants to be safe from the blows of the Mujahadeen must [disavow] the government of Ja'fari and all its crimes. Otherwise it will suffer the same fate as the crusaders.[33]

The destruction of one of Iraq's holiest Shi'ia sites, the Al-Askari Shrine in Samarra, north of Baghdad, on 22 February 2006 probably marked a turning point in the escalation of sectarian violence. Zarqawi was killed in June 2006. At the time of writing, it is not clear how this will affect the organization. Foreign fighters are said to be active mainly in the al-Qaeda brigades, although their numbers may have been exaggerated. Most estimates suggest that they account for 5 to 10 per cent of total insurgents, though they account for a higher proportion of suicide bombers. In June 2005, US officials claimed that foreign fighters accounted for fewer than 600 out of 14,000 detainees and less than 5 per cent of casualties.[34] A recent report suggested that foreign fighters were being sent back home to practise their skills learned in Iraq.[35]

A Shi'ite resistance group called Imam Ali Bin-Abi-Talib Jihadi Brigade, first reported in October 2003, also threatened to assassinate all members of the then Interim Governing Council and any Iraqi cooperating with the Coalition forces. Finally, there are various organized crime groups which operate under the cover of the insurgency, and which include many criminals who were released from prison by Saddam Hussein just before the invasion.

What these groups have in common is their opposition to the American occupation. Like the movements that have emerged in other 'new wars', they can be understood in terms of the conditions thrown up by globalization. Some are fighting to defend former power positions; others are reacting against the insecurity of the contemporary situation, both physical and material. Although both Islam and Iraqi nationalism are important ideological currents, the insurgency did not initially have a sectarian identity, even though a majority of the insurgents are Sunni. But, as the violence intensified, the notion of a struggle against the West, which mirrors the American idea of a 'War on Terror', has increasingly acquired a sectarian character, since it is largely Sunni areas that are targeted by Coalition forces. Like other new wars, the violence represents a form of political mobilization, a way of constructing Sunni or Shi'ia identities, which were less clearly delineated before the war. Indeed, it is reinforced by the political process as politicians use sectarian identities to gain votes or ministries.

The insurgents engage in a wide variety of tactics. Table 7.1, collated from the NGO Coordinating Committee in Baghdad, illustrates the pattern of targeting and casualties.

The vast majority of attacks (around 70 per cent) were directed against Coalition forces, at least up until late 2005, when sectarian attacks became more frequent. The insurgents also increasingly attack Iraqi security forces, especially the police and the newly created army; members of the Iraqi Interim Government and others considered to be collaborators; critical infrastructure, especially pipelines and power stations; international agencies and NGOs; foreign contractors; and ordinary civilians. Attacks on civilians increased from 4 per cent of all attacks to 9 per cent between the year September 2003 to October 2004 and the period January to June 2005. Weapons and equipment vary from relatively simple improvised explosive devices, with off-the-shelf systems of control and communication, to more sophisticated weapons, including RPGs, mortars, hand grenades, Kalashnikovs and light arms. Increasingly insurgents are reported to be using a more sophisticated mix of weapons. There have been around 500 suicide bombings and they are growing; more than 200 took place in the first half of 2005. The cells are highly decentralized; they often do not know their leaders or their sources of finance. They have developed sophisticated ways of bypassing Coalition intelligence through human contacts, the use of messengers, or coded Internet messages.[36]

Table 7.1 *Incidents and casualties in Iraq, 2003–5*

Target	September 2003–October 2004			January–July 2005		
	Number of incidents	*Number killed*	*Number of wounded*	*Number of incidents*	*Number killed*	*Number of wounded*
Coalition forces /Multinational forces	3227	451	1002	3984	267	675
Coalition/MNF Air Convoy	49	55	32	33	60	0
Coalition Provisional Authority	32	60	206	na	na	na
Diplomatic mission	11	7	9	2	na	2
Local authority	31	56	81	80	58	57
Contractor	113	210	203	220	148	138
Civilian	180	1981	3467	569	1800	3300
Criminal & suspect	49	1316	972	130	724	74
Iraqi Civil Defence Corps	58	191	310	na	na	na
Iraqi Security forces	na	na	na	274	581	576
Kurds Army	31	25	8	31	17	15
Police	209	480	1012	435	583	754
UN	67	2	3	na	na	na
International organizations	1	2	0	na	na	na
NGO	5	5	11	3	5	na
Journalist	8	27	38	6	na	na
Interpreter	7	17	6	7	5	2
Public property	182	5	15	180	na	na
Unspecified	143	1	1	94	na	na
Total	**4396**	**4896**	**6466**	**6136**	**4451**	**5776**

Notes: na = not available.
   Totals are from the original data; they do not add up either because some
   figures are unavailable or because some incidents are counted twice.
Source: Data from NGO Coordination Committee in Iraq, November 2004 and
   September 2005.

Although direct attacks on civilians were initially only a small proportion of the total incidents, easily the biggest share of people killed and wounded in these attacks were civilians, perhaps reflecting the lack of protection. After civilians, the highest number of casualties is in a category known as 'criminals and suspects'. These are presumably insurgents targeted in American attacks. But since it is difficult to distinguish 'criminals and suspects' from civilians, and since reports of killed insurgents are so high, these numbers probably conceal additional civilian deaths. Interestingly this category declined from 33 per cent of all deaths in the period September 2003 to October 2004 to 16 per cent in the first half of 2005; whether this is because the Americans are more careful or whether it reflects a change in counting methods is not clear. In any case American attacks in this category greatly increased again during the summer of 2005. The next highest number of casualties is Iraqi police and, since January 2005, all Iraqi security forces.

The total number of attacks has steadily increased. As can be seen from table 7.1, the total number of incidents in the first half of 2005 is considerably higher than for the whole period September 2003 to October 2004 and the level of casualties is about the same – that is to say, twice as high on a monthly basis. Some forty to sixty cities have been the scene of attacks since the second half of 2004, including many outside the Sunni triangle. Easily the most violent city is Baghdad, with twenty to forty attacks a week. Mosul is second, with four to thirteen a week.[37] The extremist groups mentioned above, especially those affiliated with al-Qaeda, appear to specialize in grisly spectacular incidents designed to gain maximum media attention, such as videos depicting the torture and beheading of hostages.

As the insurgency has spread, so has the capacity for intelligence and the penetration of Iraqi government and security agencies. This has led to increasingly effective attacks. On 23 October 2004, for example, guerrillas dressed as police officers executed forty-nine newly trained Iraqi soldiers on a remote road in Eastern Iraq. They stopped at a fake checkpoint when returning home after completing their training.

It is difficult to establish a clear pattern to these attacks. There appears to be some coordination from the pattern of violent incidents – the increase in attacks, for example, in the run-up to the elections. But there is also a degree of in-fighting, as evidenced by mysterious killings of Sunni clerics and disagreements about tactics, such as whether hostage-taking is permissible and how hostages should be treated. Although the Coalition forces continue to be the main targets, attacks on the Iraqi government and Iraqi civilians have been increasing, and these often constitute sectarian attacks. The effect of the attacks is to create a generalized sense of pervasive insecurity and fear, in which people feel forced to choose between the insurgency and the occupation, and in which those who present themselves as tough and able to act as protectors are more likely to augment their power. Population displacement has begun to take place in parts of Baghdad.

American officials claim that the insurgents have 'unlimited money' supplied by members of the former regime or by Saudi and religious charities.[38] They claim that ordinary criminals are paid to conduct attacks. According to Major General Raymond T. Odierno, commander of the US Army's 4th Infantry Division: 'When we first got here, we believed it was about $100 to conduct an attack and $500 if you are successful. We now believe that it's somewhere between $1000 and $2000 if you conduct an attack and between $3000 and $5000 if you are successful.' According to him, 70 to 80 per cent of captured insurgents were ordinary criminals.[39]

It may be the case that former Ba'athists and some of the Islamic groups have substantial funding, but it is also clear that there is widespread looting, hostage-taking and convoy-hijacking for money. Illicit sales of oil are also widespread.[40] Some of it may be purely criminal – the absence of law and order being conducive to criminal activities – but it is probable that this is the method through which various groups are able to fund themselves. Since infrastructure has suffered from decades of neglect and deliberate destruction, and since the lack of security prevents any substantial new investment, the violence contributes to a typical new-war criminalized economy in which income often depends on violent methods.

On the American side there are, of course, some 160,000 Coalition troops currently in Iraq, including 8600 British troops and a very small number from twenty-one other countries (twenty-eight at the time of the invasion).[41] The

Americans have made widespread use of 'non-state actors'. Estimates of private American security contractors range from 6000 to 60,000 individuals, of which the majority are Iraqis, and twenty-two to forty private companies.[42] Some retired soldiers do undertake military and security work; there are said to be some 5000 foreign mercenaries working for security companies. Most private contractors do support jobs such as logistics, training, communications and intelligence, catering and laundry.[43] Indeed, the combination of regular troops and private contractors is reminiscent of the networks of regular troops and paramilitary groups in many 'new wars', where the latter are often used to carry out tasks that fall outside the laws of war; hence when the scandals about torture in the Abu Ghraib prison became public, it was evident that private contractors had carried out some of the most dubious practices.

In addition, the Iraqi army and police are now being established. As of October 2005, total Iraqi security forces amounted to 196,600, of which 91,100 were the armed forces under the control of the Ministry of Defence, 70,000 were police, including highway patrols, and an additional 40,000 were under the control of the Ministry of Interior.[44] These numbers are beginning to rise, although the process of rebuilding Iraqi security forces has been precarious and has had many ups and downs. Recruits are threatened by insurgents, and during major attacks, such as in Fallujah in November 2004, many troops disappeared or colluded with the insurgents. In Senate hearings in February 2005, Paul Wolfowitz acknowledged that many new Iraqi soldiers fail to return to their posts after receiving pay cheques. Many of the party militias have been absorbed into the security forces, especially the police, and this does raise issues of divided loyalties – as British forces discovered in Basra, where captured insurgents actually included a member of the police force. There remains a gap between actual forces and the desired end strength; as of September 2005 this stood at 271,041, in other words a shortfall of around 75,000, or around half of the actual forces. Moreover, General Richard Myers, the chairman of the Joint Chiefs of Staff, has said that only about a third of the total are trained and equipped to 'go anywhere and meet any threat';[45] however, this may not be so important, since it is presence on the ground that provides reassurance.

American tactics are aimed at defeating the insurgency. Rumsfeld has stressed that this is a 'battle of wills' which the United States has to win. Hence, the tactics include classic counter-insurgency techniques of the type known as 'search and destroy': the detention of large numbers of potential insurgents, forced interrogation techniques to extract information, and the attempts to destroy the safe havens of the insurgents through the attacks on places such as Fallujah, Samarra, Najaf, or al-Sadr City. According to one American soldier: '[I] don't think we will put much energy into trying the old saying "win hearts and minds". I don't look at it as one of the metrics of success.'[46] Table 7.1 shows that, in the category 'criminals and insurgents', there is a very high ratio of people killed to number of attacks. Whereas over the period as a whole the ratio of American soldiers killed to attacks on American convoys is only 0.06, the ratio of 'criminals and suspects' killed in American attacks is 11.3. In other words, the Americans are nearly 200 times more efficient at killing than the insurgents.

Because it is difficult to distinguish insurgents from the civilian population, it is civilians that appear to be the main victims of attacks and of detentions, despite American disclaimers. The attacks on all sides have resulted in very high civilian casualties – probably the best estimate up to October 2005 is around 28,000.[47] They also result in large numbers of displaced persons as civilians flee the fighting, are made homeless by the destruction of their houses, or leave their homes out of fear of sectarian attacks. The attack on Fallujah in November 2004, for example, resulted in some 150,000 displaced persons.

Since the insurgents are able to disappear before these attacks and are able apparently to hide or even exist openly in large parts of Iraq, the main effect of these attacks is to increase the sense of insecurity and injustice and to substantiate claims that this is a war of the West against Islam. The effect of killing so many civilians and of razing cities such as Fallujah is to recruit more sympathizers to the insurgents' cause. Indeed, at the very moment of the attacks on Fallujah in November, the insurgents seem to have been able to orchestrate a wave of attacks throughout the Sunni triangle. Moreover, since most American operations take place in Sunni areas and cause high levels of collateral damage to people and property, these attacks are portrayed by insurgents as attacks on the Sunni community.

The Iraqi administration and the Coalition forces are, of course, funded by government revenue, including the funds made available under the oil-for-food programme and seized assets from the former regime. Undoubtedly, some of these funds find their way into the new war economy. But one might also put forward the argument that the war economy contributes to growing material insecurity in the United States and the weakening of state institutions and legitimacy, thus contributing to the conditions that give rise to the ideology of war. Where this new version of old war differs from, say, World War II is that it does not require sacrifice from the American population. They do not have to pay additional war taxes; indeed, the war is accompanied by tax cuts. Nor are they conscripted to fight in the war, and American casualties, although mounting, are still rather low by historical standards. The American war effort is funded from the American deficit, which in turn is funded by foreign borrowing. Any attempt to reduce the size of the deficit is likely to be achieved largely through cuts in social security rather than through cuts in war spending (although overall defence spending will have to be reined in) or through increases in taxation. Unlike World War II, where everybody was mobilized for the war effort, more and more people are politically and socially excluded.

In addition to the Americans and the insurgents, it is important to mention a range of other private security groups that exist in Iraq and compound the absence of any monopoly of legitimate violence. Dozens of armed groups attached to the political parties involved in the Interim Government are still in existence, protecting the various villas and houses requisitioned by party leaders as well as being involved in other security tasks. They include the Kurdish Peshmerga attached to the Kurdish Democratic Party (PDK) and the Patriotic Union of Kurdistan (PUK), who still play a significant role in maintaining law and order in Northern Iraq; the various militia attached to the religious parties, who were already in existence during the former regime; tribal armed militias; and new groups such as the militia attached to the Iraqi National Congress (INC), which was trained by the Americans in Hungary.[48] These groups are busily engaged in creating facts on the ground in order to shape the future political arrangements.

Effectively, what is happening in Iraq is that the United States is being drawn into a genuinely new type of war. The Americans' belief that they are fighting an old war, adapted and improved by the advent of new technology, actually prevents any strategy towards Iraq that might lead to stability. As in other new wars, the warring parties are both caught up in their own narratives about what they are trying to achieve, and their respective narratives feed on each other. The Americans believe that they are leading a struggle for democracy, and the more they confront resistance, especially of the more spectacular type, the more those who support the war are convinced of the rightness of what they are doing and the more the polarized atmosphere within the United States contributes to the strength of war party. As long as they and others believe in the narrative, it does not matter that the insurgency grows. On the contrary, it perpetuates and substantiates the idea of a long war. At the same time, the more that American behaviour exacerbates the sense of insecurity and humiliation, the more the insurgency grows and the more those that promulgate an idea of a war of the West against Islam, or who identify the Iraqi government, Shi'ites and Kurds with the West in order to promote a sectarian war, gain the upper hand.

As in other new wars, the victims are the civilians, who suffer the vast bulk of the casualties, who are detained by the Americans or taken hostage by the insurgents, and who are displaced from their homes as a consequence of the fighting or the efforts by both sides to establish secure areas. Despite the American attacks on the insurgents and the insurgents' attacks on the Americans, the warring parties rarely directly engage each other; instead the victims are Iraqi civilians or those associated with the nascent Iraqi security forces. This is perhaps the distinguishing characteristic of new wars. Unlike in Bosnia, deliberate attacks on civilians are rare, although they are increasing as the war acquires a sectarian character. But, as in Chechnya, it becomes increasingly difficult to distinguish between ethnic cleansing and counter-insurgency. Civilians are killed, detained, tortured, or displaced from their homes because it is so difficult to distinguish combatants from non-combatants. Civilians are also caught in the crossfire because, unlike Coalition troops, they have no protection.

Each stage of the conflict accelerates the process of unravelling state institutions and shared norms and rules, both inside Iraq and, indeed, within an increasingly polarized United States. In particular, it is the prospect of Iraqi democracy that is being defeated in this war. Those who hope for peaceful ways of managing disagreements through elections and debates have to choose between association with the insurgents, dominated both by repressive Ba'athism and conservative Islam or, worse, al-Qaeda, or associating with the Coalition, which discredits them in the eyes of many of their fellow citizens.

Was There or is There an Alternative?

In the West, there have been big debates about the goals of the war in Iraq and the rightness or wrongness of those goals. Those who favoured the war claimed that it was intended to get rid of weapons of mass destruction (WMD) accumulated by Iraq, to defeat terrorism, or to bring democracy to Iraq. Those who opposed the war claimed that this was an imperial war designed to expand American power and, in particular, to control sources of oil.

The argument that I have put forward here is that the technique of 'old war' was a very bad way to achieve any of these goals. Indeed, the war may have achieved the opposite of all of them. No one has been able to find any WMD, although recently the IAEA (the International Atomic Energy Agency) has expressed deep concern about the looting of 377 tons of explosive in the period since the invasion, implying that the war may have contributed to proliferation.[49] Nor has anyone found any links between Saddam Hussein and al-Qaeda. However, since the war, there have been many attacks by al-Qaeda, and al-Qaeda groups are now present in Iraq and are 'exporting' terrorists. As for democracy, the 'new war' is destroying step by step whatever prospects there might have been because it has fostered extreme sectarian politics. And if the American goal had been to expand bases and to secure oil supplies, surely a deal with Saddam Hussein would have been an easy and safer option. For now the oil infrastructure has been run down and destroyed; it will be a long time before oil production regains its pre-war levels, if ever, and the American bases are surrounded by hostile territory.

My argument is, rather, that the purpose of the war was war; it was designed to keep alive an idea of old war on which American identity is based, to show that old war could be upgraded and relatively pain free in the twenty-first century. I do not want to suggest that this was cynical manipulation; on the contrary, the conservatives in the Bush administration believe in American power and their mission to spread the American idea. My point is rather that they are caught up in a narrative of their own making, which resonates well with the American public and is reinforced by the American media. And it can be argued that this belief is mirrored by a similar belief among some elements of the insurgency, particularly those who espouse the idea of a global jihad, of Islam against the West.

So was there and is there an alternative to war? The most important strategy in my type of new war, as I argued in the previous chapter, is the restoration of legitimate political authority. This is no less true in Iraq than in other new wars, both before and after the invasion.

In the period before the invasion, the best justification for war was regime change. Saddam Hussein's regime was one of the most brutal in the world – millions had died from his maniacal foreign adventures, from the suppression of uprisings in the North and the South, and from purges and repression, as well as economic devastation. So was there another way to achieve regime change? From discussions with the opposition inside Iraq, I believe that there was a real possibility of 'opening up' the regime rather in the way that happened in Eastern Europe in the 1980s as a result of a combination of pressure from outside, based on the Helsinki Final Act, and pressure from below.[50]

There was much more going on inside Iraq than was realized. Indeed the expatriate opposition and Saddam Hussein had a shared interest in suppressing this reality. First, there were underground movements and parties – these included the Al Da'wa Party (Shi'ite Islamist), the Communist Party, the General Union of Students (GUSIA), and the League of Iraqi Women, who did a lot to support the widows of the victims of Saddam's regime. Second, there were various efforts to create public spaces. For example, the Hewar (dialogue) gallery was established by a well-known artist who left the Ba'ath Party at the time of the invasion of Kuwait. It became a place where artists could exhibit their work and find foreign buyers, and it had a café where they could meet and talk. It included artists such as the Najeen (survivors) group, who openly opposed the regime. Likewise, a group known as the Wednesday group, composed of current and ex-Ba'athists, met every Wednesday to discuss political and intellectual issues, even after one of their members was arrested and executed.[51]

Most interestingly, perhaps, was the way in which the mosques, both Sunni and Shi'ite, were leveraging Saddam's new emphasis on religion to create more open space within the mosques, in a strategy reminiscent of the Catholic Church in Poland. In language that reminded me of Eastern Europe, members of the Council of Sunni Clerics that I met in May 2004 told me how they had come to the conclusion that they could never defeat Saddam Hussein through a coup; instead, from 1999 onwards they developed a strategy, together with their Shi'ite counterparts, of slow strangulation.

This opening up 'from below' could have been supported from outside, along lines that were actually proposed by underground groups before the war. They favoured the lifting of overall sanctions, to be replaced by targeted sanctions, as well as pressure on Saddam Hussein to respect those provisions in the ceasefire resolution after the 1991 war, which involved respect for human rights and political pluralism. They suggested that the 'oil-for-food' programme could have been run directly by the United Nations, as in the North, rather than being mired in the nefarious manipulations of Saddam's government. They argued that an international presence did improve the domestic situation and that the weapons inspectors could have been augmented by human rights monitors, according to the terms of UN Security Council Resolution 689. At the time such proposals were accused of naïveté, but that was also true of efforts to bring change to Eastern Europe in the 1980s.

There have also been moments in the aftermath of the invasion when there were genuine opportunities to establish a legitimate Iraqi government. Immediately after the invasion, had the Coalition:

- not dissolved the army
- rapidly introduced a system of transitional justice so that the criminals of the previous regime could have been separated from ordinary Ba'athists, who had often been forced to join the party, and who largely comprised the expert class in Iraq
- consulted with different political, civil, religious and tribal groups on the ground instead of relying primarily on a collection of expatriate consultants and advisors and
- allowed the Interim Governing Council to exercise real power

then, there might have been a chance that the insurgency could have been avoided. In the aftermath of the invasion, there was a myriad of civic initiatives – neighbourhood watch groups protecting their communities against looting, museum employees protecting valuable artefacts, various forms of social and humanitarian initiatives. Subsequently, debate and dialogue blossomed among students, women's groups, newly formed democracy groups, or religious institutions, but many of those engaged in this debate felt marginalized and neglected by the Coalition authorities.[52]

Another moment was in the spring of 2004, when the United Nations Special Representative Lakhtar Bahimi was asked to make recommendations for the transfer of power. He consulted widely and came up with a set of proposals that did have a real chance of mobilizing widespread support. However, in the event, under American pressure, the new Interim Government was dominated by pro-American expatriates, and the new American Embassy, which replaced the Coalition Provisional Authority, continued to interfere with day-to-day government.

Yet another opportunity was the elections in January 2005. They took place relatively peacefully, and, even though Sunni groups boycotted the election, the turnout was 60 per cent – much higher, of course, in the North and South. The Shi'ite list, the United Iraqi Alliance, won 48 per cent of the vote. Had they formed a government quickly, reached out to the Sunni community, and set a timetable for the withdrawal of the multinational forces, they might have been able to establish a legitimate political authority, and this could have been a way to deal with all but the most extreme parts of the insurgency. That did not happen. The process of forming a government was slow and tortuous, and the constitution, drawn up with the cooption of some Sunnis, turned out to be a sectarian and Islamist document. Despite an overall yes vote in the referendum on the constitution on 15 October 2005, it was overwhelmingly rejected by the Sunni community, thus further polarizing Iraqi society. The subsequent elections in December 2005 further entrenched sectarian positions, and the tortuous process of trying to form a government has inflamed sectarian violence.

At the time of writing, sectarian strife seems likely to increase. In the previous chapter, I proposed a strategy for 'new wars' based on 'islands of civility'. These islands exist both in the largely peaceful regions that constitute at least twelve of the eighteen governorates but also among certain groups of people all over the country. These include religious leaders, such as the Ayatollah Sistani, or members of the Association of Muslim Scholars (Sunni clerics who have condemned attacks on civilians), women's groups that remain strong, students, and other independent intellectuals. The spaces in which they meet and talk need to be protected and their ideas and proposals need to be heard and taken seriously, if only to keep alive the seeds of an inclusive cosmopolitan politics.

A serious political strategy would have to be accompanied by a serious security strategy and an economic strategy as well. The Coalition forces are discredited. A timetable for withdrawal needs to be decided; if the forces were withdrawn, much of the fighting would die down, since they are the main targets of attack. This is especially true in the South, where attacks on British forces are the main source of violence. But as sectarian violence increases some military forces are needed. These could be Iraqi forces or international forces trusted by Iraqis. The key point is that they have to be used in a way that is neither classic war-fighting nor classic peacekeeping. Rather they would need to be used in support of law-enforcement. In new wars, all sides violate the laws of war and human rights law. The task of legitimate security forces is to protect people, provide public security so that a political process can get going, and act in support of the rule of law. For this role, forces are needed that are made up of a combination of soldiers, police, and civilians with the capacity to undertake various humanitarian and legal activities.[53]

During 2005, the Americans did introduce a change of strategy, which superficially has some similarity to the notion of 'islands of civility', but it is a military rather than a political strategy. This is the strategy of 'clear, hold, and build', based on what was known as the 'grease spot' strategy.[54] The idea is to focus on the spaces that are relatively peaceful and to expand them. The problem is the 'clear' part. The tactics used by American forces to defeat insurgents often involve killing civilians, thereby undermining the prospects for inclusive politics. Fallujah has had to be 'cleared' twice, and even now there are continuing attacks on American forces.

In the period preceding the war, forces of this kind should have been available to protect people in the event of an uprising similar to that which occurred in 1991. In that year, international forces did successfully establish a safe haven for Kurds in the North. But in the South the Shi'ite uprising was brutally suppressed. An intervention in the event of such an uprising would be defensive rather than offensive, designed to protect people rather than topple a regime, to stabilize the situation rather than defeat an enemy.

In the period after the war, the primary task should have been the provision of public security. This is the lesson of all recent international interventions. In Bosnia and Kosovo, the failure to provide public security, immediately following the ceasefires, led to reverse ethnic cleansing of Serbs and allowed widespread criminality. In Afghanistan, the failure to provide public security outside Kabul allowed the warlords to regain their fiefdoms. And in Iraq, the failure to provide public security allowed widespread looting, which, along with the dissolution of the army and the de-Ba'athification policy, was one of the disastrous mistakes of the Coalition, despite Donald Rumsfeld's oft-quoted laconic remark that 'stuff happens'.[55] The primary task after the war should have been the protection of individuals and communities and the restoration of law and order, rather than the hunt for war criminals and insurgents. Of course, the latter was necessary, but as a means to protect people rather than as a primary goal. To some extent, the British forces in the South did adopt such an approach, and this, in part, explains the relative quiescence of the South. However, such an approach has to be accompanied by efforts to restore political legitimacy, and British forces remain relatively isolated and vulnerable to the spread of the insurgency because of the lack of legitimacy in the country as a whole.

Finally, of course, there has to be an economic strategy as well. Here, the priority is to create legitimate autonomous ways in which individuals and families can make a living, both as a basis for democratic empowerment and so that they face a material alternative both to criminality and to collaboration (either with the government before the invasion, or with the insurgency now). Before the war, the blanket application of sanctions and, later, allowing the Iraqi government to administer the oil-for-food programme compounded the sense of despair and powerlessness. In the post-war period, generating employment and local economic activity, using Iraqi contractors where possible, and restoring basic services were all priorities, but huge sums were wasted on Western contractors. It is also critical to develop transparent and fair procedures for the distribution of oil revenues.

It is hard to be optimistic at the current juncture. The insurgency is escalating – more attacks, more casualties, more groups and more names are reported daily. The idea that Bush is a successful wartime leader, pioneering the new technology-intensive form of warfare, contributed to his election victory in 2004 and to a second term, in which the more hawkish elements of the administration were reappointed and promoted. The American pursuit of a moral crusade reinforces the insurgents' notion of a global jihad. The new American Strategic Plan envisages a 'long war' against terror.[56] Indeed, the new war in Iraq could be viewed as the stage for a global new war, which will be hard to contain as the ideas and experiences spread and hard to end because of the bitterness, fear and hate that are mobilized in war.

But how long can the narrative of imagined old war be sustained in the context of a real new war? American casualties, though low by the historical standard of war, are mounting. As of October 2005, there had been 2147 coalition troop deaths: 1953 Americans, 96 Britons, 13 Bulgarians, 2 Danes, 2 Dutch, 2 Estonians, 1 Hungarian, 26 Italians, 1 Kazakh, 1 Latvian, 17 Poles, 1 Salvadorean, 3 Slovaks, 11 Spaniards, 2 Thais and 18

Ukrainians.[57] Nor is it evident that deficit financing of the war can be kept up indefinitely; already the dollar has undergone one major decline. The military is overstretched, and disillusion and dissatisfaction among servicemen and women, especially reservists, who have been called up for much longer than they expected, is growing. Hurricane Katrina drew attention to the neglect of domestic services. Democrat politicians have finally begun to criticize the war and call for withdrawal.

Will reality bring about a questioning of the story of old war and its contemporary relevance? Are there other actors, the United Nations, the European Union, together with Iraqi civil society, developing some kind of alternative strategy, based on the principles outlined above, which could offer a convincing alternative storyline, one that might actually avert a global new war?

8

Governance, Legitimacy and Security

Liberal writers of the late eighteenth and nineteenth centuries had a teleological view of history. They believed that the zone of civility would, inevitably, extend itself in time and space. In his book *Reflections on Violence*,[1] John Keane contrasts their optimism with the pessimism of twentieth-century writers such as Zygmunt Bauman or Norbert Elias, who considered that barbarism was the inevitable concomitant of civility. For these writers, violence is embedded in human nature. The cost of allowing the state to monopolize violence is the terrible barbarity of twentieth-century wars and totalitarianism.

The end of the Cold War may have marked the end of statist barbarism on this scale. Certainly, the threat of modern war and, in particular, of nuclear war – the absolute expression of twentieth-century barbarism – has receded. Does this mean that violence can no longer be controlled, that the new type of warfare described in the previous chapters is likely to be pervasive, an ongoing characteristic of the post-modern world? The implication of the argument so far is that it is no longer possible to contain war geographically. Zones of peace and zones of war exist side by side in the same territorial space. The characteristics of the new wars I have described – the politics of identity, the decentralization of violence, the globalized war economy – can be found in greater or lesser degree all over the world. Moreover, through transnational criminal networks, diaspora networks based on identity, the explosive growth of refugees and asylum-seekers, as well as the global media, these characteristics have a tendency to spread. Terrorist attacks in New York, Madrid, London and other cities, conflicts in places such as Bosnia and Somalia, and even the virtual old-style wars conducted through air strikes are all manifestations of the new types of organized violence.

But if it is not possible to contain the new wars territorially, is it possible to envisage ways in which they might be contained politically? Globalization, after all, is a process which involves integration and inclusion as well as fragmentation and exclusivism. A new cosmopolitan politics, based on goals such as peace, human rights or environmentalism, is emerging side by side with the politics of particularism. Are the pessimists right? Is violence inherent in human society? Or could the new cosmopolitan politics offer a basis for restoring legitimacy at both local and global levels? Can we conceive of a world in which violence is controlled on a transnational scale, in which the monopoly of legitimate violence is reclaimed by global or transnational institutions, and in which the abuse of power by those same institutions can be checked by an alert and active cosmopolitan citizenry?

As I argued in chapter 2, military power in the post-war period was to a large degree transnationalized. The rigidification of the alliances in Europe and the establishment of integrated command systems, together with a global network of military connections through military assistance, arms sales and training, effectively meant that most countries, apart from the superpowers, abandoned the unilateral capacity to wage wars. Although there was some renationalization of armed forces in the aftermath of the Cold War, a whole set of new arrangements were also put in place – multinational peace-keeping, arms-control agreements involving mutual inspection teams, joint exercises, new or renewed organizations such as the WEU, Partnership for Peace, NATO Coordination Council (NACC) – which constitute an intensification of transnationalization in the military sphere. The promulgation of the 'War on Terror' could be regarded as a reassertion of sovereignty, but the United States is discovering in Afghanistan and Iraq how difficult it is to act unilaterally. During the Cold War, the boundaries of violence were extended to the edges of the two blocs; or, to put it another way, pacification was achieved throughout the bloc system. The question is whether this transnational agglomeration of military power can lead to global pacification. Can we conceive of pacification without territorial boundaries?

There is no self-evident answer. In every era there is a complex relationship between processes of governance (how human affairs are managed), legitimacy (on which the power to govern is based) and forms of security (how organized violence is controlled). On the one hand, the ability to maintain order, to protect individuals in a physical sense, to provide a secure basis for administrative capacities, to guarantee the rule of law, and to protect territory externally are all primary functions of political institutions from which they derive legitimacy. Moreover, the character of these institutions is largely defined in relation to the way in which these functions are undertaken and which aspects of security are accorded priority. On the other hand, it is not possible to provide security in the sense defined above without some underlying legitimacy. There has to be some mechanism, whether it is religious injunction, ideological fanaticism or democratic consent, which explains why people obey rules and why, in particular, agents of organized violence – soldiers or policemen, for example – follow orders.

In chapter 2, I described the way in which the evolution of modern (old) war was linked to the emergence of the European nation-state, in which internal pacification was associated with the externalization of violence and legitimacy derived from notions of patriotism embedded in the actual experience of war. The term 'national security' was largely synonymous with external defence of national borders. In the post-war period, the internal/external distinction extended to bloc boundaries, and ideological identities – notions of freedom and/or socialism – drawn from the experience of World War II supplanted but did not displace national identities as a basis for bloc legitimacy. Bloc security also meant external defence of the blocs.

Today, there is great uncertainty about future patterns of governance and the direction of security policies. In the National Security Strategy, the US administration sets out a vision of defending America through defeating 'rogue states', who harbour terrorists and acquire weapons of mass destruction, through traditional military means.[2] The Europeans, by contrast, have proposed a European Security Strategy, which emphasizes the need for preventive engagement and multilateralism.[3] But do either of these approaches address the real sense of insecurity experienced by millions of people in the new war zones? The national monopoly of legitimate organized violence has been eroded from above by the transnationalization of military forces. It has been eroded from below by the privatization of organized violence which is characteristic of the new wars. Under what conditions are existing or new security institutions able to eliminate or marginalize privatized forms of violence and to restore trust in institutions?

My argument is that this depends on political choice and how we choose to analyse the nature of contemporary violence and what conception of security we adopt. Traditional political science rooted in nineteenth- and twentieth-century experience is able to predict only a new variant of the past or else the descent into chaos. Precisely because the dominant stream of political science thinking was directed towards the existing system of governance, providing a form of justification or legitimation of that system and at the same time a basis for offering advice about how to operate within the system, it gives rise to a kind of fatalism or determinism about the future. In contrast, critical or normative approaches to political science allow for human agency. They are based on the assumption that people make their own history and can choose their futures, at least within a certain framework that can be analysed.

In what follows, I outline some possible ways of thinking about security which derive from competing political visions of the future based on differing perceptions of the nature of contemporary violence. One of these visions is a restoration of world order based on the reconstruction of some kind of bloc system in which cleavages based on identity supplant cleavages based on ideology. This approach draws on realist assumptions about international relations in which the main actors are territorially based political authorities and new wars are treated as a variant of old wars – geo-political conflicts. The most well-known example of this type of thinking is in Samuel Huntington's *The Clash of Civilizations*, where he proposes a variant of the bloc system based on cultural identity instead of ideology.[4] This vision is closest to that put forward by the current American administration and, perhaps, also by al-Qaeda.

A second vision can be described as neo-medievalism[5] or as anarchy, and draws on a post-modern rejection of realism.[6] Proponents of this line of thought recognize that the new wars cannot be understood in old terms, but at the same time are unable to identify any logic in the new wars. They are treated as a Hobbesian 'warre' against all.[7] This vision is, essentially, a counsel of despair, an admission of our inability to analyse global developments. Finally, a third vision is based on a more normative approach, drawing on the argument put forward for cosmopolitanism in the previous chapter.

The Clash of Civilizations

Huntington's thesis is a variant of the bloc system in which the source of legitimacy is cultural identity – loyalty to what he defines as historic civilizations. His book has received so much attention because it expresses what many believe to be the unstated convictions of parts of the political establishment, particularly those whose livelihood depended on the Cold War – an attempt to re-create the comfortable certainties of the bipolar world and to construct a new threat to substitute for communism. The 'War on Terror' could be said to represent a paradigm of the Huntington approach. Islamic terrorism is compared to the totalitarian movements of fascism and communism.[8] The democratic liberal and, implicitly, Christian West has to oppose this movement militarily in the same way as it opposed fascism and communism in World War II and the Cold War in an ongoing confrontation that, according to Donald Rumsfeld, may last for fifty years. By making the 'War on Terror' commensurate with the Cold War, the disparate band of fanatics, criminals and alienated young men that is known as al-Qaeda has been elevated into a formidable enemy on a par with Germany or the Soviet Union.

Huntington argues that we are entering a multi-civilizational world in which culture rather than ideology will be the bonding mechanism for societies and groups of states. As many critics have pointed out, he is rather vague about what is meant by culture, although clearly, for him, religion is a key defining element. Thus, the West is Christian, but only Catholic and Protestant. He is adamant that Turkey cannot be allowed to join the EU because it is Muslim, and he considers that the membership of Greece, an Orthodox country, is a mistake; according to Huntington, Greece is definitely not part of Western civilization. It is also clear that, for him, states are the key guarantors of civilizations. He emphasizes the role of 'core states', e.g. the USA for the West and China for Asia.

He defines some six or seven civilizations (Sinic, Japanese, Hindu, Islamic, Western, Latin American and, possibly, African). But he sees the dominant cleavage which shapes global order as running between the West and either Islam or Asia. Islam is viewed as a threat because of population growth and what he sees as the Muslim 'propensity for violence'. Asia is viewed as a threat because of rapid economic growth organized around what he calls the 'bamboo network' of ethnic Chinese. For Huntington, the West is defined as American political creed plus Western culture. He takes the view that Western culture is decaying and must defend itself against alien cultures; in particular, the USA and Europe must stick together as they did in the Cold War period.

The main source of violence comes from what Huntington calls 'fault-line wars'. He argues that communal conflicts are a fact of contemporary existence; in other words, he accepts the primordialist conception of the new conflicts. According to him, they are increasing in scale partly because of the collapse of communism and partly because of demographic changes. (He thinks that the war in Bosnia was mainly a consequence of the higher birth rate of Muslims.) When communal conflicts involve different civilizations, as in Bosnia–Herzegovina, they become fault-line wars, calling into being what he calls the kin-country syndrome. Hence, Russia was brought into the Bosnian conflict on the Serbian side, Germany on the Croatian side and the Islamic states on the Bosnian side. (He is a little puzzled by US support for Bosnia, which does not quite fit the thesis, but it can be explained away in terms of the mistaken legacy of a universalizing political ideology.) In other words, the new wars are to be subsumed into a dominant civilizational clash and superpower patrons are to be re-created on a cultural rather than an ideological basis.

Huntington is highly critical of a global universalizing mission, describing himself as a cultural relativist, and, at the same time, deeply opposed to multiculturalism. He argues that the USA no longer has the capacity to act as a global power, citing the overstretch of US forces at the time of the Gulf War, and that its task is to protect Western civilization in a multi-civilizational world. He also considers that human rights and individualism are purely Western phenomena and we have no right to impose Western political values on societies to whom this is alien. At the same time, he argues that the USA has the task of preserving Western culture domestically. Hence, what he envisages is a kind of global apartheid in which relatively homogeneous civilizations held together from above by core states become mutual guardians of international order, helping each other through their mutual confrontation to preserve the purity of their respective civilizations. In other words, he is proposing a form of bloc political mobilization based on exclusive identity: 'In the greater clash, the global "real clash" between Civilization and Barbarism, the world's great civilizations . . . will . . . hang together or hang separately. In the emerging era, clashes of civilization are the greatest threat to world peace, and an international order based on civilizations is the surest safeguard against world war.'[9]

A major problem for Huntington is the fact that the Muslim world has no core state capable of keeping order. Just as the USA needed the Soviet Union to sustain the bipolar order of the Cold War years, so the Huntington scenario requires a stable enemy. The absence of a core Muslim state is more than just a problem for the argument, for it has something to do with the fragility of the entire theoretical framework. For Huntington, it is geo-politics as usual. In his framework, states retain the monopoly of legitimate organized violence. Civilizational security is provided by core states and, at least implicitly, supplies the basis for the legitimacy of civilizational blocs. But is this realistic?

Huntington does not ask why the Soviet Union collapsed or what are the factors that characterize the current transition period. Words such as 'globalization' or 'civil society' simply do not enter the Huntington vocabulary. For him, history is about changing state relations; models of state structures can be constructed without any regard to changing state–society relations. Seemingly random developments such as population growth or urbanization are invoked to explain particular phenomena such as the growth of fundamentalism or the strength of China. But there is no questioning of the content of govern-ance, of how political institutions change in character, and little explanation about how the world moves from today's uncertainty to the new civilizational order. It is assumed that territorial defence of civilizations is the way to maintain order; it ignores the complexities of forms of violence which are neither internal nor external, public nor private.

The problem has become apparent in the wars in Afghanistan and Iraq. Al-Qaeda is not a state and Iraq and Afghanistan were not powerful military enemies but, as became evident afterwards, on the verge of state failure. The defeat of the Taliban or of Saddam Hussein did not mean the defeat of al-Qaeda. On the contrary, even though the training camps were destroyed and some key leaders killed or captured, the al-Qaeda idea is as strong as ever, fed by the notion of an ongoing civilizational conflict. The instability in Afghanistan and especially in Iraq provides a fertile environment for terrorism – undermining the notion of civilizational order.

The Coming Anarchy

In contrast to Huntington's thesis, the strength of the anarchy argument is that it takes account of the break with the past and the difference between old and new wars. Robert D. Kap-lan's book *The Ends of the Earth: A Journey at the Dawn of the 21st Century* is a good example of this type of thinking. It is a kind of political travel book, which contains compelling descrip-tions of social life as it exists today on the ground. His conclu-sions are thus derived from direct experience of contemporary realities. Kaplan draws attention to the erosion of state author-ity in many parts of the world and the myopia induced by a state-centric view of the world:

> What if there are really not fifty-odd nations in Africa as the maps suggest – what if there are only six, or seven, or eight real nations on the continent? Or, instead of nations, several hundred tribal entities? . . . What if the territory held by guerrilla armies and urban mafias – territory that is never shown on maps – is more significant than the territory claimed by many recognized states? What if Africa is even further away from North America and Europe than the maps indicate?[10]

In Sierra Leone, he discovers the breakdown of the monopoly of organized violence, the weakening of the distinction between 'armies and civilians, and armies and criminal gangs'.[11] In Pakistan, he discovers a 'decomposing polity based more on criminal activities than effective government'.[12] In Iran, he speculates about a new type of economy based on the bazaar. His journey gives him scope to describe the growing scarcity of resources, widespread environmental degradation, the pressures of urbanization and the new class of restless, unemployed young urban dwellers attracted to the certainties of religious fundamentalism. He talks about global inequalities of wealth and about the global communications revolution which has made these disparities so visible. He describes the growth of NGOs as 'the international army of the future'.[13] He dwells on the impact of modern technology on traditional societies – on radio, for example, as magic in Africa.

In his original article in the *Atlantic Monthly*, Kaplan coined the phrase the 'coming anarchy' to depict a world in which civil order had broken down. In West Africa, he observed a return to nature and to Hobbesian chaos which he argued prefigured the future elsewhere in the world. Referring to Africa, Kaplan told a BBC interviewer in March 1995:

> You have a lot of people in London and Washington who fly all over the world, who stay in luxury hotels, who think that English is dominating every place, but yet they have no idea what is out there. Out there is that thin membrane of luxury hotels, of things that work, of civil order, which is proportionately getting thinner and thinner and thinner.[14]

In his book, the thesis is somewhat modified. He also finds islands of civility, in Eritrea, in Risha valley in India, or in the slums of Istanbul, where local people have succeeded in establishing or maintaining new or traditional forms of self-management. He is doubtful about whether these relatively isolated examples can provide models for other regions, arguing that their success depends largely on whether or not they have inherited certain civic-minded traditions, on what is or is not inherent in local culture. He goes on to argue:

> The map of the world will never be static. The future map – in a sense, the 'last map' – will be an ever-mutating representation

of cartographic chaos: in some areas benign, or even productive, and in some areas violent. Because the map will be always
changing, it may be updated, like weather reports, and transmitted daily over the internet in those places that have reliable
electricity or private generators. On this map, the rules by
which diplomats and other policymaking elites have ordered
the world these past few hundred years will apply less and less.
Solutions in the main, will have to come from within the
affected cultures themselves.[15]

Kaplan's argument is essentially determinist. While he rightly
dismisses geo-political solutions of the Huntington type drawn
on the state-centric assumptions of the past, he implicitly
shares Huntington's hypothesis that the prospects for governance depend on the essentialist assumptions about culture.
Because he witnesses collapsing states and because he cannot
envisage alternative forms of authority at a global level, his
scenario contains no security and no legitimacy except in
certain arbitrary instances. Like Huntington, Kaplan laments
the passing of the Cold War, suggesting that we may, in future,
come to see it as an interlude between violence and chaos, like
the Golden Age of Athenian democracy. He concludes his book
with an admission of helplessness: 'I would be unfaithful to
my experience if I thought we had a general solution to these
problems. We are not in control. As societies grow more popu-
lous and complex, the idea that a global elite like the UN can
engineer reality from above is just as absurd as the idea that
political "science" can reduce any of this to a science.'[16]

Cosmopolitan Governance

In contrast to the above approaches, the project for cosmopolitan governance or human governance, as Richard Falk calls it,[17]
breaks with the assumption of territorially based political entities. It is a project which derives from a humanist universalist
outlook and which crosses the global/local divide. It is based
on an alliance, as described in chapter 6, between islands of
civility, noted by Kaplan, and transnational institutions. There
are no boundaries in a territorial sense. But there are political
boundaries – between those who support cosmopolitan civic
values and who favour openness, toleration and participation,

on the one hand, and those who are tied to particularist, exclusivist, often collectivist political positions, on the other. In the
nineteenth century, the dominant international cleavages were
national, tied to a territorial definition of nation. These were
replaced in the twentieth century by ideological cleavages
between left and right or between democracy/capitalism and
socialism, which also became tied to territory. The cleavage
between cosmopolitanism and particularism cannot be territorially defined, even though every individual particularism
makes its own territorial claim.

This is not a project for a single world government. The
Kantian notion of cosmopolitan right was based on the assumption of a federation of sovereign states; cosmopolitan right was
essentially a set of rules agreed by all the members of the federation. Essentially, what is proposed is a form of 'global over-
watch'. It is possible to envisage a range of territorially based
political entities, from municipalities to nation-states to conti-
nental organizations, which operate within a set of accepted
rules and to certain standards of international behaviour. The
job of international institutions is to ensure implementation of
those rules, particularly as regards human rights and humanitarian law. Just as it is increasingly accepted that governments
can intervene in family affairs to stop domestic violence, so a
similar principle would be applied on a global scale.

In some senses, a cosmopolitan regime already exists.[18] Transnational NGOs monitor and draw public attention to abuses of
human rights, to genocide and other war crimes, and international institutions do respond in different ways. What has been
lacking up to now has been enforcement. The argument here
is that some form of cosmopolitan law-enforcement, as elaborated in chapter 6, would underpin a cosmopolitan regime. In
effect, it would fill the security vacuum and enhance the legitimacy of international institutions, enabling them to mobilize
public support and to act in other fields, for example, the environment or poverty. Of course, international institutions would
need to increase their accountability and transparency, to
develop democratic procedures for authorizing the use of legitimate force. Recent proposals for United Nations reform, including the endorsement of the 'Responsibility to Protect', the
establishment of a standing police force and a peace-
building commission, agreed at the UN Summit in 2005, are

tentative steps in this direction. The point is, surely, that, just as the development of the modern state involved a symbiotic process through which war, administrative structures and legitimacy evolved, so the development of cosmopolitan governance and, indeed, democracy is already taking place through a similar, although evidently fragile, process involving growing administrative responsibility for upholding cosmopolitan norms.

What are the implications of this approach for the debate about European security? Any security organization has to be inclusive rather than exclusive. An organization with boundaries is one which implicitly emphasizes external defence against a common enemy rather than cosmopolitan law-enforcement. In the construction of the European Union, there has always been a tension between different conceptions of Europe. One conception is Europe as a superpower in the making. There has always been a strand of Europeanism which sees the project as a way of reversing the decline of Europe's Great Powers. Many European politicians have long favoured a common defence policy because they believed that Europe had the potential to become a superpower rivalling the United States. Such a policy would build European security capabilities on the same model as those of the member states, only bigger and better. Such a conception envisages the strengthening of integrated European military forces on a traditional defence model so that the EU can be either a partner or a competitor to the United States. According to this approach, the main threats to Europe, as for the United States, are states which possess weapons of mass destruction and/or harbour terrorists. The main doctrinal changes required relate to technology, from platform-centric warfare to network-centric warfare.[19] But external defence of the EU, or indeed of NATO, will not protect EU countries from the spread of new wars, rather it will treat those countries outside the boundaries as potential enemies. Those countries that are poorer, with less well-established political institutions, that are perhaps Muslim and/or Orthodox, would be designated as outsiders. This is unlikely to create a new civilizational order on the Huntingtonian model. On the contrary, exclusion is likely to contribute to the conditions that give rise to the new type of warfare which could easily spread and which could nurture terrorism.

The other conception has always been Europe as a 'peace project'. This is an Enlightenment idea – many of the great liberal thinkers (Abbé St Pierre, Jeremy Bentham and Kant) developed perpetual peace projects, which were essentially proposals for European integration. In the same spirit, the founders of what was to become the European Union wanted, in the immediate aftermath of World War II, to preclude another war on European territory. This continues to be a strong motive in the minds of European citizens: when asked what the European Union means to them personally, the third answer that comes up in the Eurobarometer survey, right after the euro and freedom of movement, is 'peace'. Indeed, 8 per cent of respondents consider 'maintaining peace and security in Europe' to be a priority of the EU. It is also considered to be the most effective of EU policies.[20] In a globalizing world, the 'peace project' has to be understood as a process rather than an end goal. The coming together of legal relations and a civil space has had to be reproduced and extended to keep the process going. In the interdependent post-Cold War environment, the peace project can succeed only as a global project and not as a merely European one. Thus this conception of Europe would favour the construction of a European capacity for cosmopolitan law-enforcement as a contribution to global security.[21]

The advantage of NATO was that it became the instrument through which military forces were transnationalized; it provided a basis for transnational pacification. This is probably the most important reason why a war between France and Germany is now unthinkable. The disadvantage was that it kept alive the prospect of bloc war. A cosmopolitan approach to European and, indeed, global security would try to bring together potentially conflicting countries and to spread as far as possible the transnationalization of armed forces. This could be under the umbrella of the United Nations as well as regional organizations such as the EU, NATO or the African Union. The important point is not the name of the organization but how the security task is reconceptualized. A cosmopolitan approach to security encompasses political and economic approaches to security, as described in chapter 6. The task of the agents of legitimate organized violence, under the umbrella of transnational institutions, is not external defence, as was the case for national or bloc models of security, but cosmopolitan law-enforcement.

Conclusion

Table 8.1 provides a schematic description of the relationship between patterns of governance and forms of security and how this relationship would vary according to the competing visions I have described.

Which of the last three scenarios – clash of civilizations, coming anarchy, cosmopolitan governance – will the future hold? Prediction is not possible. The answer depends on the outcome of public debates, on the effectiveness of institutions, on political choices being made at various levels of society and in different places – the response to terrorism, whether in London, Darfur or Iraq, the efforts to solve long-standing conflicts in Israel/Palestine or Kashmir, the future of international administrations in Bosnia or Kosovo, or the commitment to development as an alternative to the globalized war economy. Will Bosnia continue to be divided into Huntington-style statelets or be ruled by an international administration, or will it eventually be transformed into a functioning democracy? Is Iraq an example of Kaplan's anarchy or is it degenerating into a Huntingtonian civilizational war? Can there be an alternative cosmopolitan intervention that would help to establish democracy and the rule of law? The 'War on Terror', the paradigm of the Huntington visions, is floundering. It has not brought a sense of security either to the Middle East or to Europe and the United States. Yet insecurity does not necessarily lead to a different approach. It may indeed foster more and more extreme positions, leading to a new war on a global scale in which identity politics, attacks on civilians and the shadowy economic underside of globalization are all mutually reinforcing. Will the outcome be a form of anarchy punctured by fortified islands of civility? Or can a cosmopolitan approach offer a way to bridge the gap between zones of war and zones of civility, an alternative to the 'War on Terror'?

Critics of the cosmopolitan approach might argue that it is a modernist/universalist project on an even more ambitious scale than earlier modernist projects such as liberalism or socialism, and thus contains within it a totalitarian claim. Moreover, given the secular character of the concept and the explicit rejection of identity-based forms of communitarianism, it might be argued that the concept is open to more severe

Table 8.1 *Patterns of governance*

Patterns of governance	*Political institutions*	*Source of legitimacy*	*Mode of security*
States system	Nation-states	Nation-building, patriotism	External defence, internal pacification
Cold War	Nation-states, blocs, transnational institutions	Ideology – freedom or socialism	Deterrence, bloc cohesion
Clash of civilizations	Nation-states, civilizational blocs	Cultural identity	Civilizational defence at home and abroad
Coming anarchy	Pockets of authority	Non-existent	Fortified islands of civility amidst pervasive violence
Cosmopolitan governance	Transnational institutions, nation-states, local government	Humanism	End of modern war, cosmopolitan law-enforcement

charges of utopianism and inconsistency than were earlier modernist projects. I take the view that public morality has to be underpinned by universalist projects, although those projects are periodically changed by circumstances; they always produce unintended consequences and have to be revised. Thus, they can never be universalistic in practice, even if they make universalistic claims. Such projects, like liberalism or socialism, are validated by circumstances, at least for a time, or discredited. The eighteenth-century idea that reason is immanent in nature implied that rational (moral) behaviour can be learned through experience; there is a reality in which there are better or worse ways of living and that how to live in these different ways can be learned through experience – for example, the experience of happy or unhappy families or of war and peace. These lessons are never learned for ever because reality is so complicated and the exact set of circumstances in which a particular rationality seems to work cannot be reproduced. But they can be learned for a while and in approximate circumstances.

In today's reflexive era, a cosmopolitan project is, of its nature, tentative. We are likely to live permanently with contending approaches, although the character and assumptions of the different approaches are bound to keep changing. It may be that no solution will be found in Iraq and that Bosnia will be permanently divided and run by an international protectorate, but the wars in Iraq and Bosnia may well represent for some time to come a new narrative, a way of telling the story of our political differences.

The optimistic view of current developments is the obsolescence of modern war. War, as we have known it for the last two centuries, may, like slavery, have become an anachronism. National armies, navies and airforces may be no more than ritual vestiges of the passing nation-state. 'Perpetual peace', as envisaged by Immanuel Kant, the globalization of civility, and the development of cosmopolitan forms of governance are real possibilities. The pessimistic view is that war, like slavery, can always be reinvented. The capacity of formal political institutions, primarily nation-states, to regulate violence has been eroded and we have entered an era of long-term low-level informal violence, of post-modern warfare. In this book, I have argued that both views are correct. We cannot assume that either barbarism or civility is embedded in human nature. Whether we can learn to cope with the new wars and veer towards a more optimistic future depends ultimately on our own behaviour.

Notes

Preface

[1] Human Security Centre, *Human Security Report* (2005), http://www.humansecurityreport.info/; Nils Petter Gleditsch, Peter Wallensteen, Mikael Eriksson, Margareta Sollenberg and Håvard Strand, 'Armed conflict 1946–2001: a new dataset', *Journal of Peace Research*, 39/5 (2002), pp. 615–37; *Armed Conflict Dataset Codebook*, http://www.prio.no/cwp/armedconflict/current/Codebook_v3-2005.pdf; Project Ploughshares, http://www.ploughshares.ca/.

[2] United States Department of State, *Patterns of Global Terrorism*, http://www.state.gov/s/ct/rls/pgtrpt/ [annual report].

[3] Mary Kaldor and Diego Muro, 'Religious and nationalist militant groups', in Mary Kaldor, Helmut Anheier and Marlies Glasius, *Global Civil Society 2003*, Oxford: Oxford University Press, 2003.

[4] See, for example, Roland Paris, *At War's End: Peace-Building after Civil Conflict*, Cambridge: Cambridge University Press, 2004; Francis Fukuyama, *State-Building: Governance and World Order in the 21st Century*, Ithaca, NY: Cornell University Press, 2004.

Chapter 1   Introduction

[1] The research project was undertaken for the United Nations University's World Institute for Development Economics Research (UNU/WIDER). The results are published in Mary Kaldor and

Basker Vashee (eds), *Restructuring the Global Military Sector, Volume I: New Wars*, London: Cassell/Pinter, 1997.

2 David Keen, 'When war itself is privatized', *Times Literary Supplement* (December 1995).

3 Mark Duffield, 'Post-modern conflict: warlords, post-adjustment states and private protection', *Journal of Civil Wars* (April 1998); Michael Ignatieff, *The Warrior's Honor: Ethnic War and the Modern Conscience*, London: Chatto & Windus, 1998.

4 Chris Hables Gray, *Post-Modern War: The New Politics of Conflicts*, London and New York: Routledge, 1997.

5 See, for example, the various chapters including my own chapter 'Elaborating the "new war" thesis', in Jan Angstrom and Isabelle Duyvesteyn, *Rethinking the Nature of War*, London and New York: Frank Cass, 2005; see also Errol A. Henderson and David Singer, '"New wars" and rumours of "new wars"', *International Interactions*, 7/2 (2002); Stathis N. Kalyvas, '"New" and "old" civil wars: a valid distinction?', *World Politics*, 54 (October 2001).

6 Martin Shaw, 'War and globality: the role and character of war in the global transition', in Ho-Won Jeong (ed.), *Peace and Conflict: A New Agenda*, Aldershot: Ashgate, 2000.

7 See David Jablonsky, *The Owl of Minerva Flies at Night: Doctrinal Change and Continuity and the Revolution in Military Affairs*, US Army War College, Carlisle Barracks, PA, 1994; Elliott Cohen, 'A revolution in warfare', *Foreign Affairs* (March/April 1996); Robert J. Bunker, 'Technology in a neo-Clausewitzean setting', in Gert de Nooy (ed.), *The Clausewitzean Dictum and the Future of Western Military Strategy*, The Hague and London: Kluwer Law International, 1997.

8 Jean Baudrillard, *The Gulf War*, London: Power Publishers, 1995.

9 See Malcolm Waters, *Globalization*, London: Routledge, 1995; David Held, *Democracy and the Global Order: From the Modern State to Cosmopolitan Governance*, Cambridge: Polity, 1995.

10 See Mary Kaldor, Ulrich Albrecht and Asbjörn Eide, *The International Military Order*, London: Macmillan, 1978.

11 Anthony Giddens makes a similar argument about the new political cleavage between cosmopolitanism and fundamentalism. See Anthony Giddens, *Beyond Left and Right: The Future of Radical Politics*, Stanford, CA: Stanford University Press, 1994.

12 On the concept of the mode of warfare, see Mary Kaldor, 'Warfare and capitalism', in E. P. Thompson et al., *Exterminism and Cold War*, London: Verso, 1981.

13 See, for example, David Keen, *Conflict and Collusion in Sierra Leone*, Oxford: James Currey, 2005.

14 In addition to the research project undertaken for UNU/WIDER, I and my colleagues at the Sussex European Institute undertook a research project in 1995 on Balkan reconstruction for the European Commission. See Vesna Bojičić, Mary Kaldor and Ivan Vejvoda, 'Post-war reconstruction in the Balkans', *SEI Working Paper*, Brighton: Sussex European Institute, 1995. A shorter updated version is published in *European Foreign Affairs Review*, 2/3 (Autumn 1997).

Chapter 2   Old Wars

1 According to Clausewitz: 'War belongs not to the province of Arts and Sciences but to the province of social life . . . It would be better instead of comparing it with any Art, to liken it to business competition, which is also a conflict of human interests and activities.' *On War* (first pubd 1832), Harmondsworth: Penguin, 1968, p. 202.
2 Clausewitz, *On War*, p. 101.
3 Martin van Creveld, *The Transformation of War*, New York: Free Press; Oxford: Maxwell Macmillan International, 1991.
4 John Keegan, *A History of Warfare*, London: Hutchinson, 1993, p. 12.
5 Michael Roberts, 'The military revolution 1560–1660', in David B. Ralston, *Soldiers and States: Civil–Military Relations in Modern Europe*, Boston: Heath & Co., 1966, p. 18.
6 Max Weber, *The Theory of Social and Economic Organization*, trans. and ed. A. M. Henderson and Talcott Parsons, New York: Free Press, 1947, p. 326.
7 Van Creveld, *Transformation of War*, p. 41.
8 I am indebted to Robert Neild for some of these points. See *Public Corruption: The Dark Side of Social Evolution*, London: Anthem Press, 2002.
9 See Charles Tilly, *Coercion, Capital and European States AD 990–1990*, Oxford: Blackwell, 1990; Michael Mann, *States, War and Capitalism*, Oxford: Blackwell, 1988.
10 Anthony Giddens, *The Nation-State and Violence*, Cambridge: Polity, 1985.
11 Theda Skocpol, *States and Social Revolutions*, Cambridge: Cambridge University Press, 1979.
12 'Abstract and judgment of Saint-Pierre's project for perpetual peace' (1756), in Stanley Hoffman and David P. Fidler, *Rousseau on International Relations*, Oxford: Oxford University Press, 1991, pp. 90–1.

[13] 'Perpetual peace' (1795), in *Kant's Political Writings*, ed. Hans Reiss, Cambridge: Cambridge University Press, 1992.

[14] Clausewitz, *On War*, p. 119–20.

[15] See Richard Simkin, *Race to the Swift: Thoughts on Twenty-First Century Warfare*, London: Brasseys, 1985.

[16] Clausewitz, *On War*, p. 102.

[17] The St Petersburg Declaration of 1868, which limited weapons that cause unnecessary suffering, reads as follows:

> Considering that the progress of civilization should have the effect of alleviating as much as possible the calamities of war;
> That the only legitimate object which states should endeavour to accomplish during war is to weaken the military forces of society;
> That for this purpose it is sufficient to disable the greatest possible number of men;
> That this object would be exceeded by the employment of arms which uselessly aggravate the sufferings of disabled men or render their death inevitable;
> That the employment of such arms would therefore be contrary to the laws of humanity.

Quoted in Michael Howard, 'Constraints on warfare', in Michael Howard, George J. Andreopoulos and Mark R. Shulman (eds), *Constraints on Warfare in the Western World: The Laws of War*, New Haven, CT, and London: Yale University Press, 1994.

[18] This crime against humanity, as it was labelled after the war, did not technically count as a violation of the nineteenth-century laws of war, as Adam Roberts points out, since it took place in occupied territory. See Adam Roberts, 'Land warfare: from Hague to Nuremberg', in Howard, Andreopoulos and Shulman, *Constraints on Warfare*.

[19] See Ernest Gellner, *The Conditions of Liberty: Civil Society and its Rivals*, London: Hamish Hamilton, 1994.

[20] Edward N. Luttwak, 'Towards post-heroic warfare', *Foreign Affairs*, 74/3 (1995).

[21] Gabriel Kolko, *A Century of War: Politics, Conflicts, and Society since 1914*, New York: New Press, 1994.

[22] This is explored in my book *The Baroque Arsenal*, London: Andre Deutsch, 1982.

[23] See, for example, Lawrence Freedman, *The Evolution of Nuclear Strategy*, London: Macmillan, 1981.

[24] The issue has been extensively discussed in the pages of the American journal *International Security*. Key studies include Michael Doyle, 'Liberalism and world politics', *American Political Science Review*, 80/4 (December 1986); and Bruce Russett, *Grasp-*

ing the Democratic Peace: Principles for a Post-Cold War World, Princeton, NJ: Princeton University Press, 1993.

25 Claus Offe, 'Western nationalism, Eastern nationalism, and the problems of post-communist transition', *Europe and the Balkans International Network*, Bologna, 1996.

26 Van Creveld, *Transformation of War*, p. 16.

Chapter 3   Bosnia–Herzegovina: A Case Study of a New War

1 He said: 'I understand your frustration but you have a situation that is better than ten other places in the world . . . I can give you a list.' Quoted in David Rieff, *Slaughter House: Bosnia and the Failure of the West*, New York: Vintage, 1995, p. 24.

2 *Final Report of the Commission of Experts Pursuant to Security Council Resolution 780 (1992)*, S/1994/674, 27 May 1994, vol. I, annex IV, par. 84.

3 The story is contained in a collection of Ivo Andrić's short stories published in *The Damned Yard and Other Stories* (London and Boston: Forest Books, 1992). At the end of the story, the young man volunteers to fight in the Spanish Civil War, where he is killed in an air raid. 'Thus ended the life of a man who ran away from hatred', says Andrić. Does this mean that hatred is everywhere? Or that, in volunteering to fight in Spain, he had some hopes of overcoming hatred?

4 Perhaps this was because the perception corresponded to the world view of European politicians themselves. David Owen's book is peppered with remarks that suggest that he himself categorizes people in national terms. Thus, for example, Cosić, the then Yugoslav president, is described as showing 'some of the qualities that have made and will in future make Serbs a substantial people'. The challenge for the negotiations, he says, is to devise a structure which preserves the integrity of Bosnia–Herzegovina but allows the Serbs to 'preserve and safeguard their national identity'. See David Owen, *A Balkan Odyssey*, London: Victor Gollancz, 1995, pp. 48, 67.

5 'Croats belong to a different culture – a different civilisation from the Serbs. Croats are part of Western Europe, part of the Mediterranean tradition. Long before Shakespeare and Molière, our writers were translated into European languages. The Serbs belong to the East. They are Eastern people, like the Turks and Albanians. They belong to the Byzantine culture . . . Despite similarities in language, we cannot be together.' Quoted in Leonard J. Cohen, *Broken Bonds: Yugoslavia's Disintegration and Balkan Politics in Transition*, Oxford and Boulder, CO: Westview Press, 1995, p. 211.

6 See for example, A. D. Smith, *Theories of Nationalism*, London: Duckworth, 1971.

7 According to Sead Fetahagić, a member of Circle 99, the association of independent intellectuals in Sarajevo: 'Many of us are opposed to this multiculturalism because multiculturalism has accepted the manner in which the West has accepted it – one culture alongside another culture alongside a third culture. But we in Bosnia–Herzegovina have always had one culture. I have been brought up within the Serb, Croat, Muslim, Jewish, Czech, European and American culture. We think that one culture exists and not several which are developed one next to the other.' 'The Force of Irreality', *hCa Quarterly*, 15/16 (Winter/Spring, 1996). Likewise, according to a sociological study undertaken in 1939, 'a feeling of real ethnic and characterological unity remains alive alongside all the historical and national-political differentiation'; quoted in Cohen, *Broken Bonds*, pp. 19–20.

8 See Ernest Gellner, *Nations and Nationalism*, Oxford: Blackwell, 1983.

9 See Ivan Vejvoda, 'Yugoslavia 1945–91 – from decentralisation without democracy to dissolution', in D. A. Dyker and I. Vejvoda, *Yugoslavia and After: A Study in Fragmentation, Despair and Rebirth*, London and New York: Longmans, 1996.

10 For a more extensive discussion of this, see Susan Woodward, *Socialist Unemployment: The Political Economy of Yugoslavia 1945–90*, Princeton, NJ: Princeton University Press, 1995; Vesna Bojičić and Mary Kaldor, 'The political economy of the war in Bosnia–Herzegovina', in Mary Kaldor and Basker Vashee (eds), *Restructuring the Global Military Sector*, Vol. 1: *New Wars*, London: Cassell/Pinter, 1997.

11 See David Dyker, 'The degeneration of the Yugoslav Communist Party as a managing elite – a familiar East European story?', in Dyker and Vejvoda, *Yugoslavia and After*.

12 See Mark Thompson, *Forging War: The Media in Serbia, Croatia, and Bosnia–Herzegovina*, London: Article XIX, 1994.

13 See James Gow, *Legitimacy and the Military: The Yugoslav Crisis*, London: Pinter, 1992.

14 See Milos Vasić, 'The Yugoslav Army and the post-Yugoslav armies', in Dyker and Vejvoda, *Yugoslavia and After*.

15 Rieff, *Slaughter House*, p. 103.

16 'To invite the émigrés back to the homeland for a great meeting was risky to the point that even those people who were later in my leadership waited till the last minute to see whether we would be arrested or not. This is why that was a turning point in my life in terms of decision-making . . . Great deeds, both in individual

creative terms, and especially in social innovation, and even militarily, are created on the razor's edge between the possible and the impossible.' Quoted in Laura Silber and Alan Little, *The Death of Yugoslavia*, London: Penguin, 1995, p. 91.

[17] Xavier Bougarel, 'Etat et communautarisme en Bosnie–Herzegovina', unpublished MS; English version in Dyker and Vejvoda, *Yugoslavia and After*.

[18] Private interview with the author.

[19] For example, one of its editorials said: 'Instinctively every Muslim would wish to save his Serb neighbour instead of the reverse, however, every Muslim must name a Serb and take an oath to kill him.' 1 April 1993, quoted in Mazowiecki Report E/CN.4/1994/3, 5 May 1993.

[20] I am indebted to my doctoral student Neven Andjelić for detailed information about the pre-war peace movement. See *Bosnia–Herzegovina: The End of a Legacy*, London: Frank Cass, 2003.

[21] According to one of his fellow students:

> Many people will tell you now that they saw the war coming then, but I didn't and I don't think Suada [the student who died] did either . . . As a medical student scheduled to graduate in May, Suada could easily have stayed away from the demonstration that day. She wasn't from Sarajevo. She wasn't even Bosnian . . . It was not an angry crowd . . . The people around us, most of them young, were good-humoured and eager to make their point in a peaceful way. I was about fifty metres from the bridge when a few shots – maybe five or six – rang out. Everybody began to run. Once we got to cover behind a building, I was incredibly angry. It had never occurred to me that someone would open fire on a group of unarmed demonstrators. Strange to say, war still didn't seem inevitable. It was only a few days later that there seemed no turning back, that we began to speak of Suada as the first person killed in the Bosnian war. What had seemed a random act of violence, a great personal tragedy, slowly took shape in our minds as the first incident in a far greater drama: Europe's worst war in fifty years.

Quoted in Silber and Little, *The Death of Yugoslavia*, pp. 251–2.

[22] 'Dans un ultime sursaut, la société civile bosniaque naissante a tenté d'évincer le communautarisme de la sphère politique. Un moment destabilisées, les parties nationalistes se vengent en faisant entrer la guerre dans la vie quotidienne.' Bougarel, 'Etat et communautarisme'.

[23] *Report on the Situation of Human Rights in the Territory of Former Yugoslavia*, United Nations, E/CN.4/1992/S–1/9, New York, 28 August 1992, par. 17.

[24] Stockholm International Peace Research Institute, *SIPRI Yearbook 1992: World Armaments and Disarmament*, Oxford: Oxford University Press, 1992.

[25] Ibid.

[26] The same company has been used since the Dayton Agreement to train the army of the Federation of Bosnia–Herzegovina. See David Shearer, *Private Armies and Military Intervention*, Adelphi Paper 316, London: International Institute for Strategic Studies, 1998.

[27] *Final Report of the Commission of Experts.*

[28] This was a point generally missed by those who advocated lifting the arms embargo on Bosnia–Herzegovina as a solution to the war. Whatever symbolic significance this may have had, it would have had little practical significance, since whether or not the Bosnian army received arms depended on the attitude of the Croatian government. Perhaps the most positive consequence would have been the circumventing of illegal arms dealers in Zagreb.

[29] Reports in both the Croatian and the Serbian press refer to cooperation between the JNA and Croat factories to produce M-84 tanks. There were also reports that all three sides in Bosnia–Herzegovina cooperated in the production of ammunition because even the 7.62 mm rifle bullet contained components that were produced by the different sides. See Milan Nikolić, 'The Burden of the Military Heritage', unpublished paper produced for WIDER, Helsinki, 1993.

[30] *Final Report of the Commission of Experts*, Annex IV, 'Ethnic Cleansing', par. 238.

[31] His doctoral thesis, which he completed in 1976, was on Marxist justifications for war.

[32] *Final Report of the Commission of Experts*, Annex IV, 'Ethnic Cleansing', par. 103.

[33] Ibid., Annex III A, 'Special Forces', par. 68.

[34] See Vasić, 'The Yugoslav Army', p. 129.

[35] Silber and Little, *The Death of Yugoslavia*, p. 270.

[36] Shems Hadj-Nassar, 'Has Rape been Used as a Systematic Weapon of War in the Conflict in the Former Yugoslavia?', unpublished Master's thesis, University of Sussex, 1995.

[37] Ethnic cleansing continued in Banja Luka and in Bijeljina and Janja right up to the end of the war. UNHCR reported one man arriving in Tuzla at the end of 1994: 'There are no more children, no more friends, no more information, no more life, no more Mosques and no more graveyards.' UNHCR, *Information Notes on Former Yugoslavia*, 11/1994, Zagreb, November 1994.

[38] Mazowiecki Report E/CN.4/1994/3, 5 May 1993.

[39] *Final Report of the Commission of Experts*, Annex III A, 'Special Forces', par. 70.

[40] At Dretelj, 'Victims stated that they were subjected to sexual torture, beaten with truncheons and sticks, burned with cigarettes and candles, and forced to drink urine and eat grass. One victim reported that she was held in a room with three other professional women for ten days during which time women in the room were raped repeatedly.' Ibid., par. 67.

[41] Vasić, 'The Yugoslav Army', p. 134.

[42] *Final Report of the Commission of Experts*, Annex III, par. 239. Interestingly, during the war in Croatia, an internal JNA memo stated that Arkan and Šešelj were dangerous to 'military morale' and that their 'primary motive was not fighting against the enemy but robbery of private property and inhuman treatment of Croatian citizens'. Ibid., par. 100.

[43] Xavier Bougarel, *L'Anatomie d'un conflit*, Paris: La Découverte, 1995.

[44] *Final Report of the Commission of Experts*, Annex III, par. 102.

[45] Ibid., Annex IV, par. 142.

[46] Alex de Waal, 'Contemporary warfare in Africa', in Kaldor and Vashee (eds), *Restructuring the Global Military Sector*.

[47] This was a German initiative supported only reluctantly by the other European countries. In fact, under German pressure, the EU appointed the Badinter Commission to report on the criteria for recognition for all Yugoslav successor states. In the event, only Macedonia and Slovenia met the criteria for satisfactory arrangements for minorities, but Macedonia's recognition was delayed because of Greek objections.

[48] Owen himself suggests that a settlement could have been reached much earlier had the international community been more united and had the negotiators had the full backing of the Americans. He blames the lack of American support for the failure to impose the Vance–Owen Plan in the summer of 1993. It is certainly true that when the Americans took charge much more was achieved, as in the case of the Washington Agreement and the Dayton Agreement. But this argument misses the politics of the period; there was great reluctance to impose partition. A different proposal, say a protectorate, might have mobilized international support. By the time the Dayton Agreement was reached, most people had given up on the alternatives to partition.

[49] See Pierre Hassner, 'Ex-Yougoslavie: le tournant?', *Politique Internationale* (Autumn 1995).

[50] As Carrington recalls: 'When I talked to Presidents Tudjman and Milošević, it was quite clear to me that both of them had a solution which was mutually satisfactory, which was that they were going to carve it up between them. They were going to carve

Bosnia up. The Serb [areas] would go to Serbia and the Croat [areas] to Croatia. And they weren't worried too much, either of them, about what was going to happen to the Muslims.' Quoted in Silber and Little, *The Death of Yugoslavia*, p. 210.

51 Owen insists that he did treat Izetbegović differently because he was the president, but this was not the public impression, and that, after all, was what mattered.

52 UN Department of Public Information, *United Nations Peace-Keeping Information Notes: Update December 1994*, DPI/1306/Rev.4, New York, March 1995, p. 104.

53 SCR 836 extended the mandate of UNPROFOR 'to deter attacks against the safe areas . . . to promote the withdrawal of military and para-military units other than those of the Government of the Republic of Bosnia and Herzegovina and to occupy some key points on the ground.' It authorized UNPROFOR 'acting in self-defence, to take all the necessary measures, including the use of force, in reply to bombardments against the safe areas by any of the parties or to armed incursion into them or in the event of any deliberate obstruction in or around those areas to the freedom of movement of UNPROFOR or of protected humanitarian convoys.' And it decided that 'Member States, acting nationally or through regional organisations or arrangements [i.e. NATO], may take, under the authority of the Security Council and subject to close co-ordination with the Secretary-General and UNPROFOR, all necessary measures through the use of air power, in and around the safe areas in Bosnia and Herzegovina to support UNPROFOR.' UN Department of Public Information, *The United Nations and Former Yugoslavia*, DPI/1312/Rev.2, New York, 15 March 1994, p. 136.

54 This was a proposal put forward at the beginning of the war by the Bosnian peace movement. It was discussed as a proposal for negotiation; the idea was that Izetbegović would have been satisfied by preserving the integrity of Bosnia and Herzegovina and that the Serbs would have been satisfied by the removal of the SDA from power. It was considered seriously in the autumn of 1992 but rejected on the ground that it would have been too costly in both military and financial terms.

55 Mazowiecki Report, E/CN 4/1994/110, 21 February 1994, par. 347.

56 Quoted in Rieff, *Slaughter House*, p. 211.

57 Owen, *A Balkan Odyssey*, p. 354. This was not the case for men on the ground whom I talked to.

58 Allied Forces Southern Europe, Public Information, *Fact Sheet: Operation Deliberate Force*, Naples, 6 November 1995.

59 Formally, Bosnia was divided into two entities – Republika Srpska and the Federation of Bosnia and Herzegovina – but the latter was partitioned between the Croats and the Muslims.
60 Gerald Knaus and Felix Martin, 'Lessons from Bosnia and Herzegovina: Travails of the European Raj', *Journal of Democracy*, 14/3 (2003), http://www.journalofdemocracy.org/articles/KnausandMartin.pdf. See also the website of the European Stability Initiative: www.esiweb.org.

Chapter 4   The Politics of New Wars

1 Ernest Gellner, *Nations and Nationalism*, Oxford: Blackwell, 1983.
2 Paul Hirst and Grahame Thompson, *Globalization in Question: The International Economy and the Possibilities of Governance*, Cambridge: Polity, 1996.
3 C. Freeman, J. Clarke and L. Soete, *Unemployment and Technical Innovation: A Study of Long Waves and Economic Development*, London: Frances Pinter, 1982; C. Perez-Perez, 'Micro-electronics, long waves, and world structural change', *World Development*, 13/3 (1985).
4 See Margit Mayer, 'The shifting local political system in European cities', in Mick Dunford and Grigoris Kafkalas (eds), *Cities and Regions in the New Europe: The Global–Local Interplay and Spatial Development Strategies*, London: Belhaven Press, 1992; also Manuel Castells and Peter Hall, *Technopoles of the World: The Making of Twenty-First-Century Industrial Complexes*, London: Routledge, 1994.
5 For information on transnational movements and NGOs, see the annual publication *Global Civil Society*, published by Oxford University Press in 2001, 2002 and 2003, and by Sage for 2004/5 and 2006/7.
6 Nikolai Bukharin, *Economics of the Transformation Period*, New York: Bergman, 1971.
7 Robert Reich, *The Work of Nations: Preparing Ourselves for 21st Century Capitalism*, London: Simon & Schuster, 1993, p. 97.
8 Alberto Melucci, *Nomads of the Present: Social Movements and Individual Needs in Contemporary Society*, London: Hutchinson Radius, 1989.
9 Alain Touraine, *The Post-Industrial Society*, New York: Random House, 1971.
10 Reich, *The Work of Nations*, p. 178.

[11] Giddens calls these symbols 'disembedding mechanisms'. The key characteristic of modernity was what he calls 'time–space distantiation', in which social relations can be constructed with 'absent' others. He defines globalization as a stretching of time–space distantiation. See Anthony Giddens, *The Conditions of Modernity*, Cambridge: Polity, 1990.

[12] This definition was developed by Radha Kumar. See Mary Kaldor and Radha Kumar, 'New forms of conflict', in *Conflicts in Europe: Towards a New Political Approach*, Helsinki Citizens' Assembly Publication Series 7, Prague, 1993.

[13] See Mary Kaldor and Diego Muro, 'Religious and nationalist militant networks', in Mary Kaldor, Helmut Anheier and Marlies Glasius, *Global Civil Society 2003*, Oxford: Oxford University Press, 2003.

[14] In his analysis of conflicts involving political Islam, Mohamed El Said Said distinguishes between Islam based on missionary politics and Islam based on identity politics. The Iranian revolution is an example of the former, while Islamic movements in India are an example of the latter. See 'Conflicts involving Islam', in Mary Kaldor and Basker Vashee (eds), *Restructuring the Global Military Sector*, Vol. 1: *New Wars*, London: Cassell/Pinter, 1997.

[15] I am indebted to Ivan Vejvoda for this point.

[16] The term is used by Katherine Verdery in 'Nationalism and national sentiment in post-socialist Rumania', *Slavic Review* (Summer 1993).

[17] Ibid., p. 82. See also Robert M. Hayden, 'Constitutional nationalism in the formerly Yugoslav republics', *Slavic Review*, 51 (1992).

[18] This argument is also developed by Katherine Verdery. See, in particular, 'Ethnic relations, economies of shortage and the transition in Eastern Europe', in C. M. Hann (ed.), *Socialism: Ideals, Ideology and Local Practice*, London: Routledge, 1993.

[19] See, for example, Andrei Amalrik, *Will the Soviet Union Survive Until 1984?*, London: Penguin, 1970; or Hélène Carrère d'Encausse, *Decline of an Empire: The Soviet Socialist Republics in Revolt*, New York: Newsweek, 1979.

[20] Teresa Rakowska-Harmstone, 'The dialectics of nationalism in the USSR', *Problems of Communism*, 23/1 (1974).

[21] In many cases, these titular nationalities were artificial. Tadjikistan, for example, is an invented territorial unit. The Tadjik language is a Persian dialect spoken in parts of Iran and Afghanistan which was given a Cyrillic alphabet. The main Tadjik centres of civilization, Samarkand and Bukhara, ended up outside the borders of Tadjikistan, in Uzbekistan.

22 Victor Zaslavsky, 'Success and collapse: traditional Soviet nationality policy', in Ian Bremmer and Ray Taras (eds), *Nations and Politics in Soviet Successor States*, Cambridge: Cambridge University Press, 1993.

23 See, for example, Peter Lewis, 'From prebendalism to predation: the political economy of decline in Nigeria', *Journal of Modern African Studies*, 34/1 (1996); Obi Igwara, 'Holy Nigerian nationalisms and apocalyptic visions of the nation', *Nations and Nationalism*, 1/3 (1995); and Kisangani N. F. Ermizet, 'Zaire after Mobutu: a case of a humanitarian emergency', *WIDER Research for Action 32*, Helsinki: UNU/WIDER, 1997.

24 See Cynthia Brown and Farhad Karim (eds), *Playing the 'Communal Card': Communal Violence and Human Rights*, London and New York: Human Rights Watch, 1995.

25 For a description of this phenomenon in various places, see the Médecins Sans Frontières report on world crisis intervention, *Life Death and Aid*, London: Routledge, 1993. In Liberia, Charles Taylor's National Patriotic Front of Liberia is described as marching on the capital: 'Constantly drunk or high on Marijuana, wearing wigs, wedding dresses or welder's goggles, they acted out the profound identity crisis in which their shattered world has led them' (p. 56).

26 Rakiya Omaar and Alex de Waal, *Rwanda: Death, Despair and Defiance*, London: Africa Rights, 1994, p. 35.

27 Šumit Ganguly, 'Explaining the Kashmir insurgency: political mobilisation and institutional decay', *International Security*, 21/2 (1996).

28 Radha Kumar, 'Nationalism, nationalities and civil society', in *Nationalism and European Integration: Civil Society Perspectives*, Helsinki Citizens' Assembly Publication Series 2, Prague, 1991.

29 See Oliver Roy, *The Failure of Political Islam*, London: Taurus, 1994; see also Ernest Gellner, *Postmodernism, Reason and Religion*, London and New York: Routledge, 1992.

30 A. D. Smith, *Nations and Nationalism in a Global Era*, Cambridge: Polity, 1996.

31 Kwame Anthony Appiah, 'Cosmopolitan patriots', *Critical Inquiry* (Spring 1997), p. 618.

32 See Robert D. Kaplan, 'The coming anarchy', *Atlantic Monthly* (February 1994).

Chapter 5   The Globalized War Economy

1 Jeffrey Herbst, 'Responding to state failure in Africa', *International Security*, 21/3 (1996–7), pp. 121–2.

[2] Cynthia Brown and Farhad Karim (eds), *Playing the 'Communal Card': Communal Violence and Human Rights*, London and New York: Human Rights Watch, 1995.

[3] Maggie O'Kane, 'The terrible day when Frenki's Boys came calling', *The Guardian* (19 June 1999).

[4] David Keen, 'When war itself is privatized', *Times Literary Supplement* (December 1995).

[5] For details on this story, see David Shearer, *Private Armies and Military Intervention*, Adelphi Paper 316, London: International Institute for Strategic Studies, 1998.

[6] International Institute for Strategic Studies, *Military Balance 1996–7*: London: Brasseys, 1997, p. 237.

[7] Quoted in Richard Simkin, *Race to the Swift: Thoughts on Twenty-First Century Warfare*, London: Brasseys, 1985, p. 311.

[8] The great exception, widely quoted, was the British experience in Malaya. However, the revolutionary movement was quite limited, consisting mainly of the Chinese minority. Nevertheless, what is interesting is the way in which, in contrast to other counter-insurgency practices, the British copied revolutionary tactics by trying to win 'hearts and minds' through the promise of independence and using similar military tactics to the guerrillas. See ibid.

[9] Brown and Karim, *Playing the 'Communal Card'*, p. 9.

[10] Quoted in Irving Lewis Horowitz, *Taking Lives: Genocide and State Power*, 4th edn, New Brunswick, NJ: Transaction Books, 1997. According to Horowitz, genocide is a state activity and is contrasted with vigilantism, which is carried out by private groups, e.g. the Ku Klux Klan.

[11] For the earlier figures, see Dan Smith, *The State of War and Peace Atlas*, London: Penguin Books, 1997. The figure for the 1990s is my own calculation; see Mary Kaldor, 'Introduction', in Mary Kaldor and Basker Vashee (eds), *Restructuring the Global Military Sector*, Vol. 1: *New Wars*, London: Cassell/Pinter, 1997.

[12] UNHCR, *The State of the World's Refugees: In Search of Solutions*, Oxford: Oxford University Press, 1995. UNHCR, *Global Refugee Trends*, Geneva, 17 June 2004.

[13] These figures can be found in the regular *World Refugee Survey* published in Washington, DC, by the US Committee on Refugees.

[14] Myron Weiner, 'Bad neighbours, bad neighbourhoods: an inquiry into the causes of refugee flows', *International Security*, 21/1 (1996).

[15] See Lotta Harbom and Peter Wallensteen, 'Armed conflict and its international dimensions, 1946–2004', *Journal of Peace Research*, 42/5 (2005).

[16] Mark Duffield, 'The political economy of internal war: asset trans-fer, complex emergencies and international aid', in Joanna Macrae and Anthony Zwi (eds), *War and Hunger: Rethinking International Responses*, London: Zed Press, 1994.

[17] David Keen has described the way in which the famine in Southern Sudan was caused by cattle-raiding by Baggara militia-men in the North supported by the Sudanese government as a way of weakening the SPLA (Sudan People's Liberation Army) which operated from the South: 'For young Baggara men, particularly those severely hit by economic marginalisation and drought, raiding offered the prospect of increasing their meagre capital stock.' David Keen, 'A disaster for whom? Local interests and international donors during famine. Among the Dinka of Sudan', *Disasters*, 15/2, (1991), p. 155.

[18] 'Central Asia's narcotics industry', *Strategic Comments*, 3/5 (1997); 'Colombia's escalating violence: crime, conflict and politics', *Strategic Comments*, 3/4 (1997).

[19] See Mary Kaldor, Terry Karl and Yahia Said, *Oil Wars*, London: Pluto Press, forthcoming.

[20] Duffield, 'Political economy of internal war', p. 56.

[21] Keen, 'When war itself is privatized'.

[22] John Simpson, *In the Forests of the Night: Encounters in Peru with Terrorism, Drug-running and Military Oppression*, London: Arrow Books, 1994.

[22] Keen, 'When war itself is privatized'.

[24] A Norwegian psychologist describes a session with 'Ivan', a boy from Bosnia–Herzegovina:

> How can one talk to a nine year old child about the fact that his father shot his best friend?
>
> I asked him for his own explanation, and he looked me right in the eyes and said 'I think they have been drinking something that has been poisoning their brains.' But he suddenly added, 'But now they are all poisoned, so I'm sure it is in the drinking water, and we really have to find out how to clean the polluted water reser-voirs.' When I asked him if children were as much poisoned as adults he shook his head and said 'No, not at all. They have smaller bodies, so they are less contaminated, and I have discovered that small children and babies who mostly drink milk, they are not poisoned at all.'
>
> I asked him if he had ever heard the word politics. He almost jumped and looked at me and said, 'Yes. That's the name of the poison.'

Quoted in Dan Smith, *State of War and Peace*, p. 31.

[25] Several writers refer to the predatory character of contemporary war economies. See Xavier Bougarel, *L'Anatomie d'un conflit*, Paris:

La Découverte, 1995, whom I quote in chapter 3. See also R. T. Naylor, 'The insurgent economy: black market operations of guerrilla organizations', *Crime Law and Social Change*, 20 (1993); and Peter Lewis, 'From prebendalism to predation: the political economy of decline in Nigeria', *Journal of Modern African Studies*, 34/1 (1996).

26 Michael Cranna (ed.), *The True Cost of Conflict*, London: Earthscan, 1994.

27 See Vesna Bojičić, Mary Kaldor and Ivan Vejvoda, 'Post-war reconstruction in the Balkans', *European Foreign Affairs Review*, 2/3 (1997).

28 By the end of 1986, the USA had supplied some $3 billion worth of aid. Some was diverted by the CIA to Nicaragua and Angola; some was diverted by Pakistani military intelligence for its own use and for the black market; some was sold by political leaders; and some was diverted by the arms suppliers through inflated invoices and pilfered cargoes. According to Naylor ('The insurgent economy', p. 19): 'The result was that not only did international aid organizations have to scour the bazaars to buy back the diverted food, clothing, tents and medicine, but those Afghan rebel chiefs who actually did fight sometimes had to use the profits of the heroin traffic to buy weapons that had already been paid for by the US and Saudi Arabia.'

29 Duffield, 'Political economy of internal war', p. 57.

Chapter 6   Towards a Cosmopolitan Approach

1 Noam Chomsky, *The New Military Humanism: Lessons from Kosovo*, London: Pluto, 1999.

2 See Michael Walzer, *Just and Unjust Wars: A Moral Argument with Historical Illustrations*, Harmondsworth: Penguin, 1980.

3 Hannah Arendt, *Reflections on Violence*, London and New York: Harcourt, Brace, 1979, pp. 50–1.

4 'Perpetual Peace' (1795), in *Kant's Political Writings*, ed. Hans Reiss, Cambridge: Cambridge University Press, 1992.

5 'The law of armed conflict had the purpose of restricting the uses of violence between states and, in the case of civil wars, between governments and rebels. Human rights law had (among other things) the purpose of averting and restricting the uses of violence by governments towards their subjects whether formally in rebellion or not; a field of conflict for which international law, by definition, brought no remedies.' Geoffrey Best, *War and Law Since 1945*, Oxford: Clarendon Press, 1994.

6 On the references to humane or cosmopolitan law, see J. Pictet,

'International humanitarian law: a definition', in UNESCO, *International Dimensions of Humanitarian Law*, Dordrecht: Martinus Nijhoff, 1988.

[7] For good introductions to the literature, see Oliver Ramsbotham and Tom Woodhouse, *Humanitarian Intervention in Contemporary Conflict: A Reconceptualization*, Cambridge: Polity, 1996; Ian Forbes and Mark Hoffman, *Political Theory, International Relations and the Ethics of Intervention*, London: Macmillan, 1993.

[8] Adam Roberts, *Humanitarian Action in War*, Adelphi Paper 305, Oxford: Oxford University Press for the International Institute for Strategic Studies, 1996.

[9] See Radha Kumar, 'The troubled history of partition', *Foreign Affairs*, 76/1 (1997).

[10] Mary Kaldor, 'A decade of humanitarian intervention: the role of global civil society', in Helmut Anheier, Marlies Glasius, and Mary Kaldor (eds), *Global Civil Society 2001*, Oxford: Oxford University Press, 2001.

[11] Davin Bremmer, 'Local peace and the South African transition', *Peace Review*, 9/2 (1997).

[12] William Warfield, 'Moving from civil war to civil society', *Peace Review*, 9/2 (1997).

[13] Ed Garcia, 'Filipino zones of peace', *Peace Review*, 9/2 (1997).

[14] *Times Literary Supplement* (21 February 1997).

[15] Quoted in ibid., p. 30.

[16] Alex de Waal, *Famine Crimes: Politics and the Disaster Relief Industry in Africa*, Bloomington and Indianapolis: Africa Rights and the International African Institute/Indiana University Press, 1997, p. 178. See also Mohamed Sahnoun, *Somalia: The Missed Opportunities*, Washington, DC: US Institute for Peace, 1994.

[17] See, for example, William J. Durch (ed.), *The Evolution of UN Peacekeeping: Case Studies and Comparative Analysis*, New York: St Martin's Press, 1993; Ministry of Defence, *Wider Peacekeeping*, London: HMSO, 1995; Mats R. Berdal, *Whither UN peacekeeping?*, Adelphi Paper 281, London: International Institute for Strategic Studies, 1993.

[18] See, for example, John Mackinlay and Jarat Chopra, *A Draft Concept of Second Generation Multinational Operations*, Providence, RI: Thomas J. Watson Jr. Institute for International Studies, 1993.

[19] Charles Dobbie, 'A concept for post-Cold War peace-keeping', *Survival* (Autumn 1994).

[20] 'Torture, rape, pillage and even cannibalism by ECOMOG supported factions hurt ECOMOG's general political acceptance.' Herbert Howe, 'Lessons of Liberia: ECOMOG and regional peace-keeping', *International Security*, 21/3 (1996–7), p. 163.

21 Quoted in African Rights, *Somalia and Operation Restore Hope: A Preliminary Assessment*, London: African Rights, 1993, p. 28.

22 Roberts, 'Humanitarian action', p. 51.

23 John Mackinlay, 'Improving multifunctional forces', *Survival* (Autumn 1994). In fact, Mackinlay is himself confused. He goes on to say: 'Where force is used, impartiality [here he means neutrality] may seem to have been lost, especially by the party concerned. If legitimacy is intact, however, the appearance of impartiality can be restored.' What is important here is legitimacy in the eyes of the local population. It may not be possible to restore neutrality, which he refers to as impartiality, since the warring parties are no respecters of rules. The point is to retain impartiality from the point of view of the victims.

24 Quoted in Dobbie, 'A concept', p. 137.

25 Ioan Lewis and James Mayall, 'Somalia', in James Mayall (ed.), *The New Interventionism 1991–4: United Nations Experience in Cambodia, Former Yugoslavia, and Somalia*, Cambridge: Cambridge University Press, 1996, p. 117.

26 There have been reports of human rights abuses by UN personnel in Cambodia, Bosnia–Herzegovina, Somalia and Mozambique. Abuses have included rape, killings and involvement in child prostitution in Mozambique. See, for example, African Rights, *Somalia: Human Rights Abuses by the UN Forces*, London: African Rights, 1993.

27 *Doctrine of the International Community*, speech by Tony Blair at the Economic Club, Chicago, 24 April 1999, http://www.pm.gov. uk/output/Page1297.asp.

28 See Ministry of Defence, *Lessons from the Crisis*, Cmnd 4724, London: HMSO, 2000; House of Commons, Select Committee on Defence, *Fourteenth Report, Session 1999–2000*, London: HMSO, 2000.

29 The number of deaths is widely disputed. These figures represent the best estimate of the IICK based on the collation of a wide range of reports from NGOs and other sources. See Annex 1, 'Documentation on human rights violations', *The Kosovo Report: The Report of the Independent International Commission on Kosovo*, Oxford: Oxford University Press, 2000.

30 Mark Duffield, 'Relief in war zones: towards an analysis of the new aid paradigm', *Third World Quarterly* (1997).

31 Alvaro de Soto and Graciana del Castillo, 'Obstacles to peace-building', *Foreign Policy*, 94 (Spring 1994).

32 African Rights, *Somalia and Operation Restore Hope*.

33 Frances Stewart and Valpy Fitzgerald, *War and Underdevelopment*, Oxford: Oxford University Press, 2001.

34 See the annual *Conversion Survey* on *Global Disarmament, Demilitarisation and Demobilization* of the Bonn International Conversion Centre, www.bicc.de.

35 Alex de Waal, 'Contemporary warfare in Africa', in Mary Kaldor and Basker Vashee (eds), *Restructuring the Global Military Sector*, Vol. 1: *New Wars*, London: Cassell/Pinter, 1997, p. 331.

Chapter 7   The 'New War' in Iraq

1 George W. Bush, 'President Bush announces major combat operations in Iraq have ended: remarks by President Bush from the USS *Abraham Lincoln*', 1 May 2003.

2 Ibid.

3 Max Boot, 'The new American way of war', *Foreign Affairs* (July/August 2003).

4 See Mary Kaldor, *Imaginary War: Understanding the East–West Conflict*, Oxford: Blackwell, 1990.

5 Ibid., chapters 11 and 12.

6 See Lawrence Freedman, *The Revolution in Strategic Affairs*, Adelphi Paper 318, London: International Institute of Strategic Affairs, 1998.

7 In the aftermath of 9/11, the military recruited the University of Southern California's Institute of Creative Technology to involve Hollywood in imagining terrorist worst-case scenarios. See James Der Derian, '9/11: Before, After and Between', in Craig Calhoun, Paul Price and Ashley Timmer (eds), *Understanding September 11*, New York: New Press, 2002, p. 180.

8 According to Max Boot, the *New York Times* report left out the phrase 'a bit', thereby exaggerating American difficulties. See Boot, 'The new American way of war'.

9 Elliott A. Cohen, 'A tale of two secretaries', *Foreign Affairs* (May/June 2002), p. 39.

10 Donald H. Rumsfeld, 'Transforming the military', *Foreign Affairs* (May/June 2002), p. 21.

11 Donald H. Rumsfeld, Testimony to the Senate Armed Services Committee, 9 July 2003.

12 Kersti Hakansson has demonstrated this point in a comparison of tactics in Vietnam and Afghanistan. See 'New wars, old warfare? Comparing US tactics in Afghanistan and Vietnam', in Jan Angstrom and Isabelle Duyvesteyn, *The Nature of Modern War: Clausewitz and his Critics Revisited*, Stockholm: Swedish National Defence College, Department of War Studies, 2003.

13 Bush, 'Major combat operations in Iraq have ended'.
14 George W. Bush, West Point graduation speech, 1 June 2002.
15 Bush, 'Major combat operations in Iraq have ended'.
16 See Ahmed S. Hashim, *The Sunni Insurgency in Iraq*, Center for Naval Warfare Studies, 15 August 2003, http://www.mideasti. org/articles/doc89.html.
17 See Yahia Said, 'Civil society in Iraq', in Helmut Anheier, Marlies Glasius and Mary Kaldor, *Global Civil Society 2004/5*, London: Sage, 2005, p. 6.
18 Quoted in Toby Dodge, 'Cake walk, coup or urban warfare', in Toby Dodge and Steven Simon (eds), *Iraq at the Crossroads: State and Society in the Shadow of Regime Change*, Adelphi Paper 354, Oxford: Oxford University Press for the International Institute for Strategic Studies, 2003, p. 62.
19 See Dilip Hiro, *Iraq: A Report from the Inside*, London: Granta Books, 2003.
20 As elsewhere, contemporary tribes are largely a colonial construction. After the Iraqi rebellion against the British in 1920, the British administration adopted a very similar strategy, abolishing elected municipal councils and replacing them with tribal councils (*majlis*) presided over by tribal sheikhs appointed by the British political officer. See Judit Yaphe, 'War and occupation in Iraq: what went right? What could go wrong?', *Middle East Journal*, 37/3 (2003).
21 Faleh A. Jabar, 'Clerics, tribes, ideologues and urban dwellers in the South of Iraq – the potential for rebellion', in Dodge and Simon, *Iraq at the Crossroads*, p. 173.
22 See *Comprehensive Report of the Special Advisor to the DCI on Iraq's WMD*, Washington, DC: Central Intelligence Agency (30 September 2004).
23 Reportedly Wolfowitz was thrown by the question. It was considered unfair because 20,000 is a more usual estimate of the numbers involved in the insurgency; even so, it is difficult to believe that all those 15,000 killed were part of the insurgency. See *Strategic Comments*, 11/1 (2005).
24 See *Strategic Survey 2004–5*, London: International Institute for Strategic Studies, 2004.
25 Report on a visit to Baghdad, 3–9 December 2004.
26 Hashim, *The Sunni Insurgency in Iraq*. See also Samir Haddad and Mazin Ghazi, 'An inventory of Iraqi resistance groups: "Who kills hostages in Iraq?"', *Al Zawra* [Baghdad] (19 September 2004).
27 Quoted in Hashim, *The Sunni Insurgency in Iraq*.
28 Haddad and Ghazi, 'An inventory of Iraqi resistance groups'.
29 Hashim, *The Sunni Insurgency in Iraq*.

30 Anthony H. Cordesman, 'The developing Iraqi insurgency: status at end 2004', working draft, Washington, DC: Center for International and Strategic Studies (updated December 2004).

31 Said, 'Civil society in Iraq'.

32 See Anthony H. Cordesman, *New Patterns in the Iraqi Insurgency: The War for a Civil War in Iraq*, Washington, DC: Center for Strategic and International Studies (27 September 2005).

33 *A Face and A Name: Civilian Victims of Insurgent Groups in Iraq* London and New York: Human Rights Watch, October 2005.

34 Cordesman, *New Patterns in the Iraqi Insurgency*.

35 'Foreign fighters leaving Iraq to export terror', *The Guardian* (3 October 2005).

36 See Cordesman, 'The developing Iraqi insurgency'.

37 Ibid.

38 *New York Times* (22 October 2004).

39 Quoted in Bruce Hoffman, *Insurgency and Counterinsurgency in Iraq*, Santa Monica, CA: Rand Corporation, 2004.

40 In the South, pipelines are directly tapped into by smugglers, which allows tankers to top off their loads at will. Since this generally can happen only with the cooperation of oil ministry employees, it is evident that corruption in the industry is rampant. In April the Iraqi oil ministry sacked more than 450 employees suspected of selling fuel on the black market, and one oil ministry official discovered more than twenty illegal taps on one pipeline alone. Interview with representative of Iraq Oil Workers' Union from Basra, London, June 2005.

41 See the multinational forces website: www.mnf-iraq.com; see also www.globalsecurity.org.

42 These numbers are collated from various press sources and websites.

43 When I was in Baghdad in May 2004, Turkish laundry workers were billeted at my hotel. It was decided that the previous method of sending coalition laundry to Kuwait was too expensive and it was too dangerous for Iraqi laundry workers.

44 See the official US Defense Department website: www. defendamerica.mil.

45 See Anthony H. Cordesman, *Iraqi Force Development: A Current Status Report, July 2005 – February 2006*, Washington, DC, Center for Strategic and International Studies, 2006.

46 Quoted in Andrew F. Krepinevich, 'How to win in Iraq', *Foreign Affairs* (September/October 2005).

47 There are two main sources for civilian casualties. One is iraqbodycount.org, which is based on reports of violent incidents in the media. The estimates for October 2005 range from 26,457 to 29,795. The other is the epidemiological study reported in the

British medical journal *The Lancet*, which is widely considered the best method for estimating casualties. This study was based on the sampling of clusters of households in all the governorates of Iraq. Excluding the Fallujah cluster, which had greater casualties than elsewhere (accounting for two-thirds of violent deaths), the study found the rate of casualties to be much higher than actually reported to the press. It estimated an additional 98,000 deaths, excluding Fallujah, throughout Iraq, compared with a similar period before the war. The biggest cause of death was violent incidents, accounting for some 24 per cent of the total; of these the majority, or 23,500, were caused by American air strikes. If one adds in Fallujah and the extra deaths since the study was completed, a total of around 28,000 seems fairly low. See Les Roberts, Riyadh Lafta, Richard Garfield, Jamal Khudhairi and Gilbert Burnham, 'Mortality before and after the 2003 invasion of Iraq: cluster sample survey', *The Lancet* (29 October 2004).

[48] Mary Kaldor and Yahia Said, *Impressions from a Visit to Iraq, April 28 to May 10 2004*, London School of Economics and Political Science, Centre for the Study of Global Governance, 2004.

[49] Anthony H. Cordesman, *Al Qaqaa and the Military Realities in Iraq*, Washington DC: Center for Strategic and International Studies, 2004.

[50] Mary Kaldor, 'In place of war: open up Iraq', *Open Democracy* (13 February 2003).

[51] Yahia Said, 'Civil society in Iraq'.

[52] Ibid.; Kaldor and Said, *Impressions from a Visit to Iraq*; Mary Kaldor and Yahia Said, *Regime Change in Iraq*, Discussion Paper 26, London School of Economics and Political Science, Centre for the Study of Global Governance, 2003.

[53] For a detailed discussion of what this might mean, see *A Human Security Doctrine for Europe: The Barcelona Report of the Study Group on European Security Capabilities* (15 September 2004).

[54] See Krepinevich, 'How to win in Iraq'.

[55] *Newsweek* reported on 21 July 2003 that the Mukhabarat, the secret police, issued instructions 'to do what is necessary after the fall of the Iraqi leadership to American-British-Zionist Coalition Forces'. The document reportedly outlined eleven steps to be taken, including the looting and burning of government institutions, sabotaging power plants and oil infrastructure, and creating chaos by utilizing stolen weapons.

[56] Chairman of the Joint Chiefs of Staff, *National Military Strategic Plan for the War on Terror*, Washington, DC, 1 February 2006.

57 See http://edition.cnn.com/SPECIALS/2003/iraq/forces/
   casualties/.

Chapter 8   Governance, Legitimacy and Security

1 John Keane, *Reflections on Violence*, London: Verso, 1996.
2 http://www.whitehouse.gov/nsc/nss.html.
3 http://ue.eu.int/uedocs/cmsUpload/78367.pdf.
4 Samuel P. Huntington, *The Clash of Civilizations and the Remaking
   of World Order*, New York: Simon & Schuster, 1996; also 'The
   clash of civilizations?', *Foreign Affairs* (Summer 1993).
5 The neo-medievalism thesis is usually accredited to Umberto Eco,
   Travels in Hyperreality, London: Picador, 1987. For a description,
   see Barry Smart, *Postmodernity*, London: Routledge, 1996. It
   should be distinguished from Bull's New Medievalism, which
   referred to the idea of overlapping political sovereignties and is
   closer to the cosmopolitan governance approach. Hedley Bull, *The
   Anarchical Society: A Study of Order in World Politics*, London:
   Macmillan, 1977.
6 Robert D. Kaplan, 'The coming anarchy', *Atlantic Monthly* (February 1994); and Robert D. Kaplan, *The Ends of the Earth: A Journey
   at the Dawn of the 21st Century*, London: Papermac, 1997.
7 According to Martin van Creveld: 'Truth to say, what we are
   dealing with here is neither low-intensity conflict nor some bastard
   offspring of war. Rather it is WARRE in the elemental Hobbesian
   sense of the word, by far the most important conflict of our time.'
   Van Creveld, *The Transformation of War*, New York: Free Press;
   Oxford: Maxwell Macmillan International, 1991, p. 22.
8 For an elaboration of this argument, see Paul Berman, *Terror and
   Liberalism*, London: Norton, 2003.
9 Huntington, *The Clash of Civilizations*, p. 321.
10 Kaplan, *The Ends of the Earth*, p. 6.
11 Ibid., p. 45.
12 Ibid., p. 329.
13 Ibid., p. 432.
14 Quoted in David Keen, 'Organized chaos: not the new world we
   ordered', *World Today* (January 1996).
15 Kaplan, *The Ends of the Earth*, p. 337.
16 Ibid., p. 436.
17 Richard Falk, *On Humane Governance*, Cambridge: Polity, 1995.
18 David Beetham, 'Human rights as a model for cosmopolitan
   democracy', in Daniele Archibugi and David Held (eds), *Reimag-
   ining Political Community: Studies in Cosmopolitan Democracy*,
   Cambridge: Polity, 1998.

[19] See *European Defence: A Proposal for a White Paper Report of an Independent Task Force*, Paris: European Union Institute for Strategic Studies, May 2004.

[20] European Commission, *Eurobarometer 60: Public Opinion in the European Union, Autumn 2003*, http://europa.eu.int/comm/public_opinion/archives/eb/eb60/eb60_rapport_standard_en.pdf (2004).

[21] *A Human Security Doctrine for Europe: The Barcelona Report of the Study Group on Europe's Security Capabilities*, Barcelona, September 2004, http://www.lse.ac.uk/Depts/global/Publications/HumanSecurityDoctrine.pdf

Index

Page references for notes are followed by n.

Short Loan Collection